1–2 PETER, JUDE

WORD and SPIRIT COMMENTARY ON THE NEW TESTAMENT

VOLUMES NOW AVAILABLE

Acts Robert P. Menzies and Craig S. Keener
Romans Sam Storms
2 Corinthians Ben Witherington III
Colossians and Philemon Holly Beers
1–2 Peter, Jude Craig S. Keener

1–2 PETER, JUDE

Craig S. Keener

Baker Academic
a division of Baker Publishing Group
Grand Rapids, Michigan

Published by Baker Academic
a division of Baker Publishing Group
Grand Rapids, Michigan
BakerAcademic.com

Printed in the United States of America

Library of Congress Cataloging-in-Publication Data
Names: Keener, Craig S., 1960– author
Title: 1–2 Peter, Jude / Craig S. Keener.
Other titles: First–Second Peter
Description: Grand Rapids, Michigan : Baker Academic, a division of Baker Publishing Group, 2025. | Series: Word and spirit commentary on the New Testament | Includes bibliographical references and index.
Identifiers: LCCN 2025013828 | ISBN 9781540963871 paperback | ISBN 9781540969576 casebound | ISBN 9781493451753 ebook | ISBN 9781493451760 pdf
Subjects: LCSH: Bible. Peter—Commentaries | Bible. Jude—Commentaries | LCGFT: Commentaries.
Classification: LCC BS2795.52 .K44 2025 | DDC 227/.9206—dc23/eng/20250616
LC record available at https://lccn.loc.gov/2025013828

In the commentary on 1 Peter, unless otherwise indicated, Scriptures are from the NIV. In the commentary on 2 Peter and Jude, unless otherwise indicated, Scriptures are the author's own translation.

Italics in Scripture references have been added for emphasis.

Baker Publishing Group publications use paper produced from sustainable forestry practices and post-consumer waste whenever possible.

25 26 27 28 29 30 31   7 6 5 4 3 2 1

To my mentors in ministry in the Black church,
where I learned how justice, compassion,
and preaching Jesus belong together:
Alyn Waller, Carl Kenney, Jacqueline Reeves,
Frank Reid, and Jeremiah Wright

Contents

Series Preface

In the foreword to Roger Stronstad's 1984 volume *The Charismatic Theology of St. Luke*, Clark H. Pinnock wrote, "The young Pentecostal scholars are coming!"[1] That was a generation ago, and now the Pentecostal scholars are here, many of them having grown up alongside the explosive global growth of charismatic and Pentecostal traditions. Such growth has been well documented,[2] with the number of adherents estimated at more than half a billion. In many places, Bible teaching has not been able to keep pace with this growth. Because of this reality, there is a clear need for a balanced commentary series aimed at Christians who identify as Spirit-filled, including renewalists, charismatics, and Pentecostals, as well as others who want to learn more from this sphere of the church.

Because so many within these traditions often use wider evangelical literature, this series is sensitive to those intellectual and academic standards. However, others mistrust what they see as "purely intellectual" approaches, and they will find that this series also focuses on how the same Spirit who inspired the text speaks and works today. In this way, the series offers a conversation for the church rather than operating primarily as a forum for discussion among scholars.

The commentary proper in each volume engages the biblical text both in its ancient setting and with regard to its message for Spirit-filled Christians

1. Clark H. Pinnock, foreword to *The Charismatic Theology of St. Luke*, by Roger Stronstad (Hendrickson, 1984), vii.

2. For example, Peter L. Berger, "Four Faces of Global Culture," in *Globalization and the Challenges of a New Century: A Reader*, ed. Patrick O'Meara, Howard D. Mehlinger, and Matthew Krain (Indiana University Press, 2000), 425; Robert Bruce Mullin, *A Short World History of Christianity* (Westminster John Knox, 2008), 211 (cf. 276); Mark A. Noll, *The New Shape of World Christianity: How American Experience Reflects Global Faith* (IVP Academic, 2009), 32.

today. The commentaries often integrate exegesis and application, as readers in charismatic and Pentecostal traditions tend to move naturally between these categories rather than separate them. In other words, such readers traditionally blend the ancient and modern horizons so as to read themselves within the continuing narrative of salvation history—that is, as part of the ongoing biblical story (not part of ancient culture but as theologically/spiritually/eschatologically part of God's same church).

As part of the blending of horizons, distinctive interests for Spirit-filled audiences are addressed when relevant. These include, but are not limited to, the reality of the new birth, healing and other miracles, spiritual gifts, hearing God's voice, the working of the Spirit in daily life, and spiritual warfare. Not all biblical text, and thus not all exposition, focuses on these points alone, and our authors do not artificially impose these topics on passages that do not naturally address them. In other words, our authors observe how God works in the biblical texts and how Christians can expect God to be working today, even if in new or culturally surprising ways.

However, each author also writes from within a charismatic, renewalist, or Pentecostal context across the broad spectrum of the Spirit-focused tradition, and the authors often refer to such spaces in their writing. The range of voices includes denominational Pentecostals, Reformed charismatics, charismatic Methodists, and others. They also reflect a range of cultures, including Spirit-filled voices from multiple continents.

The authors "preach" their way through the texts, hosting a conversation both as trusted insiders for their own home traditions and as hospitable guides for others who wish to listen again alongside the ancient audiences for the Spirit's voice in our time and contexts. The commentaries are written with other distinctives of the tradition(s), including the incorporation of testimony and sidebars that feature connections to Pentecostal/charismatic/revival history, teaching, and practice.

Other sidebars focus on biblical background and lengthier points of application. The series has adopted the New International Version (NIV) as the default text, as it is widely used in contexts that identify as Spirit-filled. However, our authors will often reference other translations, including their own. Quoted biblical texts from the passage under discussion will be highlighted in bold. Greek words are transliterated.

We offer this series to the church, and we pray that it testifies to the creative work and restorative goodness of the triune God.

Holly Beers, Westmont College
Craig S. Keener, Asbury Theological Seminary

Acknowledgments

Special thanks to editors Holly Beers and Bryan Dyer for welcoming this contribution to the series, to James Korsmo as my editor, and to my PhD student E. J. Davila for doing the Scripture and ancient references index.

Abbreviations

Old Testament

Gen.	Genesis	2 Chron.	2 Chronicles	Dan.	Daniel
Exod.	Exodus	Ezra	Ezra	Hosea	Hosea
Lev.	Leviticus	Neh.	Nehemiah	Joel	Joel
Num.	Numbers	Esther	Esther	Amos	Amos
Deut.	Deuteronomy	Job	Job	Obad.	Obadiah
Josh.	Joshua	Ps(s).	Psalm(s)	Jon.	Jonah
Judg.	Judges	Prov.	Proverbs	Mic.	Micah
Ruth	Ruth	Eccles.	Ecclesiastes	Nah.	Nahum
1 Sam.	1 Samuel	Song	Song of Songs	Hab.	Habakkuk
2 Sam.	2 Samuel	Isa.	Isaiah	Zeph.	Zephaniah
1 Kings	1 Kings	Jer.	Jeremiah	Hag.	Haggai
2 Kings	2 Kings	Lam.	Lamentations	Zech.	Zechariah
1 Chron.	1 Chronicles	Ezek.	Ezekiel	Mal.	Malachi

New Testament

Matt.	Matthew	Eph.	Ephesians	Heb.	Hebrews
Mark	Mark	Phil.	Philippians	James	James
Luke	Luke	Col.	Colossians	1 Pet.	1 Peter
John	John	1 Thess.	1 Thessalonians	2 Pet.	2 Peter
Acts	Acts	2 Thess.	2 Thessalonians	1 John	1 John
Rom.	Romans	1 Tim.	1 Timothy	2 John	2 John
1 Cor.	1 Corinthians	2 Tim.	2 Timothy	3 John	3 John
2 Cor.	2 Corinthians	Titus	Titus	Jude	Jude
Gal.	Galatians	Philem.	Philemon	Rev.	Revelation

Deuterocanonical Works and Septuagint

Bar.	Baruch	3 Macc.	3 Maccabees	Tob.	Tobit
1 Esd.	1 Esdras	4 Macc.	4 Maccabees	Wis.	Wisdom
Jdt.	Judith	Sir.	Sirach (Ecclesiasticus)		
1–2 Macc.	1–2 Maccabees	Sus.	Susanna		

Ancient Texts, Text Types, and Versions

LXX Septuagint

MT Masoretic Text

Mishnah, Talmud, and Related Literature

b. Babylonian Talmud
bar. baraita
m. Mishnah
par. parashah
pq. pereq
t. Tosefta
y. Jerusalem Talmud

Modern Versions

ASV American Standard Version
BBE Bible in Basic English
ESV English Standard Version
KJV King James Version
NASB New American Standard Bible
NET New English Translation
NIV New International Version
NJB New Jerusalem Bible
NRSV New Revised Standard Version

Secondary Sources: Major Reference Works

BDAG Bauer, Walter, Frederick W. Danker, William F. Arndt, and F. Wilbur Gingrich. *Greek-English Lexicon of the New Testament and Other Early Christian Literature.* 3rd ed. Chicago: University of Chicago Press, 2000

CIJ *Corpus Inscriptionum Judaicarum.* Edited by Jean-Baptiste Frey. 2 vols. Pontifical Biblical Institute, 1936–52

I. Eph. *Die Inschriften von Ephesos.* Edited by Hermann Wankel et al. 8 vols. in 10. Habelt, 1979–84

LCL Loeb Classical Library

LSJ Liddell, H. G., R. Scott, and H. S. Jones. *A Greek-English Lexicon.* 9th ed. with rev. suppl. Clarendon, 1996

OTP *The Old Testament Pseudepigrapha.* Edited by James H. Charlesworth. 2 vols. Doubleday, 1983, 1985

PGM *Papyri Graecae Magicae: Die griechischen Zauberpapyri.* Edited by Karl Preisindanz. 2nd ed. Teubner, 1973–74

P.Mich. *Michigan Papyri.* 19 vols. in 20. University of Michigan Library, 1931–99

General

AT author's translation
cf. *confer*, compare
chap(s). chapter(s)
col(s). column(s)
e.g. *exempli gratia*, for example
esp. especially
ET English translation
frg. fragment
Gk. Greek
i.e. *id est*, that is
Lat. Latin
lit. literally
v.(v). verse(s)
// parallel text(s)

1 Peter

Introduction

Even a casual glance at this commentary will reveal that I have treated 1 Peter differently from 2 Peter and Jude.[1] For the latter two I have provided my own translations and much fuller documentation from primary sources, which I have neglected in 1 Peter for the sake of space. This is because my translation and documentation for 1 Peter are already available in another commentary, for those who wish to pursue it,[2] whereas the same is not true for these other works. For 1 Peter my brief quotations therefore use the NIV to save space.

Authorship

I regard Jesus's disciple Peter as the author of 1 Peter. Although this position once commanded nearly unanimous consensus, scholars highly debate it today, not least because the style of the letter seems too advanced for a Galilean fisherman. Still, Peter had been preaching in Greek for more than three decades at this point, and we should not assume that the movement he led would leave him entirely to his own skills to compose the work. Like most ancient authors, literate or not, Peter would have dictated his ideas to a scribe.

More to the point here, supportive members of the movement surely would also have volunteered to help shape his language more eloquently.[3] Josephus, for

---

Scripture quotations in the commentary on 1 Peter are from the NIV unless otherwise noted.

1. These three letters belong to a collection today called General Epistles, Catholic Epistles, or (with Slater, "Misnomer," esp. 5) "Judeo-Christian literature" (though more broadly that could apply to the entire New Testament); or perhaps, non-Pauline epistles.

2. Keener, *1 Peter*.

3. For varying levels of scribal involvement in composition, see esp. Richards, *Secretary*; Richards, *Letter Writing*.

example, used style assistants, as did Cicero.[4] We do not know for certain who may have helped Peter, but among those explicitly present with him were Mark and Silvanus (1 Pet. 5:12–13), both of whom came from respected and probably educated backgrounds (Acts 12:12–13; 16:37). Silvanus, known to participate in letter writing (1 Thess. 1:1; 2 Thess. 1:1), certainly helped at some stage in the process (1 Pet. 5:12). Some scholars even find elements of style similar to earlier letters in the composition of which Silvanus participated.

Some scholars complain that 1 Peter sounds too Pauline; others respond that Silvanus could also account for alleged Paulinisms (cf. 2 Cor. 1:19; 1 Thess. 1:1; 2 Thess. 1:1). The question of Silvanus's participation aside, however, Peter himself knew Paul (Gal. 2:11–14), and clearly they shared some key beliefs (see Gal. 2:16).

Outside of New Testament studies, historians of antiquity usually depend heavily on objective, external evidence. A key list for attesting the ancient author Plutarch's works, for example, stems from a century or two after Plutarch, yet historians of antiquity rely heavily on it. Meanwhile, *all* external evidence supports Peter as the author of 1 Peter—starting from within a generation of the letter. Living memory normally is defined as the period when those who knew eyewitnesses were still living, or quantified as a period of sixty to eighty years. The major weaknesses of oral tradition are much less relevant within this shorter time frame.

Christians accepted 1 Peter as authentic from its earliest attestation.[5] Writing in the early second century, Polycarp clearly echoes 1 Peter, as may the *Didache* (1.4), Clement of Rome, and possibly Ignatius of Antioch.[6] These early authors hardly would quote from 1 Peter as authoritative if they believed it to be spurious. Likewise, Eusebius, who had the text of Papias available (Eusebius, *Ecclesiastical History* 3.39.1), reports that Papias quoted 1 John and 1 Peter (3.39.17). Very early evidence, therefore, strongly supports the view that the letter is indeed from Peter.

Date

Evidence supporting Peter as author also suggests a date in the early 60s of the first century. If the letter is from Peter, it must come from shortly before Nero's persecution (64–67, when Peter reportedly was martyred in Rome) rather than later persecutions under Domitian (ruled 81–96) or Trajan (ruled 98–117). Peter warns of impending persecution; he does not claim current state persecution in Asia Minor.

4. Josephus, *Against Apion* 1.50; Cicero, *Epistles to Friends* 16.10.2.

5. Eusebius, *Ecclesiastical History* 3.3.1, 4; 3.25.2; cf. perhaps 2 Pet. 3:1.

6. See Berding, *Polycarp and Paul*, 201–2; Keener, *1 Peter*, 17–23. For example, Polycarp, *To the Philippians* 2.2 cites nine successive Greek words verbatim from 1 Pet. 3:9.

Message

The letter is explicit about an audience in Asia Minor (today's Türkiye); most scholars believe that the letter was sent from Rome (cf. 1 Pet. 5:13). At the proud heart of a vast empire, Rome's male aristocrats detested local Romans (often Roman women) who adopted foreign religious practices, including Judaism. Still less popular, Christians appeared as a messianic, apocalyptic, charismatic Jewish sect. A Christian writer in Rome by 62, such as Peter, might well see the handwriting on the wall; a mere spark could ignite a firestorm of persecution. Soon after, when an actual fire in AD 64 burned Rome but spared Nero's gardens, many people blamed the emperor for the fire. Needing an unpopular scapegoat without a significant local constituency, Nero accused Christians, and he proceeded to burn many alive to light his imperial gardens at night.[7]

The letter of 1 Peter often focuses on suffering (2:19–20; 3:9, 14, 17; 4:1, 13, 15, 19; 5:9–10), including that of Christ (1:11; 2:21, 23; 3:18; 4:1, 13). It does so in light of *hope*—that is, God's good promise for our future (1:3, 13, 21; 3:15). Enduring unmerited suffering for the sake of subsequent glory also follows the model, and shares the experience, of Christ (1:11, 21; 2:21; 3:17–18; 4:1, 13; 5:1). Like Christ, we endure unjust sufferings when we cannot avoid them, depending on God's vindication (2:18–25; 5:6). Suffering honors Christ so long as we suffer for doing right rather than for doing wrong (2:12, 19–20; 3:13–18; 4:14–18; cf. 2:15).

This message is of vital importance for today's church. Christians in many regions face persecution and even martyrdom for Christ's name, proving their faith in his promises.[8] In the Western world, however, many of us lack a good theology of suffering, whether it is directly *for* Christ or simply *with* Christ as part of life in a difficult world.

Outline

1. Letter address (1:1–2)
2. Praising God for salvation (1:3–12)
3. Live for God's eternal values (1:13–2:3)
   - A. Live wholly for God (1:13–16)
   - B. Ransomed from the world by the precious Lamb (1:17–21)
   - C. Transformed by God's eternal message (1:22–2:3)

7. Tacitus, *Annals* 15.44.

8. See P. Marshall, *Their Blood Cries Out*; Marshall, Gilbert, and Shea, *Persecuted*; for particular cases, Ibraheem with Bach, *Shackled*; Panahi, *I Didn't Survive*.

4. God's people (2:4–10)
5. Honoring Christ where you are exiled (2:11–17)
   A. Do not act as the world does (2:11–12)
   B. Submit to the world's authorities (2:13–17)
6. Slaves to slaveholders (2:18–25)
7. Wives and husbands (3:1–7)
8. General exhortation before God (3:8–12)
9. Better to suffer unjustly than justly (3:13–17)
10. Christ's suffering and exaltation (3:18–4:2)
11. Live for God's assessment, not the world's (4:3–6)
12. Serve fellow believers (4:7–11)
13. Suffering for Christ (4:12–19)
14. Servant leaders and mutuality (5:1–7)
15. General exhortation (5:8–11)
16. Epistolary postscript/closing (5:12–14)

Recommended Resources

Balch, David L. *Let Wives Be Submissive: The Domestic Code in 1 Peter*. Society of Biblical Literature Monograph Series 26. Scholars Press, 1981.

du Toit, Sean. *1 Peter*. New Covenant Commentary Series. Cascade Books, 2025.

Elliott, John H. *1 Peter: A New Translation with Introduction and Commentary*. Anchor Bible 37B. Doubleday, 2000.

Jobes, Karen H. *1 Peter*. Baker Exegetical Commentary on the New Testament. Baker Academic, 2005.

Keener, Craig S. *1 Peter: A Commentary*. Baker Academic, 2021.

Kelly, J. N. D. *A Commentary on the Epistles of Peter and Jude*. Thornapple Commentaries. Baker, 1981.

Martin, Troy W. *Metaphor and Composition in 1 Peter*. Society of Biblical Literature Dissertation Series 131. Scholars Press, 1992.

Reese, Ruth Anne. *1 Peter*. New Cambridge Bible Commentary. Cambridge University Press, 2022.

Watson, Duane F., and Terrance Callan. *First and Second Peter*. Paideia. Baker Academic, 2012.

Williams, Travis B., and David G. Horrell. *A Critical and Exegetical Commentary on 1 Peter*. 2 vols. International Critical Commentary. T&T Clark, 2023.

Letter Address (1:1–2)

First Peter 1:2–25 highlights the future consummation of salvation brought about by Christ and inherited through new birth by the gospel (1:23–25). This salvation rests on Christ's sacrificial suffering (1:19; cf. 1:11; 2:24), his resurrection (1:3, 21), and his future revealing (1:7).

The first two verses of 1 Peter constitute the epistolary prescript and introduce some key themes of the letter, such as resident aliens, God's plan, obedience, and Christ's sacrifice. Ancient letters typically began by naming the sender, then the recipient(s), followed by a greeting and a prayer for the recipient's well-being. All the regions named in 1:1 are provinces in Roman Asia Minor.

The audience's identity as **exiles scattered** (1:1) reflects their continuity with the Jewish community after the exile. Jewish people dispersed outside the Holy Land recognized themselves as God's **chosen** people (1:2), but they often lived as resident aliens in the predominantly gentile cities where they settled. Whereas

Roman Asia Minor

my wife, who is from Central Africa, received a green card and US citizenship fairly quickly after our marriage, Jewish residents in gentile cities often remained "resident aliens" there for generations, vulnerable to discrimination. Peter, however, refers to a spiritual rather than ethnic diaspora, and he transfers these images to all who now follow Israel's God in Christ (1:17; 2:11; cf. 5:13). They are God's people residing as aliens in a culture foreign to their divine origin.

Their spiritual identity as **chosen according to the foreknowledge** (1:2) reflects not the pagan idea of arbitrary fate but the providential, benevolent Jewish understanding of God. Most Jewish groups affirmed human responsibility alongside God's sovereignty. God knowing and God choosing or bringing about are closely connected here (as in Acts 2:23; Rom. 8:29; 11:2), as in earlier Scripture (see LXX Gen. 18:19; Jer. 1:5; Amos 3:2). Reacting against determinism, most early church fathers predicated predestination on **foreknowledge** in the sense that God's "choice depends on our foreseen response to his invitation."[9] Reacting against the idea that humans can make themselves righteous, Augustine and his Western heirs underlined God's sovereign choice. Both approaches offer insights, but Peter's setting and focus differ. Though he would both affirm God's sovereignty and invite conversion, his primary point is simpler. Like other New Testament writers, he uses our chosenness to remind us of the special privilege that God has given us in Christ.

The mention of **God the Father**, the **Spirit**, and **Jesus Christ** together in 1:2 probably reflects a trinitarian understanding, as in, for example, 1 Cor. 12:4–6; 2 Cor. 13:14 (note also Matt. 28:19; Eph. 4:4–6). **Grace** [*charis*] adapts the conventional greeting *chairein*; **peace** [*eirēnē*] reflects the standard Jewish greeting *shalom*, "May it be well with you," implicitly invoking God's blessing (as in today's "God bless you"; cf. Num. 6:26).

Praising God for Salvation (1:3–12)

In Greek, 1 Pet. 1:3–12 is one elaborate "periodic" sentence, a sophisticated literary form that required of its author intense attention. Believers have been reborn into a living hope (1:3), an imperishable inheritance (1:4), and a prepared salvation (1:5).

"Blessed be" or **praise be to** is a common blessing form that appears more than forty times in the Old Testament, usually for God, and appears pervasively in a later mishnaic tractate, Berakot, devoted to such Jewish blessings. Peter praises God's saving acts. **God** the **Father** of **Jesus** births us into new life

9. Edwards, *Galatians*, xix. See, e.g., Origen, *Commentary on Romans* 7.7.5; 8.29; Ambrosiaster, *Commentary on Romans* 8.29; Theodoret of Cyrrhus, *Commentary on Romans* 8.29–30.

through Jesus Christ's **resurrection** to eschatological life. That is why Peter describes this eschatological expectation as **living** (cf. 1:23; 2:5). Resurrection would inaugurate eternal life (Dan. 12:2), and Jesus's resurrection has confirmed the promised future resurrection of all his followers (1 Cor. 15:20, 23). Our spiritual **birth** from God creates a new and virtuous nature within us, one that will live forever, like God (see comment on 1:23; 2 Pet. 1:4).

Being born to God (1 Pet. 1:3) also confers on God's new children an **inheritance** (1:4). The inheritance rightly belongs to the obedient children (1:14) born to the Father (1:3, 23). Jewish tradition widely reapplied the biblical language of "inheritance" to our future hope (cf. already LXX Isa. 57:13; 58:11; 60:21; 65:9; Ezek. 36:12; 47:14, 22–23). In Jewish tradition the righteous expected to "inherit" God's "promises" and to "inherit" eternal life. The promise of inheriting the "land" (e.g., Pss. 25:13; 37:9, 11, 22, 29, 34) came to be understood as inheriting the "earth" (the same Hebrew term). Early Christians sometimes expressed this hope as "inheriting" (or, for the rebellious, not inheriting) the kingdom.

Our **inheritance** is imperishable and guarded for us (1:4) because we ourselves are protected by God for ultimate **salvation** (1:5, 9). **Heaven** (1:4) is the divine realm articulated in spatial terms; any **inheritance** there is secure (Matt. 6:20 // Luke 12:33–34; Mark 10:21).[10] In 1 Pet. 1:5, perhaps because early Christians saw themselves as already *in* the "last days" (e.g., 1:20; cf. Acts 2:17), Peter describes the future consummation not as the last days but as **the last time** (1:5) (cf. "the last day" in John 6:39–40, 44, 54; 12:48).

In Jewish thought, distress tested one's character to see if one would sin; suffering thus often functioned as testing or **trials** (1:6). Jewish pietists believed that God would reward the righteous who, though suffering, praised God. Peter encourages those who are suffering by reminding them of their future hope; it is easier to endure suffering when we remember that it is temporary—**a little while** (1:6; cf. 5:10) (as in the line from an old hymn: "Just a few more weary days and then . . .").

Fire refines and tests the genuineness of metals; **gold** may endure testing by **fire**, but **faith** that is tested by **fire** proves far more permanent and will be honored once Christ returns (1:7). This is because believers were bought not with perishable silver or "gold" (1:18), valuable merely outwardly (3:3), but with the far more precious blood of Christ (1:19).[11] God's people are tested as if **refined by fire** (cf. Ps. 66:10; Isa. 1:25; 48:10; Zech. 13:9). Just as testing refines **gold** and improves the final product as pure gold, so testing improves those who persevere through it. As in the old adage, how we respond to hardship determines whether it makes us bitter or better.

10. See also *4 Ezra* 7.77; *2 Baruch* 14.12; *t. Pe'ah* 4.18.

11. For God's gifts being worth incomparably more than gold or silver, see, e.g., Ps. 119:127; Prov. 3:14; 8:19; 22:1.

Believers do not see Jesus Christ **now** (1:8), in contrast to when he will be **revealed** (1:7). Because of trust in him, however, we **rejoice**, even in the face of sufferings (1:6; cf. Luke 6:22–23; Acts 5:41; 16:25; Rom. 5:3; James 1:2). Scripture and Jewish tradition associated **joy** (1:8) with worship,[12] and joy often characterizes charismatic worship in the Spirit today. The **joy** is **inexpressible** because words are not adequate to articulate it (cf. 1 Cor. 2:9–10, 13; Eph. 3:19; Phil. 4:7); we might express it to some degree affectively in tongues (cf. 1 Cor. 14:2, 14–15) or wholly inarticulately (cf. Rom. 8:26).

In 1:9, Peter speaks of the "future outcome" (**end result**) of our **faith**. Here Peter returns to the final, end-time salvation through trust promised in 1:5 (since this will include bodily resurrection, **souls** here means eternal "lives," not a Platonic idea of souls apart from bodies).

Peter says that the prophets prophesied about **grace** involving the **salvation** that they were trying to understand (1:10). **Grace** is a recurrent theme in 1 Peter (cf. 1:2; 4:10; 5:5, 10), including with respect to future **salvation** (1:10, 13; 3:7), and is a key subject of Peter's message (5:12). The prophets looked forward to the messianic era in which we now live (cf. Matt. 13:17 // Luke 10:24).[13] The prophets were trying to understand what person or what sort of time **the Spirit of Christ** within them was announcing (1 Pet. 1:11); God's Spirit inspires prophecy (e.g., Num. 11:25; 1 Sam. 19:20). That the Spirit "of Jesus" or "of Christ" (Acts 16:7; Rom. 8:9b) is the Spirit of God (Acts 16:6; Rom. 8:9a; 1 Pet. 1:12) underlines Jesus's divinity. The prophets did not understand everything, but they predicted the Messiah's sufferings and subsequent exaltation, and they knew that their message would serve most fully the future era when these matters would be fulfilled (1 Pet. 1:12). Angels knew more than the prophets, but Jesus's coming has revealed even more than they knew (cf. 1 Cor. 6:3).

Live for God's Eternal Values (1:13–2:3)

Live Wholly for God (1:13–16)

In 1 Pet. 1:13–2:3, Peter repeatedly grounds moral exhortations in God's action in Christ. For example:

- We must remain sober (1:13) because ("therefore" in 1:13a) of God's grace in Christ (1:10–12).

12. See, e.g., Pss. 5:11; 20:5; 27:6; 31:7; 32:11; 33:1–3; 35:9; 43:4; 47:1; 63:7; 67:4; 68:3–4; 71:23; 81:1; 84:2; 90:14; 92:4; 95:1; 98:4; 132:9, 16.

13. Later rabbis also often affirmed that the prophets prophesied for the end of the age and the messianic era; the Dead Sea Scrolls share this end-time perspective.

- We must love (1:22) because we have obeyed the truth (1:22) of the gospel (1:23–25), which has transformed us.
- We must put away former sinful ways (2:1) because ("therefore" in 2:1a) of the transforming gospel (1:23–25) and because we have tasted the Lord's kindness (2:3).

In Greek, 1:13 speaks of "girding up the loins" of our **minds**, the way one would have to pull up a long garment to run without tripping. It thus connotes readiness and devotion to God's promise of Christ's coming. Considering the **grace** experienced most fully at Christ's future revealing (1:13; cf. 1:7) urges a perspective that evaluates the present in light of its eternal significance.[14] Missions leader C. T. Studd expressed well the importance of an eternal perspective: "Only one life, 'twill soon be past; only what's done for Christ will last."[15] May we devote ourselves and all our resources for God's kingdom.

The theme of obedience in 1:14 revisits its mention in 1:2 and anticipates it in 1:22. **Obedient children** (1:14) imitate and become like their parents (1:15–16); here we become like our Father, God (1:17). Unconverted gentiles' passions and **ignorance** (1:14) contrast with our engaged **minds** now (1:13).[16]

Instead of being conformed to a pattern formed by passions (1:14; cf. 2:11), we should **conform** to the pattern of God (1:15–16), also exemplified as the pattern of Christ (3:17–18; 4:1, 13). God's holiness separates him from what is profane; for God's people to be **holy** (1:15) means that we are consecrated to him, separate from the values of the profane world. In principle, such consecration means that everything that we are and have, including time and money, belongs to God, and we should live accordingly. The average consumer in the United States spends over five hours per day on entertainment—about thirty-six hours per week.[17] If all Christians immersed themselves in God's Word more than entertainment, how would that reshape our thinking? If just thirty million Christians shifted two more hours a day to prayer, meeting needs in our communities for the honor of Jesus's name, or sharing Christ with their neighborhoods, that would be more than twenty billion fresh hours a year devoted to God's kingdom. Imagine what would happen if we took seriously the call, **Be holy, because I am holy** (1:16, citing Lev. 11:44–45; 19:2).

14. On this theme in Paul's letters, see Keener, *Mind of the Spirit*, 154–55, 176–79, 235, 254.

15. Quoted in Alcorn, *Heaven*, 453.

16. For the contrast between the passions and reason in ancient thought, see 1 Pet. 2:11; Keener, *Mind of the Spirit*, 19–23, 76–78.

17. The average rate is higher for men, at some 5.56 hours per day ("American Time Use Survey Summary," U.S. Bureau of Labor Statistics, June 27, 2024, https://www.bls.gov/news.release/atus.nr0.htm).

Many people in antiquity spoke of imitating deity, but the God of Israel, unlike pagan deities, is wholly just and moral. Our behavior (**all you do**, *anastrophē*) must be **holy** (1:15), so we behave (**live out**, *anastrephō*) honorably (1:17), rather than in the form of behavior (**way of life**, *anastrephō*) inherited from our (for some, some further back than others) pagan ancestors (1:18). The goal of such distinctive behavior is to win over nonbelievers, or at least vindicate God's justice in the final time (*anastrophē* in 2:12; 3:1–2, 16; "live lives," "behavior," "lives," "behavior").

Ransomed from the World by the Precious Lamb (1:17–21)

Not only has God **called** us (1:15), but also we **call on** God (1:17). If we bear the name of Christ (4:14, 16), we must live accordingly, as those consecrated to (1:15–16) God and Christ. Scripture (Deut. 10:17; 2 Chron. 19:7) and Jewish tradition heavily emphasized God's impartiality (1 Pet. 1:17). Because God **judges . . . impartially**, we must live in **reverence** (NET)—that is, the biblical fear of the Lord (cf. 2:17), keeping in mind the future judgment.

Peter uses conventional Jewish language to challenge **the empty way of life** inherited **from your ancestors**. Jewish polemic often used words such as "futile" or **empty** [*mataios*] to describe idols (1:18). Some of these were made from **silver or gold** (e.g., Deut. 29:17; Pss. 115:4; 135:15; Isa. 2:20; 31:7; Hosea 8:4; Rev. 9:20). **Redeemed** [*lytroō*] or "ransomed" (1:18) can refer to liberation more generally, but it sometimes involves a price, as it clearly does here. Because of **gold**'s worldly value, Scripture often used it in contrasts with what was much more valuable, such as God's word (Pss. 19:10; 119:72, 127) and wisdom (Job 28:19; Prov. 3:14; 8:10, 19; 16:16; 20:15; cf. 25:12) and even an honorable reputation (Prov. 22:1). But nothing could be more **precious** than the **blood** of God's own beloved Son (1:19; cf. John 1:29, 36; Acts 20:28; 1 Cor. 5:7; Rev. 5:6; 7:14). Scripture frequently mandated the sacrifice of a **lamb** (or certain other animals) for guilt or sin offerings (Lev. 4:32; 5:6–7; 14:12–13, 21, 25; Num. 6:12, 14) and for Passover (Exod. 12:5, 21). Such lambs were to be **without blemish**, hence ritually acceptable for sacrifice (e.g., Exod. 29:1, 38; Lev. 1:3, 10; 3:1, 6).

That Christ was known **before** the **world**'s beginning (1:20) suggests that God in his foreknowledge designed this plan for redemption even before sin began (cf. 2 Tim. 1:9; Rev. 13:8). **Last times** and equivalent expressions such as "last days" applied to Israel's future restoration (Isa. 2:2; Dan. 2:28; Hosea 3:5; Mic. 4:1) and the end-time suffering that preceded it (Jer. 23:20; 30:24; Ezek. 38:16; Dan. 10:14). Early Christians consistently viewed themselves as living in this period (Acts 2:17; 1 Tim. 4:1; 2 Tim. 3:1; Heb. 1:2; James 5:3; 2 Pet. 3:3; 1 John 2:18). Modern prophecy teachers are right to emphasize that we live in the "end times" but wrong when they treat that observation as only recently applicable. And those who believe that the gift of prophecy has ceased misunderstand completely New Testament eschatology: if it was already the "last days" when Peter explained tongues at Pentecost as last-day prophecy (Acts 2:17–18), it can hardly be anything other than "last days" today as well.

These gentile converts' trust in God came **through him**, Christ (1:21), and his gospel (1:23–25, esp. 1:25b). I can relate to this as a former atheist converted by an encounter with the Spirit through hearing the gospel of Christ. **Glorified him** (1:21) refers to resurrection (cf. 5:1, 4, 10; also Luke 24:26; 1 Cor. 15:40–43; Phil. 3:21) and also implies attendant honor (cf. 1:7–8; 2:12; 4:11, 16).

Transformed by God's Eternal Message (1:22–2:3)

Purified (1:22) stems from a biblical ritual image of making someone able to stand before God. It may evoke the image of blood found in 1:19, since sacrificial blood consecrates and purifies (Exod. 29:21; Lev. 8:15, 30; 16:19; Heb. 9:13–14, 22; 10:29; 13:12; 1 John 1:7) (in 1:2, Peter has already connected being "obedient" with the sprinkling of Christ's blood). **Obeying the truth** (1:22) depicts his hearers' conversion through obeying the truth of the gospel (cf. 1:2); thus Peter elaborates how that gospel message has changed them (1:23–25). For Peter, the highest expression of obeying the truth is for us to **love** one another, an emphasis consistent with Jesus's teaching (Mark 12:30–31). Jesus treated love as the highest command in the law (Matt. 22:36–40), shaping this unanimous and distinctive emphasis in early Christianity (Rom. 13:8–10; 1 Cor. 13:13; Gal. 5:14; James 2:8; *Didache* 1.2–3).

The first term of affection that Peter uses in 1:22 (*philadelphia*) especially indicates love for brothers and sisters (a familial sense obscured in the NIV's more generic **for each other**). Embracing Christ entails a new family (cf. Mark 3:34–35; 10:29–30), in which all believers are spiritual siblings, sharing the same Father (1:17, 23), with consequent claims on one another (cf. *philadelphia* in Rom. 12:10; 1 Thess. 4:9; Heb. 13:1). The emphasis on *philadelphia* seems particularly prominent in Petrine literature (1 Pet. 1:22; 3:8; 2 Pet. 1:7). **Sincere** love is *anypokritos*, "without hypocrisy," hence genuine (also Rom. 12:9; 2 Cor. 6:6).

Being **born again** from God's seed (1:23; cf. 1:3; 1 John 3:9) is equivalent to being "born from God" (John 1:13; 1 John 3:9; 4:7; 5:1, 4, 18), "born from above" (John 3:3, 7), and "born from the Spirit" (John 3:5–6, 8; Gal. 4:29). As like begets like, those born from God share his moral nature (see 2 Pet. 1:3–4). This rebirth explains the purification and sibling love in 1:22: those also spiritually born from the same Father (1:17) are spiritual siblings; also, as obedient children (1:14), we obey the truth (1:22; cf. 1:2).

Human sperm was called "seed," and gentile thinkers often spoke of divine seed as being innate in humans.[18] The New Testament, by contrast, views the divine seed not as innate in fallen humanity but as God's message (e.g., Mark 4:14; cf. *4 Ezra* 9.31, 33) that bears fruit in them (Gal. 5:22–23; 6:8). Created in God's image (Gen. 1:26–27; 9:6) as his children (cf. Gen. 5:1–3), we are being restored to that image fully in Christ (Rom. 8:29; 1 Cor. 15:49; 2 Cor. 3:18; Col. 3:10). In 1 Pet. 1:23, the most explicit characteristic of the **seed** is that it is **imperishable**, thus suggesting in general terms that we who are born from it have eternal life (cf. 1:4). In 1:24–25a, Peter demonstrates the eternal character

18. For example, Seneca, *To Lucilius* 73.16 (unless otherwise noted, all citations of Seneca refer to Seneca the Younger); Musonius Rufus, *Lectures* 2, p. 38.14; Epictetus, *Discourses* 1.9.4, 6. Note also Philo, *Life of Moses* 1.279: human souls spring from divine seed.

PENTECOSTAL INTEREST

Confessing a New Identity

Some in charismatic circles talk a lot about positive confession. So long as our faith is genuinely in what God has promised, it is biblical to express and act on that faith. Often people have confessed things that God has *not* promised, seeking to bring them to pass, but "who can speak and have it happen if the Lord has not decreed it?" (Lam. 3:37). At the same time, we charismatics (and other Christians) often fail to speak and act in faith on what God has explicitly affirmed in Scripture. We have been purified and born anew by God's own word (1 Pet. 1:3, 22–23). We need to accept for ourselves that new identity, recognizing our new allegiance to Christ, and speak and live as if that is true.

In Rom. 4:24, Paul emphasizes that God has "credited" righteousness to our account (cf. 4:3–11, 22–23, repeatedly using *logizomai*); in 6:11, he invites us to trust God's verdict so that we "count" (again using *logizomai*) ourselves as dead to sin and alive to God. That may feel hard when others view us the old way, or our memories, habits, and temptations pull us toward that old way. But God invites us to trust his transforming grace more than temptations. As we remind ourselves in faith about that new identity and fill our minds with God's values (e.g., through immersing ourselves in Scripture) rather than the world's values (e.g., through immersing ourselves in social media or worse), we continue to be transformed (Rom. 12:2; Phil. 4:8).

of God's message from Isa. 40:6–8, a passage about the good news of ultimate salvation and restoration. The **living and enduring** message in 1:23 is the transformative good news preached to the audience in 1:25.

Therefore in 2:1 predicates new behavior on the birth from God's seed stated in 1:23. We should reject vices on the basis of our new status and identity in Christ (e.g., Col. 3:3–5, 8–10). This rejection is often expressed as "putting off" (rendered in the NIV more generically as **rid yourselves of**), using a clothing metaphor (Rom. 13:12; Eph. 4:22, 25; Col. 3:8; James 1:21; cf. Heb. 12:1) that is usually matched with "putting on" the new ways (Rom. 13:12, 14; Gal. 3:27; Eph. 4:24; Col. 3:10, 12; cf. 1 Pet. 5:5).

Lists of vices, such as in 2:1, were common in antiquity, including the New Testament (e.g., Rom. 1:29–31; 1 Cor. 5:10–11; 6:9–10; Gal. 5:19–21; Eph. 5:3–5; Col. 3:5, 8). All vices listed here contrast with the love expressed in 1 Pet. 1:22. As the source of believers' birth (1:23), God is here the source of the **milk** (2:2) (cf. the analogy with Paul in 1 Cor. 3:2; 1 Thess. 2:7). Although adults in antiquity derived many dairy products from sheep and goats, newborn infants received milk from their mother (or sometimes a paid or slave nurse). In ancient usage, **pure** (lit., "without deceit," contrasting with 2:1) **milk** is unadulterated. Ancients often used **milk** as an analogy to refer to learning. Although the NIV renders *logikos* in 2:2 as **spiritual**, its meaning here is closer to "figurative" or even "rational"; playing on words, it likely relates to the *logos* ("word") in 1:23 (cf. 2:8; 3:1, 15). That is, those born from God's seed, his word (1:23), must further nurture themselves and mature by consuming God's word, so persevering toward final salvation.

We **crave** the **milk** of God's message (2:2) because we have already **tasted** how kind the Lord is (2:3). In 2:3, Peter evokes the Greek version of Ps. 34:8: "Taste and see that the Lord is kind." Aware of the verse's context, Peter resumes quoting from this psalm in 3:10–12 (Ps. 34:12–16); indeed, in Peter's next verse (2:4), he borrows an image from the Greek version of Ps. 34:5 (LXX 33:6a, different in Hebrew and English): "coming to him." Whereas the Greek version of the psalm applies the image to YHWH, Peter refers in 2:4 to Jesus, whom he recognizes to be divine.

God's People (2:4–10)

In 2:4–10, Peter reminds his audience of their new identity as a community founded on Christ, although he will soon go on to show how this alternative community must still function as resident aliens within the world (2:11–3:12). In 2:4, Peter shifts from an image of human maturation to one of architecture.

The biblically saturated wording of 2:4 anticipates the explicit biblical quotations in 2:6–7. That the stone is **living** connects this stone with the living hope (1:3), God's living message (1:23), and, in particular, the resurrection (2:24; cf. 4:6). That the stone was **rejected** by people before being exalted by God speaks of unjust suffering; Peter soon urges his hearers to share, when necessary, Christ's sufferings (2:21; 4:13–16). The stone is **chosen** (2:4, 6), like Peter's audience (1:1; 2:9). It is also invaluably **precious** (2:4, 6), like believers' faith (1:7), Jesus's blood (1:19), and believers' hearts (3:4), but its value is evident only to people of faith (2:7). Peter's **chosen** and **precious** stone anticipates his Isaiah quotation in 2:6.

The **living stones** in 2:5 are those who share Christ's risen life, and thus can function like the living stone in 2:4. Greek and Roman mythology recounts stones becoming people,[19] but (of far greater relevance here) 1 Peter uses temple imagery (2:5–8). God could raise up people for himself, without genetic lineage from Abraham, from stones (Matt. 3:9 // Luke 3:8), prepared for a new temple (cf. Mark 12:10; 13:2; 14:58). Peter will soon (in 2:9) make explicit his theological source (Exod. 19:6) for identifying believers as a consecrated community (or order) of priests (NIV: **royal priesthood**); the **spiritual house** (2:5) where we offer sacrifices is a spiritual temple.

The **spiritual house** draws on the early Christian image of God's people as a spiritual house or temple (1 Cor. 3:16–17; 6:19; 2 Cor. 6:16; Eph. 2:18–22; Rev. 3:12). This image in turn adapts an already existing Jewish image, especially in the Qumran scrolls.[20] In New Testament letters, **spiritual** usually connotes the activity of God's Spirit,[21] hence here a temple for the Spirit (1 Cor. 3:16; 6:19; Eph. 2:22; cf. John 4:21, 24). Figurative or metaphoric sacrifices appear frequently in ancient sources, including the Old Testament (e.g., 1 Sam. 15:22; Pss. 51:16–17; 69:30–31; 141:2; Mic. 6:6–8) and Jewish tradition. The New Testament notion of **spiritual sacrifices** (e.g., Rom. 12:2; 15:16; Phil. 2:17; 4:18; Rev. 5:8) would be easily intelligible. God values our worship in the Spirit (John 4:24).

In 2:6, again Peter cites **Scripture** as his authority, justifying his claim about the **precious** stone in 2:4. Here Peter quotes from Isa. 28:16, a text highlighted also by Paul for its emphasis on faith (Rom. 9:32–33; 10:11). (Early Christians may have learned this pattern of linking "stone" texts from Jesus; cf. Matt. 21:42, 44[22] // Luke 20:17–18.) However much mockers may make fun of Jesus's followers now, God will ultimately (eschatologically) vindicate whoever **trusts in him**, so we will not **be put to shame**.

19. See Keener, "Human Stones."

20. See esp. *1QRule of the Community* (1QS) 8.5–9 (which includes an allusion to Isa. 28:16); 9.6.

21. For example, Elliott, *1 Peter*, 422 (sacrifices "motivated by the Holy Spirit"); see esp. Fee, *God's Empowering Presence*, 28–31.

22. On the fair likelihood that Matt. 21:44 reflects the original reading.

Remains of stones from Jerusalem's temple thrown down after AD 70, and surviving stones in its retaining wall

But whereas Isa. 28:16 (quoted in 2:6) promises vindication to those who trust the **precious cornerstone**, the verses that Peter quotes in 2:7–8 declare the fate of those who do not trust it. Jewish interpreters often used shared key words to link verses; in 2:7 Peter quotes Ps. 118:22, another passage about a **cornerstone**. The verse's wide use in early Christian tradition (Acts 4:11 [attributed to Peter]; Eph. 2:20) probably stems from Jesus's own use (Mark 12:10).[23] The **builders** who reject the **cornerstone** in 2:7 contrast with the spiritual house's implicit builder, God, in 2:5.

In 2:8, Peter adds yet another "stone" text, Isa. 8:14, a natural text to link with the Isaian "stone" text with which he started this series (cf. similarly Luke 20:18; Rom. 9:33). Again, Peter obviously knows more of the context than he specifically quotes: the verses preceding Isa. 8:14 encourage the righteous not to fear what the wicked fear, but instead to fear the Lord (Isa. 8:12–13, which Peter later uses in 3:14–15). Isaiah's passage goes on, just before the line that Peter uses here, to speak of the Lord as a "sanctuary" for the righteous, as well as a stone of judgment to disobedient Israel. Scripture sometimes uses this term for "sanctuary" for the temple, and potentially even God's people as his sanctuary (Judah as *hagiasma* in Ps. 114:2 [LXX 113:2]).

23. Part of the festal Hallel (Pss. 113–18), the passage was especially familiar in the Passover setting in which the Gospels place it. The psalm and its usual New Testament use fit a temple setting.

For disbelievers, then, the good rock becomes an occasion to trip, to **stumble** (2:8), an image relevant to apostasy or meriting judgment.[24] Peter had once learned how he himself could function as both a positive rock and a stumbling

24. See, e.g., Ezek. 14:3, 4, 7; 18:30; 33:12; 44:12; Sir. 9:5; 25:21; 32:15; 34:7, 19; 39:24; Matt. 5:29–30; 11:6; 13:41; 16:23; 18:6–9; Mark 9:42–47; Luke 7:23; 17:1–2.

PENTECOSTAL INTEREST

Replacement Theology?

Through much of history, Christians have believed that the church replaced Israel in God's plan. The New Testament passages used to support this were meant to argue against an opposite error in the first century—namely, that gentiles were always second class and could never become part of God's people.

Paul nevertheless could see that some gentiles were in danger of viewing themselves as chosen at the expense of any promises to ethnic Israel—that is, that they replaced Israel (Rom. 11:18). Thus, in Romans, he explains that God gave the Jewish people special historic privileges (3:1–2; 9:4–5), and that although many Jews rejected the promised Messiah, others did accept him (11:1–6). Since Israel as a whole was not ready for the fulfillment of the promises, God welcomed gentiles, but to be grafted into Israel's heritage rather than to replace it (11:17–21).

Moreover, God's plan for ethnic Israelites to be saved remains and will consummate his plan (Rom. 11:12, 15, 26–31). Gentile believers are meant to play a role in this: the ingathering of gentiles promised in the Prophets (Isa. 19:25; Zeph. 3:9; Zech. 2:11; 9:6–7) would provoke Israel to jealousy (Rom. 11:11, 14; cf. 10:19), and their ingathering would precipitate Israel's conversion (11:25–26; note *houtōs*, "in this way," in 11:26). Because ancient gentile anti-Semitism infiltrated the church,[a] however, the largely gentile church claimed to replace Israel and proved a negative witness to the Jewish people. Paul's plan remains to be fulfilled: when the Jewish people see multitudes among the nations respecting their God, Scripture, and heritage instead of usurping it (cf. Zech. 8:20–23), God will turn the majority of ethnic Israel to saving faith in Christ, grafting them back into their heritage among the eschatological people of God. Presumably, Peter, who ends up in Rome at some point (see comment on 1 Pet. 5:13), knew Paul's letter to the believers there (cf. 2 Pet. 3:15–16).

a. See Brown, *Our Hands Are Stained*.

block (Matt. 16:18, 23), but here the rock of stumbling is Christ (cf. Rom. 9:33; 1 Cor. 1:23). Disbelievers **disobey the message** (2:8), in contrast to those who were reborn through it (1:23) (on disobedience, cf. 3:1, 19–20; 4:17). That non-believers **were destined for** such judgment contrasts them starkly with the ***chosen* people** in 2:9.

Chosen (see comment on 1:1–2) **people** (2:9) recalls Old Testament language for Israel, here especially Isa. 43:20 (not least since the following Isaian verse, 43:21, speaks of them declaring God's "praise"). **A royal priesthood, a holy nation, God's special possession** all reflect Israel's sacred identity in Exod. 19:5–6 (applied to all believers also in Rev. 1:6; 5:10; 20:6). On believers' consecrated status, see 1 Pet. 1:15–16; 2:5; these priests offer spiritual sacrifices (2:5). Writers commonly applied the contrast between light and darkness to good and evil, for example in the Qumran scrolls.[25] God calling his people from darkness to light (cf. Acts 26:18; Col. 1:12–13; 1 John 2:8–9) might reflect Isaian imagery (Isa. 9:2; 42:16; 58:10).

Peter further develops believers' role as a **people** (2:9) in 2:10. As signs to Israel, Hosea named a daughter "Unloved" and a son "Not My People" (Hosea 1:6, 9), a status that would be reversed when God saved his people (Hosea 1:10; 2:1, 23). Like Paul, Peter applies this language not directly to eschatologically restored Israel but to gentiles (Rom. 9:24–26). Paul does envision a future turning of the Jewish people (Rom. 11:25–26), so his point is not a permanent rejection of the Jewish people, but simply that gentiles can be grafted into Israel's heritage and thus belong to the eschatological people of God. The same approach may well be true of Peter. Peter again encourages us, affirming our new identity in Christ.

Honoring Christ Where You Are Exiled (2:11–17)

This status as God's people (2:4–10) makes us outsiders to the world (2:11), to those who still live as gentiles (2:12). Peter has emphasized our group identity in Christ (2:4–10), but now he underlines the importance of fulfilling our social obligations in the world. The eschatological people of God must still function within society, morally distinct but socially honorable.

As with the general moral exhortations in 1:13–2:3, Peter provides rationales for the more concrete social exhortations in 2:11–3:17. Here, however, most

25. For examples of the contrast between light and darkness, see *1QRule of the Community* (1QS) 3.3, 19, 25; 10.2; *1QWar Scroll* (1QM) 1.1, 11; 13.5, 15; 14.17; *4QNarrativeC*[a] (4Q462) frg. 1.9–10; *4QVisions of Amram*[f] *ar* (4Q548) frg. 1.ii 2.10–16; *11QApocryphal Psalms* (11Q11) 5.7; cf. *1QHodayot*[a] (1QH[a]) 17.26; 20.9; 21.15; *4QRule of the Community*[c] (4Q257) 3.5; *4QMysteries*[a] (4Q299) frg. 5.2; *4QWorks of God* (4Q392) frg. 1.4–6; *11QPsalms*[a] (11Q5) 26.11; *11QSongs of Sabbath Sacrifice* (11Q17) 10.5.

of the rationale seems less generically Christian (focused on the gospel) and more addressed to the audience's precarious social situation. The instructions regarding subjects of kings (2:13), slaves (2:18–25), and wives of nonbelievers (3:1–6) do not mandate maintaining monarchy, slavery, or patriarchal forms of marriage in all societies. (Indeed, attempts to resurrect those structures against current social paradigms would undercut the attempts at peace with society for which these instructions were designed.) These are *human* institutions (2:13), and Peter himself recognizes that they may act unjustly (2:19). The particular instructions do, however, illustrate the principle of honoring social roles where possible for the sake of Christian witness (2:12–13).

We might divide the exhortations among four (overlapping) categories, all "on account of the Lord" (2:13 AT):

- Counter misrepresentation by living in ways that honor God (2:12, 15; 3:1–2, 16).
- Be encouraged because God favors those who suffer unjustly (2:19–20).
- Follow Christ's example of suffering graciously (2:21–25).
- Recognize more ancient, biblical examples of submission (3:5–6).

None of this suggests that believers should seek suffering or subordination; it does, however, instruct believers locked in such situations to respond with grace rather than retaliation. Still, these four categories (of which the first and third seem most prominent) do not exhaust grounds for behavior outside 2:12–3:6. In 2:11, believers are urged to avoid fleshly lusts because they do not belong to this world. In 3:7–12, one should be gracious specifically toward a wife, and more generally toward others, or God will not hear one's prayers.

Do Not Act as the World Does (2:11–12)

Verses 11–12 are key for what follows, but they also relate to the preceding section. As members of a new people (2:9–10), Christ-followers are aliens on earth (1:1, 17; 2:11), but we should behave honorably in human societies, just as societies expected of other resident aliens (2:12–14). (For discussion of the roles of resident aliens, see comment on 1:1.) This is the first of two times that Peter "urges" (*parakaleō*) them (2:11; 5:1), and therefore an important key point in a letter the purpose of which was partly to "encourage" (*parakaleō*) them (5:12).

The Greek terms in 2:11 that the NIV renders as **foreigners** and **exiles** (which many scholars relate to the ancient concept of resident aliens) appear together only twice in the most common Greek version of the Old Testament. Abraham is a "foreigner" and "resident alien" among long-term residents of

Canaan (Gen. 23:4), and the psalmist, echoing Abraham's experience, is a "foreigner" and "resident alien" before God, like his ancestors (Ps. 39:12 [LXX 38:13]). The former term is more frequent and applies initially to the patriarchs in a land promised to them but not yet theirs (Gen. 23:4), and for Israel in Egypt (Gen. 15:13; Exod. 2:22; Deut. 23:7 [LXX 23:8]) or Moses in Midian (Exod. 18:3). The psalm depicts the fleeting character of life under God's discipline but fits well into Peter's motif that life in this world is merely transitory (cf. 1 Pet. 1:24). A similar combination declares that God's own people are just aliens (LXX: *prosēlytoi*, which came to mean "proselytes") and foreigners with him in his land (Lev. 25:23).

This world is not our home; it is, however, the arena for our only opportunity in eternity to witness to nonbelievers and to demonstrate our love for God in the face of adversity.

The NIV's **sinful desires** are more literally "fleshly" desires. Ancients often thought in terms of bodily desires, a concept we might compare with our understanding of hormones, libido, and so forth, although today we understand that mind and body are much more closely intertwined than was recognized by many ancient philosophers, especially in the Platonic tradition. Biological desires themselves serve essential functions, but like our forebears, we would agree at least in principle that they also must be governed and channeled appropriately. Virtuous thinking includes the proper governing of passions.

Some diaspora Jews used language about soul and body much the way Greeks did. The pre-Christian Wisdom of Solomon, for example, notes that "the perishable body weighs down the soul" (Wis. 9:15 AT). Josephus views the soul as afflicted by the body's defilements until freed from the body at death.[26] Despite the contrast between flesh and human soul in 1 Pet. 2:11, however, Peter elsewhere contrasts flesh and God's Spirit in a more typical Judean manner (3:18; 4:6; cf. Gen. 6:3). The Qumran scrolls develop the sense of the weakness of "flesh" in a moral direction, including its vulnerability to sin,[27] a sense that the equivalent Greek term often bears in Paul's letters.[28] Peter's language should thus not be pushed too far here. We rule our passions not because the body is bad but because providing moral guidance is not the proper function of its God-given passions.

26. Josephus, *Against Apion* 2.203. Like some Greek philosophers, he even speaks of the soul as being a portion of the divine (*Jewish War* 3.272).

27. Flusser, *Judaism*, 62–65. See *1QRule of the Community* (1QS) 3.8; 4.20–21; 9.9; 11.7, 12; *1QWar Scroll* (1QM) 4.3; 12.12.

28. James Dunn correctly notes, "It is precisely the weakness and appetites of 'the mortal body' (= the flesh) which are the occasion for sin" (*Romans*, 1:370). Likewise, "The problem with flesh is not that it is sinful *per se* but that it is vulnerable to the enticements of sin—flesh, we might say, as 'the desiring I' (7.7–12)" (Dunn, *Theology of Paul*, 67).

Ancient thinkers also often used figurative military language (**wage war**) regarding the challenge of passions, as here in 2:11.[29] Indulging fleshly passions (2:11) resembles gentile behavior (4:2–4). Self-centered passions also are not inclined to submit to or respect others (2:13–17). Abstention from some fleshly passions may inflame outsiders' hostile perceptions (4:4), but we can best respond to such perceptions, silencing hostile slanders (2:12), by self-controlled submission and respect (2:13).

Many might slander Christ-followers as **doing wrong** (2:12); this term (*kakopoios*) or its cognate surface also in 2:14; 3:17; 4:15, which together constitute 57 percent of New Testament uses. The phrase **among the pagans** is very common in the Septuagint, sometimes used of Israel's dispersion there. That others **glorify God** because of believers' **good** works may well echo Jesus's saying in Matt. 5:16. **The day he visits us** reflects a phrase in the Greek version of Isa. 10:3 that speaks of the day of judgment. By maintaining honorable behavior (Peter repeatedly uses the term *anastrophē* to refer to behavior [1:15, 18; 2:12; 3:1–2, 16]; the cognate verb in 1:17), we can challenge outsiders' slanders (again, 3:16).

Submit to the World's Authorities (2:13–17)

One should not act as the world does, as if one belongs to it (2:11–12). But neither should one provoke nongospel offense by failing to submit to its laws or by disrespecting its leaders (cf. 2:13–18; 3:1).[30] Such status may not matter in light of eternity,[31] but those who live in the world need to follow its demands that do not contradict faith. In modern idiom, believers must choose their battles, and this is not one we need to fight. If human respect does not ultimately matter, then neither does it cost us anything to offer it to those who desire it.

For Christians themselves, even those who do hold socially superior positions should use them to serve (5:3). Although believers should submit to human systems in which they are foreigners, they do so not because all these systems are intrinsically just but for the Lord's honor—**for the Lord's sake** (2:13). They do this to silence critics of the faith (2:12, 15) and bring nonbelievers to the faith (3:1; cf. 1 Tim. 3:7; 5:14; 6:1; Titus 2:5, 8, 10). Rome's greatest concern about minority cults (in which they included Jews and Christians) was their potential to subvert traditional social structures.[32] It may also be no coincidence that two

29. For example, Xenophon, *Memorabilia* 1.2.24; Seneca, *Natural Questions* 1.pref.5; 3.pref.10; Pseudo-Diogenes, *Epistles* 5. Compare the idea in Prov. 16:32b.

30. John Kloppenborg views 1 Peter as ambivalent toward the civic context ("Associations").

31. Lewis Donelson notes that the semantic range of *hōs* includes both "as" and "as if," potentially relativizing some of the praise of authority here (*I & II Peter*, 71–72).

32. See Keener, *Paul, Women, and Wives*, 139–42; esp. Balch, *Let Wives Be Submissive*, 65–80, 118.

of the major sets of household codes in the New Testament probably were sent, like 1 Peter, from Rome (Eph. 5:22–6:9; Col. 3:18–4:1), and the most explicit call to submission to authorities appears in a letter addressed to believers in Rome (Rom. 13:1–7, esp. *hypotassō* in 13:1).

After speaking of submitting to **every human** system (2:13), Peter offers examples. Ancient elites naturally promoted the ideal of submission to authorities, although even those who urged it might qualify that submission for special circumstances. Ancient writers often narrated household codes—that is, instructions for ideal relationships in households, diverse in form but functionally similar to 1 Pet. 2:18–3:7. (Unlike New Testament examples, however, most surviving examples directly instruct only the male householder.) Sometimes, as here, these household codes appear in a broader set of relational instructions that include civic duties or principles for civic management.

Aristotle instructed the male householder how to rule his wife, children, and slaves,[33] forms adopted by Jewish writers in the diaspora, probably for apologetic reasons.[34] Paul adopts the format but then transforms its approach by framing the codes with mutual submission in Eph. 5:21–6:9 (note 5:21; 6:9).

Peter's first example is that of submission to the king; this example in fact brackets the paragraph (2:13, 17). While the empire included some client kings, most people in the east would envision especially the **emperor** (which the NIV reads into both verses). Provinces, especially those whose leaders appreciated Roman rule, were often lavish in praising their **governors** (2:14). Governors **punish** and **commend** here, much as in Rom. 13:3–4.

People might slander believers as wrongdoers (1 Pet. 2:12), but by being instead good-doers we should merit "praise" (NRSV; NIV: **commend**) from governors (2:14), and so refute the false accusations (2:15). Yet, though it is **God's will** for us to **silence** accusers by **good** deeds (2:15),[35] Peter explicitly allows that God sometimes wills us to suffer for doing good (3:17; 4:19).

The Greek participle in 2:16 suggests that the thought of the preceding context continues. Although believers should **live as free** (2:16),[36] Peter speaks of moral freedom to do good; he is well aware that many of his hearers are slaves (2:18). Paul also offers the paradox of Christian freedom: slaves are freedpersons

33. Aristotle, *Politics* 1.2.1, 1253b; see also 1.2.2, 1253b; 1.5.3–4, 1259b; 3.4.4, 1278b.

34. Josephus, *Against Apion* 2.199–217 (in light of Balch, "Household Codes," 28–29, though other relationships also fall in these paragraphs [cf. Josephus, *Jewish Antiquities* 19.129–31]); Philo, *Hypothetica* 7.14 (cf. Philo, *Decalogue* 165–67; *Special Laws* 2.225–27).

35. Hearers in Greek would appreciate alliteration in 2:15: *agathopoiountas . . . aphronōn anthrōpōn agnōsian.*

36. For alliteration in 2:16, note *eleutheroi . . . epikalymma echontes . . . eleutherian.*

in Christ, and free persons are also Christ's slaves (1 Cor. 7:22). Everyone understood that people sometimes twisted liberty into license,[37] a warning reiterated by early Christians (1 Cor. 6:12–13; Gal. 5:13; Jude 4). We need to beware of voices that promise freedom to do whatever *we* want as opposed to doing whatever *Christ* wants.

As was familiar in moral exhortation, a writer could offer disconnected, short exhortations one after another. Most of those in 1 Pet. 2:17 address the same subject, **honor**. Despite the different renderings in the NIV, the Greek verb in the opening, **show proper respect to everyone**, and the closing, **honor the emperor**, is the same one (*timaō*), underlining Christians' countercultural way of seeking to respect all (for fellow believers, see Rom. 12:10; Eph. 5:21). To **fear** (revere) **God** constituted the fundamental characteristic of Jewish wisdom: living in light of the true God's reality and recognizing that we must give account for all that we do (e.g., Prov. 1:7; 2:5; 9:10). Biblically, honoring God and the king (in the Old Testament, the king of Israel) normally would coincide (Exod. 22:28; Prov. 24:21). In some cities, refraining from worshiping the **emperor** could lead to charges of disloyalty; but like Jews, Christians could honor the emperor while refraining from worshiping him. We cannot give Caesar what is God's, but surely we should give Caesar what is Caesar's.

Slaves to Slaveholders (2:18–25)

The reuse of the term rendered as **submit** (*hypotassō*) from 2:13, and perhaps also its Greek participial form here (also in 3:1), indicates a continuation of the thought from the preceding context. Typical ancient household codes advised slaveholders, not slaves. Peter's audience, however, presumably includes far more slaves than slaveholders, as well as (thus 3:1–6) a disproportionate number of wives with unconverted husbands.

Although the term for "slave" (*oiketēs*) here potentially had a wider meaning than "household slave," Peter addresses urban congregations and adapts household codes, which concerned *household* slaves. He thus addresses especially household slaves, whose conditions generally were superior to those of slaves in the fields and especially the virtual death sentence of slavery in the mines, gladiatorial combat, or galleys. A minority of household slaves even achieved some status and power, and some aristocratic women even married into slavery to improve their social status.[38] Nevertheless, Peter recognizes that

37. See, e.g., Livy, *History of Rome* 5.6.17; 27.31.6; Dio Chrysostom, *Orations* 14.3–6, 18; Josephus, *Jewish Antiquities* 4.145–49.

38. Pomeroy, *Goddesses, Whores, Wives, and Slaves*, 196.

many slaveholders practiced harsh abuses (thus the end of 2:18). Moreover, for many young women and boys, sexual abuse (at least from the slaveholder himself) remained an even graver danger for household slaves than for those in the fields.[39]

Most ancient household codes did not address slaves directly; usually these codes were written to elites who ruled slaves rather than to those who served slaveholders. But in an unjust setting in which slaves could not easily escape their holders' social control, Peter empowers slaves by affirming their own moral volition and identifying them with Christ (2:21–25).

The NIV's **fear of God** in 2:18 has added **of God** to the Greek text. In 2:18, the term for **fear** (*phobos*) is a noun cognate of the verb that Peter uses for reverencing God in 2:17; but Peter uses it also for wives' respect for their husbands (3:2) and Christians' humility (3:16), while rejecting the wrong sort of fear (3:6, 14). Here it applies to enslaved persons showing respect to their holders (with, e.g., ESV; NASB; NET; NJB; NRSV). Peter urges respect even for **harsh** holders; the term translated as **harsh** (*skolios*) nevertheless offers a moral judgment against such holders, suggesting being twisted or perverted from the right way (e.g., LXX Prov. 2:15; 16:28; Phil. 2:15). Although most thinkers agreed that we should avoid suffering when possible, some emphasized the value of suffering justly as superior to suffering unjustly.[40]

The basis for enduring unjust treatment is not that this suffering is just[41] but that one honors God (2:19), who sees and more than compensates with his **favor** (2:20 NASB). God is near the lowly and favors the oppressed, who have only him to depend on (5:5–6); God pays special attention to those who suffer wrongly (5:6–7; cf. 2 Sam. 16:10–12). Who would rather have worldly honor than God's **favor**, if we really believe in God and an eternal perspective that puts things right? Again, we must work for just conditions when possible; but when we are wronged, we know who has our back.

In 2:20, Peter addresses the harsh and unjust conditions of many enslaved persons, which are not unlike (in 2:21) the sufferings of Christ. Slaves could receive a **beating**, even in Jewish circles (Sir. 42:5). Again, Peter is not urging his audience to seek out suffering; rather, he wants to provide meaning and hope in the face of it. The **example** of Christ's suffering (2:21) stands at the center of this section.

39. See fuller discussion and documentation in Keener, *1 Peter*, 178, 185–87; at greater length, Keener, *Acts*, 2:1906–42.

40. Diogenes Laertius, *Eminent Philosophers* 2.35; Musonius Rufus, *Lectures* 3, p. 40.30; Epictetus, *Discourses* 2.2.5.

41. Contrast Aristotle, for whom by definition a slaveholder cannot be unjust to his slave, since the slave is property (*Nicomachean Ethics* 5.6.8–9, cited in Kelly, *Peter and Jude*, 116).

A Instruction for everyone (2:13–17)
  B Instruction for slaves (2:18–20)
    C Christ's example (2:21–25)
  B′ Instruction for wives (and husbands) (3:1–7)
A′ Instruction for everyone (3:8–12)[42]

Although Peter invites most explicitly slaves and wives of unbelievers to identify with Christ, the model proves relevant for all suffering believers. In most of the letter, believers face suffering for Christ; but in 2:18–3:6 and especially 2:18–20, believers may embrace Christ's model and name in any suffering that they may face, so long as it is not on account of their own wrongdoing or folly that risks dishonoring Christ's name. Identification with Christ affirms the sufferer's dignity, even if it cannot immediately resolve the sufferings.

Christ's crucifixion was potentially an uncomfortably relevant example for slaves (2:18), since slaves could be crucified, sometimes cavalierly.[43] That **Christ suffered for you** (2:21) takes for granted substitutionary atonement and reflects the early Christian theme of God's and Christ's self-sacrificial love for us (Rom. 5:5–10; 8:32, 37–39; 2 Cor. 5:14; Gal. 2:20; Eph. 5:2, 25; John 3:16; 1 John 3:16; 4:9–10; Rev. 1:5).

In 2:22, Peter cites Isa. 53:9, again supporting his case from Scripture. Because the servant in Isa. 53 suffers on behalf of his people rather than for his own sin (53:9), in contrast to Israel (cf. Isa. 40:2), early Christians naturally understood this ultimate servant as Jesus (e.g., Matt. 8:17; Acts 8:32–33; Rom. 4:25). The servant mission belonged to Israel (Isa. 41:8; 44:1–2, 21; 45:4; 48:20; 49:3), but Israel initially failed in its mission (42:18–19), so one representative leader suffered on Israel's behalf (49:5–6; 53:4–6).

In 2:23, Peter, like Paul earlier (Rom. 15:3), confirms the Gospels' accounts of Jesus enduring abuse during his passion. Though ridiculed, Jesus refused to resist (Mark 14:65; 15:17–20, 29–32). Jesus taught us to bless those who curse us (Luke 6:28; echoed in Rom. 12:14), a teaching followed by his apostles (1 Cor. 4:12). Given the context of Peter's use of Isa. 53 in 2:22, 24–25, here he may think of Isa. 53:7: twice it repeats that the suffering servant "did not open his mouth" when persecuted. Jesus both taught dependence on God as Father (e.g., Matt. 6:25–33 // Luke 12:22–31) and modeled it when **he entrusted himself** (2:23) to God in a death from which only God could raise him. Peter here reiterates that we can trust God's justice (see 1:17; 2:23; 4:5–6). Jesus's trust in the Father

42. I borrow this chiasm from J. Green, *1 Peter*, 72.

43. Terence, *Woman of Andros* 622–24; Livy, *History of Rome* 22.33.1–2; Seneca, *Mercy* 1.26.1; Martial, *Epigrams* 2.82; Juvenal, *Satires* 6.219–24.

Photo courtesy of Global Christian Relief

Hindu militants deface a church building

who judges justly echoes Jeremiah's experience when facing unjust persecution (Jer. 11:20).

In 2:23, Jesus models the teaching that Peter presents in 3:9, the wording of which likely echoes Jesus's teaching (see comment there). Some others in antiquity taught the ideal of nonretaliation, although they were a decided minority.[44] I never struck back when beaten for my witness. Indeed, in time I developed a positive relationship with one of the assailants. Likewise, putting his arm around an Ethiopian evangelist, Haji, another minister, explains, "I used to beat him." Haji led a radical Islamic group attacking Christians, but as this evangelist repaid Haji's hatred with love, he eventually won over Haji. Now Haji himself faces persecution, but he responds with joyful love.[45] Sometimes God will even make our enemies to be at peace with us (Prov. 16:7).

In 2:24, Peter adapts wording from Isa. 53, which he has just quoted in 2:22, drawing now on Isa. 53:4 and 53:11–12, both of which speak of the servant bearing our sins. Ancient hearers appreciated antithetical paradox, which Peter offers here: death brings new life, and liberation from sin brings righteousness (cf. Rom. 6:4, 11; 2 Cor. 5:14–15; Col. 3:3–5). Like Paul, Peter believes that death to sin with Christ entails not only forensic justification but also the ability to live a new, just life.

44. See, e.g., Philodemus, *Frank Criticism* col. 2a; Musonius Rufus, *Lectures* 10, p. 76.23–24; 10, p. 78.11–19; 39, p. 136.11–16; Maximus of Tyre, *Orations* 12 passim; Philostratus, *Life of Apollonius* 5.39; Diogenes Laertius, *Eminent Philosophers* 6.1.3, 7; *b. Shabbat* 88b, bar. Foundational in Scripture would be Lev. 19:18.

45. Nettleton, *When Faith Is Forbidden*, 24–25.

PENTECOSTAL INTEREST

Healing in the Atonement

Some argue that healing is in the atonement in such a way that it is not even a promise but "a statement of fact" that one may simply claim.[a] Russell Kelso Carter, author of the now famous hymn "Standing on the Promises" (1886), was an early leading defender of atonement-for-healing theology. Later, however, he became sick for three years until he finally obeyed his doctor. After this experience, he himself became a doctor and publicly changed his position in a work written in 1897. He still believed in healing and prayed for the sick, but he doubted that healing could be automatically appropriated apart from God's will.[b]

R. Kelso Carter

Matthew 8 does show that Jesus often healed people at the cost he would soon pay of his death on the cross, but Scripture does not emphasize this point in the same way as salvation from the rule of sin, as if it *always* must happen in *this* life.[c] Jesus's death purchased the renewal of all creation, but we await the fullness of some of these effects (Rom. 8:23). Bishop William Taylor affirmed that Christ's death provided "for bodily as well as spiritual restoration," but he maintained "that the work of physical redemption would not be completed until the resurrection."[d] Likewise, the Assemblies of God position paper on divine healing recognizes that Jesus's death provides for physical healing, but the present experience is proleptic and will be complete only at Jesus's return.[e]

At the same time, Jesus's sacrifice is what makes healing, deliverance, and other gifts accessible as a foretaste of the future, fuller restoration. This is why we can pray with full confidence in God's kindness and power. It is also why we should thank God when he blesses us, remembering what those blessings cost him.

a. Hagin, *What Faith Is*, 7; G. Copeland, *God's Will*, 34; Capps, *The Tongue*, 38; cf. similarly, Jeter, *By His Stripes*, 31.

b. Curtis, *Faith*, 197–99; Opp, *The Lord for the Body*, 32; Reyes, "Theological Framework," 76; Baer, "Perfectly Empowered Bodies," 150–51; Dayton, *Roots of Pentecostalism*, 129–32.

c. See Fee, *Health and Wealth Gospels*, 24–25.

d. Curtis, *Faith*, 194.

e. Assemblies of God, "Divine Healing."

At the end of 2:24, Peter again quotes from Isa. 53, here from 53:5. Although the Isaian corpus sometimes envisions physical healing (Isa. 29:18; 32:3–4; 35:5–6), an application that some early Christians drew from Isaiah (Matt. 8:16–17), the language can also envision healing in a spiritual sense (Isa. 6:10; 57:18), as often in the prophets (Jer. 3:22; 6:14; 8:11, 15; 14:19; Hosea 14:4). The context in Isa. 53 suggests that the servant's death would heal the nation from its sin (53:4–6, 8–9), and this is the sort of healing on which Peter focuses: We may live to righteousness because **"by his wounds you have been healed."** ***For*** [*gar*] **"you were like sheep going astray"** (2:24–25).

Just as Peter adapts Isa. 53:4–5 in 2:24, in 2:25 he adapts Isaiah's next verse: **You were going astray like sheep** (Isa. 53:6: "We all, like sheep, have gone astray"); he returns to the image of sheep and shepherd in 5:2. Here the **Shepherd** is also the sufferer in Isa. 53:9 (2:22), himself a lamb (Isa. 53:7; cf. 1 Pet. 1:19), who lays down his life for the sheep (cf. 1 Pet. 3:18; John 10:11, 15). As rulers of sheep, shepherds already provided a natural image for rulers in ancient Near Eastern, Hellenistic, and Jewish contexts. In Scripture, Moses, David, and others were shepherds of Israel, but by far the most common as shepherd is God. As shepherds provided a natural image of compassionate leaders, the language of **Overseer** suggests the same point even less metaphorically. Both Greeks and Jews used this leadership title; first-century Christians applied it to elders, who were also shepherds/pastors (Acts 20:17, 28; Titus 1:5, 7; 1 Pet. 5:1–2). Jewish people called God himself the ultimate overseer.[46]

Wives and Husbands (3:1–7)

As in other ancient household codes (cf. Eph. 5:22–6:9; Col. 3:18–4:1), expectations for submission relate not only to slaves but also to wives (though the Christian codes, unlike those of Aristotle, address the slaves and wives as moral agents directly). The relation of Peter's instructions to wives of unbelievers (1 Pet. 3:1–6) to the preceding instructions regarding submission to rulers (2:13–17) and slaves (2:18–25) is made explicit in 3:1 with **in the same way** [*homoiōs*].[47] All of these instructions exemplify the initial exhortation in 2:13: "*Submit* yourselves for the Lord's sake to every human authority." Peter's motivation is a specifically Christian one. These power relations are "human"

46. Wis. 1:6; *Sibylline Oracles* 1.152; Philo, *Allegorical Interpretation* 3.43; Josephus, *Against Apion* 2.160.

47. Such language could be used in analogies in ethical argumentation (e.g., Arius Didymus, *Epitome* 2.7.7d, p. 46.26–28; 2.7.11m, p. 88.10–11). Paul Achtemeier sees submission here as explaining how wives fulfill honoring all (2:17) (*1 Peter*, 209).

institutions,[48] but "for the Lord's sake," for the sake of witness (most explicit in 3:1) and silencing hostile talk (2:12), believers in these various roles **submit**. Unlike what Peter says here, other ancient codes often grounded wives' submission in the intrinsic superiority of the male gender.[49]

One must submit to the government (2:13–14) for the sake of peace, and accept society's role expectations for the same purpose. But does this submission to authorities legitimize those *particular* authority structures permanently? In other words, does Peter's letter prescribe monarchy, slavery, and patriarchal marriage structures? Or does he counsel those *within* such situations? Considering the character of ancient social structures may help readers today who respect Peter's counsel to decide whether they should consider such structures universals or merely culturally conditioned.

Although not always observed, modesty and meekness were among the chief virtues traditionally expected for women. A truly prudent wife should "yield in all things" to her husband.[50] Xenophon, one of the more progressive authors of the fifth and fourth centuries BCE, praises his wife for obeying even his mere word.[51] He notes that if a wife misbehaves, it is his own fault if he has not properly instructed her, just as it is the fault of one who tends animals if the animals are poorly trained.[52]

In the first century, Seneca the Elder advises a wife to walk around looking at the ground; if a man greeted her with too much interest, she should act confused and blush.[53] Being progressive for his era, Plutarch urges the husband to control his wife only like the soul lovingly controls the body.[54] He urges that sensible wives wait silently for their husbands' fits of rage to subside before comforting them.[55] Aelius Aristides declares that the wife "should be pleased with whatever the husband says; her place is to be 'ruled,' and he will command her; she will also seek to be girded by his nature, as a better person would treat an inferior one."[56]

An early Jewish sage instructed, "If your wife does not go as your hand directs, cut her off" (Sir. 25:26 AT) (apparently advising divorce). In Philo's ethics, the

48. In this case, not marriage itself (a divine institution), but its patriarchal form. Though, in any case, Peter in 3:1–6 explicitly addresses only wives of unbelievers.

49. For example, Aristotle, *Nicomachean Ethics* 8.11.4, 1161a; Aelius Aristides, *Defense of Oratory* 129–30, §41D.

50. Euripides, *Electra* 1052–53.

51. Xenophon, *Economics* 10.1.

52. Xenophon, *Economics* 3.10.

53. Seneca the Elder, *Controversiae* 2.7.3.

54. Plutarch, *Bride and Groom* 33, *Moralia* 142E.

55. Plutarch, *Bride and Groom* 37, *Moralia* 143C.

56. Aelius Aristides, *Defense of Oratory* 129, §41D (trans. C. A. Behr, LCL 1:357). He compares the husband's superiority to the wife with God's superiority to mortals, the ruler's to the citizen's, and the master's to the slave's (130, §41D) (undoubtedly in different ways).

wife "serves" the husband, and the husband-wife relationship is comparable to father-child and slaveholder-slave relationships[57] Josephus claims that the law of Moses regards women as inferior to men in every respect; the wife should be submissive.[58] Heeding the wife can even merit punishment.[59] Women do not control their lives, early rabbis note, since they are under others' dominion.[60]

Particularly relevant for wives with unbelieving husbands (1 Pet. 3:1) were expectations regarding religion. Writing in the late first and early second centuries AD, Plutarch advises a wife not to cultivate her own friends or religion, but to accept those of her husband.[61] In light of concerns about cults from outside the Greek and Roman sphere subverting family values, the behavior of women in such cults became an apologetic issue. A range of ancient texts reveals "that the lack of submission of wives to their husbands would be a source of slander or blasphemy against Christianity."[62]

Ironically, ancient accusations essentially invert one non-Christian feminist critique of Christianity today. These particular feminist critics often anachronistically read early Christian texts that were designed to assuage the opposite critique in order to protect a minority faith from persecution. Karen Jobes laments, "How ironic it is that words that first-century slaves and wives would have read as affirming and empowering are criticized by some today as enslaving and oppressive."[63] Shively Smith concurs: "1 Peter strategized survival for a scattered population facing real threats of verbal attack, physical harm, and the looming chance of genocide."[64] Keeping his hearers alive was itself a pragmatic form of resistance in that setting, one of the only viable forms.

The husbands in 1 Pet. 3:1 are nonbelievers (2:8; 4:17). Ideally, believers were not supposed to marry nonbelievers (1 Cor. 7:39; cf. 2 Cor. 6:14), but many were converted to faith after their marriage, or had limited input into whom they married (1 Cor. 7:12–15). In 3:1–2, Peter continues to emphasize the role of **behavior** [*anastrophē*] in favorable witness, as he did in 2:12 (also 3:16; cf. 1:15, 17–18). Wives' submission carries on the theme of submission from 2:13–17, already applied to other social subordinates (slaves) in 2:18–20. Insofar as Peter defines submission, it involves respect (3:2), gentleness (3:4), and avoiding attention-getting attire that might dishonor the husband (3:3).

57. Philo, *Hypothetica* 7.3, 14.
58. Josephus, *Against Apion* 2.200–201.
59. Josephus, *Antiquities* 1.49; 18.255.
60. *Sipra Qedoshim* par. 1.195.2.2.
61. Plutarch, *Bride and Groom* 19, *Moralia* 140D. John Elliott (*1 Peter*, 557) notes also Xenophon, *Economics* 7.8; Dionysius of Halicarnassus, *Roman Antiquities* 2.25.1; Cicero, *Laws* 2.8.19–22.
62. Balch, *Let Wives Be Submissive*, 90–92.
63. Jobes, *1 Peter*, 209.
64. Smith, *Strangers to Family*, 165.

Peter underlines the point with an extreme example (further than would usually be expected of Greco-Roman wives) of calling husbands **lord** (3:6). The forms of submission that Peter encourages here are ones that would appeal to typical nonbelieving husbands. The wife's submission to her husband contrasts with the husband being "disobedient to the message" (3:1 AT; NIV: **do not believe the word**). That is, its purpose is to prioritize bringing the nonbelieving partner to submission to Christ.

The **word** or "message" (*logos*) that the husbands disobey (3:1) is the gospel, as in 1:23–25 and especially 2:8 (where more generic unbelievers disobey the message). But because *logos* has a wider semantic range, Peter plays on another sense of it later in the verse. Husbands are not won without the gospel, as if they never heard about it even once. Otherwise, how would they know the cause of their wives' honorable behavior? Rather, they are won without continuing speech. Once people know the gospel, it is often better served by how we treat them than by pestering them when they act resistant.

In 3:2 husbands "observe" (NIV: **see**) their wives' behavior, here recalling the same verb (*epopteuō*) in 2:12, its only other use in the New Testament. Both verses suggest that observing honorable behavior typically leads to conversion or at least respect and honor. Thus it continues the thought of the context by way of a specific example.

The idea of "respect" in 3:2 (NIV: **reverence**) differs from terror or dread, which Peter expressly opposes (3:6). Negative fear could characterize an abusive relationship, which Peter certainly opposes (cf. 3:7). Whereas slaves could escape an abusive situation (2:20) only by running away or purchasing their freedom, in the Greco-Roman world nothing legally forced the wife to stay in an abusive situation.

Ancient moralists often commented on **adornment** (3:3), and how women should dress modestly in public so as not to excite male interest.[65] Another common criticism of excessive adornment was its ostentatious display of luxury rather than simplicity. Peter's disinterest in **gold** surfaced earlier (1:7, 18). Here he starkly warns against outward **adornment, such as . . . wearing . . . clothes**; pressed literally, his words could entail eschewing not only braids and **gold jewelry** but also clothing altogether. Given the Jewish shame of nakedness, and that this would entail much greater immodesty and attention-getting than the practices Peter opposes here, he certainly does not mean that (thus the NIV adds **fine** to **clothes**). Rather, he urges (in 3:4) focusing on the beauty of the heart rather than outer adornment.

65. For example, Seneca, *To Lucilius* 90.20; Juvenal, *Satires* 6.457–73; Apuleius, *Apology* 76; *Testament of Reuben* 5.1–5.

Many ancient thinkers emphasized **inner** versus outer adornment (3:4; cf. 1 Tim. 2:9–10).[66] Rather than "putting on" (*endysis*) costly outward array (3:3), believers should put on, by antithetical implication, virtues of the heart (3:4). Just like his image of putting *off* old ways (2:1), Peter's image of putting *on* virtues fits first-century Christian paraenesis (Gal. 3:27; Eph. 4:22–25; Col. 3:8–12). As always, Peter is interested in what is "imperishable" (NIV: **unfading**) (3:4; cf. 1:4, 23), which Greeks often identified with the inner person.

Being **gentle** (3:4) is appropriate for all believers (3:15), as is being **quiet** (3:4; cf. 1 Thess. 4:11; 2 Thess. 3:12; 1 Tim. 2:2), but the latter is relevant here also in the context of winning husbands **without words** (3:1). Moreover, as already noted, modesty and meekness were among the chief virtues traditionally expected of women in antiquity.[67]

Jewish tradition often appealed to the ancient matriarchs (3:5–6) as models of virtue. Note that the examples that Peter offers here are not examples of abusive relationships, in contrast to the example offered to enslaved persons. Unlike most slaves, wives in the Greco-Roman world did have the option of leaving a marriage,[68] though normally they would have to give up any children (cf. 1 Cor. 7:14).

Peter naturally appeals to the side of the evidence needed to make his point, here that the matriarchs were submissive to their husbands, as he urges Christian wives of nonbelievers to be in 3:1. Sarah obeyed Abraham and called him **lord** (3:6; cf. LXX Gen. 18:12),[69] following cultural conventions in which wives sometimes called their husbands "lord" (*ba'al*).[70] What Peter does not mention, since it is not germane to his point, is that Genesis explicitly recounts also that Abraham obeyed or complied with Sarah's words (Gen. 16:2, 5–6), once at God's command (21:12)! Peter's example need not logically demonstrate that all wives in all cultures must address their husbands as "lord," but it does make Peter's point about respect by entailing that even this degree of respect is a virtuous option in relevant cultural settings.

Ancients often spoke of people who walked in ancestors' ways as their sons or **daughters** (3:6) (on being Sarah's children, cf. Isa. 51:1–2; Gal. 4:31). The motif of "doing good" (*agathapoieō*; NIV: **do what is right**) runs throughout 1 Peter (2:14–15, 20; 3:6, 17; 4:19); for Peter, submitting to husbands constitutes one

66. For example, Justin, *Epitome* 20.4.8–12; Epictetus, *Enchiridion* 40; Plutarch, *Bride and Groom* 12, *Moralia* 139DE; Pseudo-Socrates, *Epistles* 6.

67. On silence, see, e.g., Homer, *Iliad* 1.565–69; Sophocles, *Ajax* 293; Valerius Maximus, *Deeds and Sayings* 3.8.6; Plutarch, *Bride and Groom* 32, *Moralia* 142D; Heliodorus, *Aethiopica* 1.21; Sir. 9:9.

68. Verner, *Household of God*, 40; O'Rourke, "Roman Law," 181.

69. More frequent in a later source: *Testament of Abraham* 5.12; 6.2, 8; 15.4 A; 4.2; 6.5 B.

70. Gen. 20:3; Exod. 21:3, 22; Deut. 22:22; 24:4; Prov. 31:11, 23, 28; Hosea 2:18 (ET 2:16); Joel 1:8.

example of doing good. Sarah did not **fear** in that she was also ready to press Abraham as needed, with God's approval (cf. Gen. 21:10–12).

Peter's implicit biblical basis for not fearing is Isa. 8:12–13, which he will quote in 1 Pet. 3:14. In Isa. 8:12, the Lord warns Isaiah not to "fear" what others fear or to be troubled; Peter blends this contextual allusion with exact wording from LXX Prov. 3:25: "Do not fear terror." Peter's point in 3:14, and thus likely also here, is that even if authorities prove unjust, it is Christ (3:15), not mortals, whom we fear.

As Peter elaborates the general Christian practice of submission to authorities (2:13–14) with respect to slaves (2:18) and wives of nonbelievers (3:1: *homoiōs*, **in the same way**), so he elaborates a sort of submission or humility (cf. 5:5) now with respect to husbands (3:7: *homoiōs*, **in the same way**). He may elaborate more briefly because Christian husbands were fewer than Christian wives, a situation also experienced regarding converts to Judaism in antiquity.

Despite the normal subordination of wives in antiquity, some moralists allowed a degree of mutuality, and this was particularly evident among some first-century Christians (Eph. 5:21; 6:9). Given cultural expectations and Peter's apologetic concern, it is not surprising that he does not repeat the term for "submit" (2:13, 18; 3:1) here. While supporting submission to explicitly human institutions (2:13), Peter does not fix for all cultures what such institutions must be or look like.

Nevertheless, he does speak of showing the wife "honor" (3:7, using the noun *timē*; NIV: **respect**), just as believers must show to rulers and everyone else (2:17, twice using the cognate verb *timaō*). The husband must thus **respect** his wife,[71] who shares with him the same standing before God as an heir of resurrection life. Scholars often speak of women's public honor in ancient Mediterranean society in terms of "shame" or modesty. As a rule, ancient society attributed greater honor to men than to women.[72] Honoring one's wife here is a particular expression of honoring all (2:17), which in turn expresses the respectful behavior expected of all believers of either gender (cf. 2:13–18).

What does Peter mean when he speaks of treating the wife as **the weaker partner**? Ancient sources widely portray women as weaker than men physically, intellectually, emotionally, and/or morally.[73] Peter could think of one or

71. Here mutuality goes beyond even Eph. 5:33. Kurt Schaefer views this instruction as reversing the expectations of Aristotelian codes (*Husband*, 125). At the very least, it suggests mutuality (Smith, *Strangers to Family*, 79).

72. See Ulpian's statement about universal opinion in Gardner, *Women*, 67.

73. Physically, Cicero, *For Milo* 21.55; Lucian, *Dialogues of the Dead* 414 (6.20, *Menippus and Aeacus* 2); *Letter of Aristeas* 250; intellectually, Cicero, *For Murena* 12.27; Valerius Maximus, *Deeds and Sayings* 9.1.3; in leadership, Dio Chrysostom, *Orations* 3.70; both physically and intellectually, Xenophon, *Symposium* 2.9; Livy, *History of Rome* 28.19.13; morally, Livy, *History of Rome*

more of these aspects (commentators most often think physically) in terms of her being **weaker**. The only contextual hint here, however, reflects her need, thus her social position. Socially, she was clearly the more vulnerable member, placing her, from a Christian perspective, in greater need of mercy or attention (cf. Mark 9:35–37; 1 Cor. 12:22). Whatever sphere of weakness is specifically in view, it appears that at least part of the point is that the husband should be sensitive to his wife (cf. Eph. 5:25).

As children born from God (1:3, 23), she and her husband are equally **heirs** (3:7) of the eschatological inheritance (1:4; 3:9), the eschatological grace (the NIV's **gracious gift** here is *charis*) of salvation (1:10, 13). This **gift** involves **life**, inaugurated for believers by Jesus's resurrection and consummated eschatologically at their own (1:3, 23; 2:24; 4:6).

Failure to deal graciously with his sister in Christ would **hinder** the husband's **prayers** (3:7), a dangerous situation in view of the eschatological urgency that demanded prayer (4:7). Jesus, who urges his followers to bless even those who curse us, teaches that unforgiveness can hinder prayers (Mark 11:24–25);[74] Paul recognized that unforgiveness played into Satan's schemes (2 Cor. 2:10–11). **So that nothing will hinder your prayers** (3:7) thus highlights a "spiritual warfare" aspect of marriage (cf. 5:8). Although all couples have some conflicts (Gen. 16:5; 21:9–12; 30:1–2), marital strife can reflect potential demonic input (cf. 1 Cor. 7:5; Eph. 4:26–27).

Peter will explain his own reasoning about hindered **prayers** (3:7) in 3:10–12, where he quotes Ps. 34:12–16: the Lord hears the prayers of those who seek peace, who avoid speaking evil or deceitfully, but God refuses to hear the prayers of the wicked. Dealing graciously with one's spouse is part of righteousness. Other passages suggest the same demand: God attends to the prayers of those who keep covenant with him (e.g., Prov. 15:8, 29; 28:9). Peter has natural reason to work especially from Ps. 34 here, however, since he already began quoting from it in 2:3.

General Exhortation Before God (3:8–12)

Peter concludes the entire section on relationships (2:13–3:7) with a series of related exhortations, starting with a list of adjectives describing virtues (3:8) and moving to antithetical exhortations (3:9). The adjectives (3:8) appear more generic and the antitheses (3:9) more concrete and illustrative. The adjectives

34.2.13; Tacitus, *Annals* 3.33; emotionally, Nicolaus of Damascus, *Life of Augustus* 30; Josephus, *Jewish Antiquities* 4.219; 4 Macc. 15:5.

74. Compare Matt. 6:12–15; Luke 17:4–6; 23:34; 1 Cor. 11:29–30; probably James 4:3.

begin with **like-minded** [*homophrōn*] and end with (lit.) "**humble**-minded" (*tapeinophrōn* [cf. Prov. 29:23]);[75] those who exalt themselves will not get along with others. Greek texts often emphasize being of one mind or soul, which speaks to harmonious cooperation rather than detailed uniformity of thought. Peter's "**humble**-minded" might possibly echo Ps. 34:18 (LXX 33:19), where God saves those broken in heart and "the humble in spirit" (LXX: *tous tapeinous tō pneumati*). We will not agree on every detail, but love and unity in Christ must transcend our differences.

Not repaying **evil with evil** (3:9) is consistent with Jesus's teaching (Matt. 5:39 // Luke 6:29). Although others in antiquity also taught nonretaliation, as noted earlier, the wording is so close here as to indicate that Jesus's teaching provides the basis for this and other New Testament references (Rom. 12:17; 1 Thess. 5:15). Not repaying **insult with insult** fits Jesus's teaching and example (Luke 6:28), as does repaying it with a **blessing** instead (note also Rom. 12:14; 1 Cor. 4:12; James 3:9).

Peter has already shown that this behavior follows the model of Jesus, who did not "repay insult with insult" (2:23 AT [here Peter uses the verb cognate of the present noun]). This model for relationships applies to all dealings with outsiders (2:13–17), including dealings with enslaved persons' holders (2:18–25) and unregenerate husbands (3:1–6). It applies all the more to fellow believers (2:17; 3:7–8). In support of his directive **Do not repay evil with evil** [*kakon anti kakou*] (3:9a), Peter also marshals the following psalm quotation, which three times warns against **evil** (*kakos*) (3:10–12).

If wrongdoing hinders prayers (3:7), doing right makes blessing available (the end of 3:9). Like the wives in 3:7, all believers are heirs, and thus will **inherit a blessing** (3:9), the future promise (see comment on 1:4). The **blessing** may encompass all God's future promises given to the patriarchs (e.g., Gen. 12:2–3; 22:17; 28:4), of which the eschatological Spirit supplies our foretaste (Isa. 44:3; Gal. 3:14; Eph. 1:3). Peter explains that God **called** us to or for this, language that recalls our being called to nonretaliation (with the same Greek expression in 2:21), God's calling us in Christ (1:15; 2:9), and especially here our future destiny of blessing in Christ (see 5:10).

To avoid prayers being hindered (3:7) and to receive promised blessing (3:9), one must be righteous (3:10–12). In this context, Peter presumably applies **life** (3:10) by analogy to eschatological "life" (3:7; cf. 1:3, 23), as did many of his contemporaries. (Such an application of more limited Old Testament passages about life in this age was consistent with the approach of Peter's contemporaries.)

75. The word can mean simply "humble," but I want to retain the rhetorical symmetry between the Greek nomenclature for the first and last virtues.

Keeping one's **tongue from evil** and **lips from deceitful speech** (3:10) is something that Jesus himself exemplified (2:22, using Isa. 53:9); Jesus's followers must do the same, avoiding deceit (2:1) and insults (3:9).

That one must **turn from evil and do good** [*poiēsatō agathon*] (3:11) fits Peter's regular refrain about "doing good" (*agathopoieō*) (2:14–15, 20; 3:6, 17; 4:19), just as **those who do evil** (3:12) fits that motif (2:12, 14; 3:17; 4:15). Possibly echoing the same psalm, other early Christian writers also urged their audiences to **seek peace** (3:11; cf. Rom. 14:19; 2 Tim. 2:22; Heb. 12:14).

Better to Suffer Unjustly Than Justly (3:13–17)

In 3:13, Peter expresses the norm (albeit not an inflexible rule [3:14]) that others are less likely to **harm** (*kakoō*, "do evil") us if we **are eager to do good**. This passage revisits and slightly qualifies the idea in 2:14: authorities should punish those who do wrong and praise those who do right.[76] Here, however, Peter qualifies the previous general statement. He remains aware that some authorities do "wrong" (*kakos*, from *kakoō*) to those zealous for good, and he expects that those who "do wrong" (*poieō kaka*) in this way will face divine punishment (3:12).

When believers, despite doing good (3:13), face persecution (3:14), we must recognize that it is God's will (2:15; 3:17; 4:19). Peter twice uses the term *makarios*, translated as **blessed**, both times in reference to being persecuted with Christ (3:14; 4:14). Both instances correspond to Matthean beatitudes: It is well with those who suffer for righteousness (Matt. 5:10) and with those reproached for Christ (Matt. 5:11). (Beatitudes were a common biblical and ancient Jewish rhetorical form.) Perhaps Peter also thinks of the line in LXX Ps. 34:8 that follows the one he used in 2:3: "Blessed is the one . . ."

The encouragement not to **fear** in 3:14 (cf. 3:6) uses the language of the Greek version of Isa. 8:12. Not coincidentally, Peter's next verse (3:15) echoes the Greek version of Isa. 8:13, while Peter has already quoted Isa. 8:14 in 2:8 regarding Christ as a stumbling stone. Thus, Peter's point is that even if one faces unjust treatment, one should revere the rock (Isa. 8:13–14; 1 Pet. 2:8), Christ the Lord (1 Pet. 3:15), rather than fearing the persecutors (cf. Matt. 10:28 // Luke 12:5). In light of that stone's contextual role as a sanctuary for the righteous (Isa. 8:14a), the righteous need not fear when they face crisis.

After quoting the end of Isa. 8:12 in 1 Pet. 3:14, Peter in 3:15 assumes Isaiah's next verse. Instead of fearing what those under judgment fear, they should fear the Lord himself. Isaiah 8:14 says to consecrate as holy the Lord himself; 1 Pet. 3:15 begins, "consecrate Christ as Lord in your hearts" (AT; the NIV substitutes

76. Compare again Rom. 13:3; see Winter, *Seek the Welfare*, 21.

revere for "consecrate," changing the meaning and missing the Old Testament allusion). As in 2:4a, Peter here applies Old Testament language about YHWH to Christ as divine. Rather than being intimidated (3:14), believers should boldly offer a "defense" (*apologia*; NIV: **answer**) of their faith (3:15; cf. Mark 13:9–11).

Just as all of us as believers should study Scripture, whether we are Bible scholars or not, all of us should know how, at a basic level, to explain and defend our faith when questioned. If "apologetics" becomes the exclusive realm of professional apologists and scholars, it will never reach most of those who need it. No less important is Peter's further warning at the end of 3:15 (or the beginning of 3:16 in some translations), introduced with the strong adversative conjunction "but" (*alla*): **Do this with gentleness and respect**. In contrast to much recent political discourse in the United States, Christians should engage not only inquiry but also disagreement in such a way that hearers recognize not just that Jesus is right but that he is good and makes his true followers good. Although some cultures value more forcefulness (making forceful answers appropriate and still graceful there), in general apologists should answer charges with grace (Col. 4:6; e.g., Acts 26:1–29).

In antiquity, judges and juries decided cases partly on the basis of "character" (*ēthos*). A person's past behavior shaped the believability of charges, and character witnesses mattered. One who had led a life above reproach was more difficult to convict, especially if one had never been previously charged (or at least convicted). If someone is shown to be virtuous, their accusers and slanderers will have to recognize that the accusations are false. Orators in law courts sought to deliberately shame the opposing side's client or witnesses, even reversing the opponents' own charges against them.[77] Peter's interest is not limited to legal settings or reversing charges, but Mediterranean honor-shame culture readily understood the principle that a person's vindication normally shamed their accusers (e.g., Pss. 31:17; 35:26; 119:78). Vindication often happens in this life; when it does not, it will happen at God's day of judgment.

In 3:17, Peter again allows that believers' suffering for doing good may be in accordance with God's will (2:15; 4:19). As noted earlier (and see in more detail the comments on 4:13–16), Peter reflects the widespread moral understanding that it is better to suffer for doing good than for doing wrong. When his wife or a close friend protested that Socrates was about to die an innocent man, he allegedly responded, "What? So you think it would be better for me to die a guilty one?"[78] Peter again (cf. 2:21–23) goes on to ground Christians' suffering for doing right in Jesus's example (3:18).

77. For documentation, see Keener, *Between History and Spirit*, 177–78; Keener, *Acts*, 4:3414–15.

78. My paraphrase; see Xenophon, *Apology of Socrates* 28; Valerius Maximus, *Deeds and Sayings* 7.2.ext.1d; Aelius Theon, *Progymnasmata* 3.105–6; Diogenes Laertius, *Eminent Philosophers* 2.35. Technically, Socrates answered a different question than his interlocutor asked.

Christ's Suffering and Exaltation (3:18–4:2)

Depending on how one interprets the **spirits** in 3:19, this section possibly reflects a chiastic (inverted parallel) structure (3:18–4:5).

A Your slanderers will be ashamed (3:16)
  B Suffer though innocent, in God's will (3:17)
    C For Christ suffered for the unjust (3:18)
      D He triumphed over hostile spirits (3:19)
        E Noah was saved through water (3:20)
        E′ You are saved through water (3:21)
      D′ Christ triumphed over hostile spirits (3:22)
    C′ For Christ suffered (4:1a)
  B′ Suffer in God's will (4:1b–2)
A′ Your slanderers will be ashamed (4:3–5)

Rhetorically, 3:18 displays antitheses: **the righteous for the unrighteous**, and **put to death in the body but made alive by the Spirit**. The expression *peri hamartiōn*, **for sins**, presumably means a *sacrifice* for sins, in view of the frequent use of this phrase with sacrifices (e.g., Lev. 5:6–7, 11; 7:37; and passim; Num. 7:16–87; Heb. 10:6, 8, 18; 13:11) and the association of Christ's death with sacrifice elsewhere in the New Testament (e.g., 1 Cor. 5:7; Eph. 5:2; Heb. 9:26; 10:12; probably Rom. 8:3). That Christ suffered as the righteous one (Acts 3:14; 7:52; 22:14) presupposes his sinlessness (1 Pet. 2:22; 2 Cor. 5:21; Heb. 4:15; 7:26; 1 John 3:5). His suffering for the unrighteous fits the notion of vicarious suffering, which was widely understood in antiquity.[79]

The Spirit that **made alive** Christ could refer to Christ being made alive "in the spirit" (e.g., NASB, NRSV), but this hardly sounds like the Christian doctrine of resurrection assumed in 1:21 and articulated at length in 1 Cor. 15:35–44.[80] People in antiquity widely believed in postmortem spirits, which were not unique enough to warrant proclamation as the condition of a unique exalted Lord. Nor would one speak of being **made alive** (as opposed to simply *being* alive) with reference to postmortem existence; this is instead the language of resurrection.

Instead of referring to Jesus's postmortem soul, Peter refers to God's Spirit, a conclusion supported by both earlier biblical (Ezek. 37:1–14) and early Christian

79. See, e.g., 2 Macc. 7:37–38; 4 Macc. 17:22; extensive evidence in Hengel, *The Atonement*; Kim, "Atonement in Early Rabbinic Thought"; Kim, "Atonement in Hellenistic Thought"; and esp. Gathercole, *Defending Substitution*.

80. On the bodily character of resurrection by definition in a Jewish context (e.g., 2 Macc. 7:10–11; 14:46), see Wright, *Resurrection*.

(Rom. 1:4; 8:11; probably 1 Cor. 15:44–45) contexts. Further, the context of the Noah allusion in 1 Pet. 3:20 is Gen. 6:3, which contrasts God's Spirit with humanity as flesh. Early Christian sources sometimes contrast flesh and the human spirit (Mark 14:38; 1 Cor. 5:5), but by far the dominant contrast is between flesh and *God's* Spirit (John 3:6; 6:63; Acts 2:17; Rom. 8:4–9, 13; Gal. 3:3; 4:29; 5:16–18; 6:8; Phil. 3:3; 1 John 4:2).

After being made alive (3:19a) is better rendered as "by that Spirit." Nevertheless, it does imply that Jesus's preaching to the spirits occurred *after* the Spirit raised him. But who or what were **the imprisoned spirits** (3:19)? Some major lines of interpretation are as follows:

1. Most early church fathers, including most Alexandrians such as Athanasius, believed that, between his death and resurrection, Christ preached to the dead in Hades. Many believed that this was a proclamation of salvation for the dead who had been righteous. On this view, it makes sense to associate this proclamation with 4:6. But if Peter envisions Christ preaching to the dead, why would he specify that Christ preached only to the flood generation (3:20)?
2. Augustine tentatively advanced a second view, followed by most medieval Western and most Reformation interpreters. On this view, the preexistent Christ, working through the Spirit, preached through Noah to Noah's generation. This view takes account of 3:20, but the action of 3:20 probably precedes that of 3:19 (note **long ago**, *pote*, "once"). That is, against this view, Christ's preaching comes at some time *after* the flood rather than before it.
3. Most interpreters today, including myself, argue that the risen Christ proclaimed triumph over the fallen angels who sinned in Noah's day (finding Gen. 6:4 as background for 1 Pet. 3:19–20). In a context closer than 4:6, a "fallen angels" interpretation of 3:19 fits 3:22 (especially if one accepts the chiasm suggested above). In Genesis, it was the sons of God, who surely knew God's expectations, whose sin provoked God's declaration of judgment on humanity (Gen. 6:2–3) in the same passage that speaks of his patience (6:3; cf. 1 Pet. 3:20). In that passage, humans were not "spirits," but specifically "flesh" (Gen. 6:3), in a contrast that might possibly also inform Peter's language in 3:18. Most of Peter's contemporaries understood the "sons of God" as fallen angels.

Spirits was an appropriate title for fallen angels or demons (e.g., Mark 1:27; 3:11), as is evident in pre-Christian Judean traditions regarding the fallen angels in Gen. 6 or their offspring (e.g., *Jubilees* 10.5–8; *1 Enoch* 19.1). These spirits

An artistic rendering of the demise of the evil angels

also **were disobedient**, defying God's command (*1 Enoch* 21.6; 106.13–14). The idea that the "sons of God" who sinned in Gen. 6:4 were fallen angels was widespread in Peter's day, as was the idea that they or at least many of them were bound.[81] Jude 6 envisages angels that sinned and were bound; 2 Pet. 2:4–5 concurs and seems to place this event before the flood. The judgment in Gen. 6 delayed **while the ark was being built** (3:20).

What then would be the **proclamation** (3:19) to these fallen angels? The Greek term here (*kēryssō*) could refer (e.g., in the LXX) to declaring either good or bad news. Here the news may be judgment. Moreover, even if the verb refers to the good news of Christ's exaltation, this proclamation nevertheless remains bad news to the fallen angels and their hostile intentions for humanity. Josephus thinks that the fallen angels resisted Noah's reproof.[82] More commonly, Jewish people recounted stories about Enoch announcing judgment to fallen angels;[83] those who knew the story would construe Christ's **proclamation** to spirits here as proclaiming their defeat (cf. 3:22; Col. 2:15).

God's waiting **patiently** (3:20) reveals his mercy (cf. 2 Pet. 3:9, 15), here reflecting Gen. 6:3, where God allows 120 years before the flood. The flood appears elsewhere as a prototype of the future judgment (the book of *1 Enoch*; Matt. 24:38–39 // Luke 17:26–27; 2 Pet. 2:5), and presumably so functions here. As Paul associates baptism with the exodus (1 Cor. 10:2), so Peter associates it here with the flood.[84] By undergoing water baptism now, believers are spared from the fiery cataclysm anticipated at the end. The Noah story was widely known, even among some unconverted gentiles.[85]

Noah's family was **saved** (*diasōzō*) or brought safely through water (3:20)—that is, delivered—prefiguring how believers are now "delivered" or "saved" (*sōzō*) from future destruction (3:21). Peter specifies the salvation of **only a few people** (3:20) to remind us that God does not decide by virtue of the majority, but God is with the minority remnant that is faithful to him.

The word that the NIV renders as **symbolizes** (*antitypon*) does not necessarily deny the literal meaning of what prefigures something else; most of Peter's contemporaries took the flood literally. But ancient thinkers looked for correspondences in history and could use earlier events to portend later ones, whether historically or homiletically. What did **baptism** signify? A range of ritual washings existed, but Jewish proselyte baptism offers the closest analogy

81. For example, *1 Enoch* 54.3–6; *Jubilees* 5.10; 7.21; 10.8–9; *2 Baruch* 56.12–13; Josephus, *Jewish Antiquities* 1.73.

82. Josephus, *Jewish Antiquities* 1.74.

83. *1 Enoch* 12.4–5.

84. The dove at Jesus's baptism (Mark 1:10) might similarly evoke postdiluvian restoration (Gen. 8:11).

85. See Trebilco, *Jewish Communities*, 86–93.

A mikvah, or immersion pool, used for Judean ritual washings

for baptism as an act of conversion.[86] By the late first and early second centuries even gentile writers could take their audience's knowledge of this practice for granted.[87]

Yet a mere act of washing, which anyone with water can undergo without any ritual considerations, does not effect conversion if the person washed does not mean to convert.[88] Otherwise, as some observe, you just go down a dry sinner and come up a wet one. Instead of mere **removal of** [lit., "putting off"] **dirt from the body** (3:21), we need a putting off (2:1) of fleshly desires (2:11). Rather than merely removing **dirt**, baptism acts as a **pledge of a clear conscience before God**. Scholars debate the precise sense of the term that the NIV renders as **pledge** (*eperōtēma*). Suggestions include a "request" (an unusual use of the term) for a clean conscience or the clean conscience being the "answer" (a more common use of the term) to objections to the faith. Likeliest in view of analogies in ancient contracts and elsewhere, however, is a pledge to maintain a good conscience, whether as a pledge offered when undertaking baptism (perhaps in

86. See *m. Pesahim* 8.8; *t. Avodah Zarah* 3.11.

87. Epictetus, *Discourses* 2.9.20; see also Juvenal, *Satires* 14.104; *Sibylline Oracles* 4.162–65; Justin Martyr, *Dialogue with Trypho* 29.1.

88. See *1QRule of the Community* (1QS) 3.4–6; *Didache* 7.4. Basil remarks on this verse that any grace in the water derives not from the water's nature but from the Spirit's presence (*Holy Spirit* 35.13).

response to a question) or the pledge implicitly expressed by baptism itself (cf. Exod. 24:7; Ps. 119:57). Our baptism has irrevocably committed us to Christ. Although the sense "pledge" has less lexical support than the meaning of "answer," it is the majority scholarly position and does explain the verse.

Although only Luke specifically *describes* Jesus's ascension (Luke 24:50–51; Acts 1:9–11; cf. John 20:17), his exaltation is theologically central (Acts 2:33; 5:31; Eph. 4:8–10; Heb. 4:14; 7:26; 8:1; 9:24). His having **gone into heaven** (1 Pet. 3:22) is presupposed in both his current heavenly reign (e.g., Acts 7:55–56; Rom. 8:34; Eph. 1:20; Col. 3:1–2; Heb. 1:3, 13; 8:1; 10:12; 12:2; Rev. 3:21; 5:6–14; 6:16; 7:9–10, 17; cf. Ps. 110:1) and his future coming from heaven (e.g., Phil. 3:20; 1 Thess. 1:10; 4:16; 2 Thess. 1:7; Rev. 19:11–16; cf. Phil. 2:9–10). If the traditional formula in 1 Tim. 3:16 is arranged chronologically, "seen by angels" seems to follow the resurrection, and may imply a heavenly presentation of the exalted Christ (cf. Dan. 7:13–14).

Paired with **angels**, the **authorities and powers** noted here are undoubtedly *heavenly* rulers and authorities, as in Rom. 8:38 (in a context of Jesus's enthronement in 8:34); Eph. 3:10; 6:12 (locating such rulers in "heavenly realms"); Col. 1:16; and probably 1 Cor. 15:24; Col. 2:15. Christians inherited from Jewish circles the understanding that guardian angels of nations ruled the peoples.[89] But can these angelic authorities be described as imprisoned, or are they simply *analogous* to the **imprisoned spirits** in verse 19? Some ancient Jewish sources depict fallen angels as imprisoned beneath the earth.[90] In the clearly pre-Christian *1 Enoch*, however, "the spirits of the angels" who slept with women are imprisoned until judgment day with "the powers of heaven" at the end of heaven and earth.[91] In the later *2 Enoch*, fallen angels are imprisoned and wailing in the second heaven.[92] In typical ancient Jewish cosmology, this is the level of "heaven" directly above the realm of birds. Again, at least some early Christians believed that some spirits in heavenly realms were hostile (Eph. 6:12), though they do not specify them as imprisoned.

The subjugation of angels in 1 Pet. 3:22 likely refers to the same event as the preaching to imprisoned spirits in 3:19, or at the least, refers to the same *kind* of event (Christ's triumph over fallen angels). Christians submit in this age to expected human rank and to one another (*hypotassō*: 2:13, 18; 3:1, 5; 5:5), but we

89. LXX Deut. 32:8; Dan. 10:20–21; *Jubilees* 15.31–32; 35.17; *1 Enoch* 40.9; 89.59–90.19; *1QWar Scroll* (1QM) 15.13–14; 17.7–8; *Mekilta Shirata* 2.112–19.

90. *Jubilees* 5.10; in an abyss: *1 Enoch* 21.7, 10. But as J. N. D. Kelly suggests, in *1 Enoch* 13.9–10 it sounds as if they are *on* the earth (*Peter and Jude*, 155).

91. *1 Enoch* 18.14–19.1 (*OTP* 1:23). This could be an abyss (cf. *1 Enoch* 60.7) where heaven and earth meet at the ocean.

92. *2 Enoch* 7.1–3.

also recognize that the spiritual powers behind earthly authorities have already been subjected to Christ (3:22: **submission**, using a passive form of *hypotassō*).

Christ's suffering **in his body** (4:1) refers especially to his death (see 3:17–18; cf. 2:21, 23). Because of Christ's triumph (3:18–19, 22) after he **suffered in his body** (4:1), **therefore** we should also be ready to suffer (4:1; cf. 2:21). Our suffering is a major Petrine theme (1 Pet. 2:19–21; 3:14, 17; 4:15, 19; 5:10).

Although our union with Christ includes dying with Christ to sin (Rom. 6:3–6; Col. 3:3; cf. 1 Pet. 2:24), the earliest, seminal image of sharing Christ's death involves embracing his suffering with him (Mark 8:34), applicable even to daily commitment (Luke 9:23; 1 Cor. 15:31). Once one reckons one's life as already forfeit and one's commitment is shown by testing, one will not live for other values. One who is truly prepared to die for Christ can also live for him.

When one of my doctoral professors warned that I might not be allowed to graduate because I was too "religious," I remained respectful but refused to let him intimidate me about my faith. Having converted from atheism, I knew what I believed and why, and I had already been beaten and had my life threatened before for my witness. If I would not play down my faith in order to preserve my life, I certainly would not do it to graduate. Happily, my other professors did not share their colleague's antipathy toward faith. I wonder, however, how many doctoral students over the years may have compromised their commitments in order to gain favor from worldly powers.

The Greek term used in **arm** [*hoplizō*] **yourselves** (4:1) can mean, more generally, "prepare" (cf. 1:13), but it does often appear in military contexts. Other passages in this letter also might use military metaphors (cf. 1:5; 5:4, 9; esp. 2:11). **Arm yourselves** might thus resemble Pauline images of putting on spiritual armor (2 Cor. 10:4; Eph. 6:10–20; 1 Thess. 5:8; probably Rom. 13:12; 2 Cor. 6:7).[93]

The sorts of **sin** they were **done with** (4:1) may refer especially to their pre-Christian behaviors listed in 4:3. Although some philosophers applied the language of "passions" to any emotion or desire, Jewish and Christian sources usually use this language only for illicit passions (e.g., desiring one's spouse is not sinful, but desiring someone else's is; cf. Rom. 7:7). Peter illustrates the **desires** in 4:2 (also in 1:14 and 2:11) with concrete examples in the unrestrained party lifestyle described in 4:3. Those who have counted the cost, their lives (4:1), can devote their lives to God's will rather than to what humans value.

93. On spiritual warfare in Paul's writings, see Bowens, *Apostle in Battle*; Keener, "Paul and Spiritual Warfare." For figurative armor for rhetorical "battles," see Horace, *Epodes* 1.18.15–16; Seneca the Elder, *Controversiae* 9.pref.4; Fronto, *Eloquence* 1.16; for moral or philosophic ones, Seneca, *To Lucilius* 109.8; 117.7, 25; Diogenes, *Cynic Epistles* 19; Dio Chrysostom, *Orations* 16.6; 49.10. It is prayer in Wis. 18:21.

Live for God's Assessment, Not the World's (4:3–6)

In 4:3, Peter contrasts his hearers as believers with their **past** as **pagans**; grafted into God's people in Christ (2:9), they are no longer like other gentiles (cf. 1 Cor. 5:1; 1 Thess. 4:5). Jewish (and subsequently Christian) views of gentile immorality usually were harsh. Although monotheists' denunciations of paganism often exaggerated rhetorically, the vast majority of gentiles did worship gods other than YHWH and venerated images (**idolatry**), and most gentile men did at some point in their lives engage in sexual practices that Jewish people considered immoral. **Drunkenness** was common at banquets, often along with sexual immorality; this could also occur at local taverns. Wild partying blended with **idolatry** especially during gentile festivals, although even banquets included libations to deities.

Idolatry belonged to the fabric of ancient society; besides traditional Greek deities, many cities in Asia Minor were particularly devoted to the worship of the emperor. Honoring civic cults and the emperor were patriotic duties; citizens celebrated participation in the festivities as a privilege. In the early second century, venerating the image of the emperor became a capital loyalty test for accused Christians.[94] Believing that refusal to honor deities was impious, gentiles naturally were **surprised** (4:4) at the religious exclusivism of Jews and still more (with less ethnic mooring) of Christians.

Whereas nonbelievers are **surprised** that converts no longer share nonbelievers' lifestyle (4:4), believers should not be "surprised" at nonbelievers' hostility (4:12). Jesus's followers here face verbal **abuse** (4:4), but those who abuse them will eventually **have to give account to** the one whose agents they have despised (4:5). The world might ask for an "account" (*logos*) from God's people (3:15), but it is to God that the world itself will one day render **account** (*logos*; 4:5). Jesus is also **judge** of **the living and the dead** (4:5; cf. Acts 10:42; 2 Tim. 4:1, 8), but here Peter may apply the title to God the Father (cf. 1:17; 2:23).

Because God will **judge the living and the dead** (4:5), the good news was preached to **the dead** so they might **live** though **judged** by humans (4:6). Interpreters divide as to the sense here. Traditionally, many believed that the point is that Jesus preached to the dead in Hades. This approach fits the traditional view of 3:19–20, which does appear in the fairly near context. A majority of scholars today, however, understand the verse as referring to the gospel being preached to those who are *now* **dead** (but were alive when the gospel was preached to them; cf. 1:25). Thus, those unjustly martyred by human judges will ultimately be vindicated and raised from the dead (cf. 4:5).

94. Pliny the Younger, *Epistles* 10.96.

Christ's exaltation over the angelic powers in 3:22 includes his proclamation of victory over them; 3:19 thus likely matches 3:22 rather than 4:6. Given this likelier reading of 3:19, which does not refer to the dead in Hades, there is no reason to suppose that those who embraced the gospel here are the dead in Hades. Rather, those who embraced the gospel and suffered were judged in the flesh (cf. 4:17) for Christ.

But while 4:6 probably does not refer to 3:19, it does draw on the preceding context: as Jesus was executed in the flesh but raised by God's Spirit (3:18), even so believers may be punished in the flesh (i.e., physically) but will be raised by God's Spirit (cf. Rom. 1:4; 8:10–11).[95] In contrast to 3:19, which refers to wicked people who perished in the flood in Noah's day, the people in 4:6 heard and apparently received the gospel before they died, perhaps for Christ (cf. 4:1). The latter have resurrection hope, since they will **live** by **the Spirit**. The meaning of the contrasting phrases **according to human standards** (*kata anthrōpous*, "according to humans") and **according to God** (*kata theon*, "according to God") is grammatically ambiguous. Probably the former refers to death in human terms; the latter to the difference that God makes. The **body** dies, but the **Spirit** (of God) will bring resurrection.

The point is that the righteous dead have hope, similar to what is said in Wis. 3:1–6. There, the foolish thought that the righteous had died (3:2), but in reality, "Even if in people's sight they are punished, their hope is full of immortality" (3:4 AT); God tested them like gold in a furnace, and now it will be well with them (3:5–6; cf. 1 Pet. 1:6–7; 4:12).

Serve Fellow Believers (4:7–11)

In 4:7–11, Peter provides paraenesis; 4:7–9 in particular fits the usual paraenetic format of short, grammatically independent exhortations. Whereas Peter earlier addresses respect for and submission to everyone generally (2:13–17; cf. 3:8–12), and that of enslaved persons (2:18–20) and wives of nonbelievers (3:1–6) specifically, here he focuses especially on treatment of fellow believers.

The nearness of **the end** [*telos*] or climax **of all things** encourages us regarding our future vindication (4:5–6; cf. 1:4–5, 7, 9; 5:4, 6, 10). (The term for "end" here also applies to the "outcome" of faith in 1:9, namely, ultimate salvation, and also in 4:17 to the outcome of judgment for those who disobey the gospel.) Peter proclaims an imminence that comforts and stirs us; he does not offer

95. For the Spirit here as God's Spirit, see comment on 3:18.

specific timing any more than could earlier prophets (cf. 1:10–11) (see comment on 2 Pet. 3:3–4).[96]

Similarly, just as ancient writers in general often connected the language of being **sober** (4:7) or disciplined with not being caught unexpectedly, early Christians often associated it with being ready for Christ's return (e.g., 1 Thess. 5:6–7). This association probably goes back to Jesus's own teaching (Matt. 24:42–51; Mark 13:23, 33–37; Luke 21:36). This warning appears three times in 1 Peter (1:13; 4:7; 5:8). In ancient usage, being **sober** also often included avoiding sexual laxity, lavish banqueting, and other excesses. On being **alert** and thus ready to **pray**, compare also Mark 14:38; Luke 21:36; Col. 4:2.

Love each other deeply (4:8) echoes 1:22, where Peter also urges loving one another, using a cognate form of the term that the NIV renders as **deeply** here. The priority (**above all**) of mutual love among believers fits early Christian ethics (John 13:34–35; 15:12, 17; Rom. 13:8; 1 Thess. 4:9; 1 John 3:11, 23; 4:7, 11–12; 2 John 5). Although ancient Jewish teachers widely valued love, early Christianity was the only movement in which love was consistently and pervasively hailed as the chief virtue. The following context suggests that for Peter, as elsewhere among early Christians, love is to be expressed in actions such as hospitality (1 Pet. 4:9; cf. Rom. 12:9–10, 13; Heb. 13:1–2; 3 John 5–6) and in serving one another with spiritual gifts (1 Pet. 4:10–11; cf. 1 Cor. 12:7; 12:31–13:2; 14:1; Eph. 4:16).

Peter here supports the priority of love by quoting Prov. 10:12. Interpretations vary. That **love covers over . . . sins** might mean (as probably in the proverb itself) that love does not take offense, or that one does not draw attention to others' wrongs. In this context, it might mean that God hides the less serious sins of his people when they value the greater mission of love (cf. James 5:20). Or it could mean that, like the commitment entailed in suffering for Christ, love for one another guaranteed that one would not return to the former way of sin (4:1–4).

Loving one another (4:8) entails offering **hospitality to one another** (4:9; cf. Rom. 12:10, 13; Heb. 13:1–2; a moral criterion for church leaders: 1 Tim. 3:2; Titus 1:8). **Hospitality** here translates a Greek term, *philoxenos*, that means "love for strangers"; it was as central to ancient Mediterranean culture as the pervasive honor-shame dynamic. At one festival in Rome people opened their homes even to passersby, a practice potentially dangerous in urban society today.

Hospitality was considered both a sacred duty and a privilege for the host, especially if the guest is a particularly honorable person, such as an agent of

96. For apocalyptic imminence, see, e.g., *4QPseudo-Ezekiel*[a] (4Q385) f4.2–3; *4 Ezra* 6.18; 8.61–62; *2 Baruch* 23.7.

God (cf. Mark 6:10–11). In antiquity, hospitality included lodging, food, and often being helped on one's way. Three days was a normal stay, with up to a week being acceptable. Cicero honored one guest who stayed with him for a year![97] One must provide good food and drink for even unexpected guests, though even a cup of cold water was acceptable if that was all one had to offer. Ideal hospitality treated one's guest as oneself. To refuse to accept hospitality was an insult to the host's generosity. People were obligated to cherish hospitality ties, sometimes even beyond death into the family's next generation.

As "resident aliens" in a world to which we no longer belong (1 Pet. 1:1; 2:11), we must be a welcoming family or home for one another. That not all passersby are trustworthy complicates matters today, just as it did in urban antiquity. Some in antiquity satirized Christians' gullibility, and a generation after Peter early Christians provided guidelines against abuses.[98] Nevertheless, biblical **hospitality** should provoke changes in how many of us treat fellow believers in need. Meanwhile, we should avoid **grumbling** (complaining), a key sin of Israel in the wilderness (1 Cor. 10:10).

In 4:10–11, Peter urges each of us to use our **gift**, much as does Paul in Rom. 12:6–8; 1 Cor. 12:4–11; 14:26. The Greek term translated here as "gift," *charisma*, was still rare in this period, so it is probably no coincidence that Paul uses the term in a similar way (esp. in Rom. 12:6; 1 Cor. 1:7; 12:4, 9, 28–31; cf. 1 Tim. 4:14; 2 Tim. 1:6; possibly also Rom. 1:11), suggesting a wider early Christian usage. The prophetic element in 1 Pet. 4:11 is another indication that we may read Peter's use of the term *charisma* in the light of wider early Christian usage; prophecy is one of the few gifts invariably among Paul's lists of *charismata*.

We can become too proud or too demeaning of our own gift. As a Bible scholar, I recognize that the work I do needs to be done, but I marvel at the gifts given to those on the front lines. Although I have prophesied, I am not in the same league as some people who have prophesied to me, such as Mesfin Negusse, Julian Adams, Kim Maas, and others. Although I have witnessed some healings, I marvel at many of the accounts of healings from Randy Clark and Ken Fish. Although I have led people to Christ one on one, I am amazed at the frontline ministries of Daniel Kolenda and Rolland and Heidi Baker. That each of these brothers and sisters whom I respect so highly has also expressed appreciation for my ministry as a scholar encourages me that my mostly behind-the-scenes ministry, too, has a place.

Some gifts look bigger than others, and some are rarer than others, but we all need one another in Christ's body. *Your* gifts are needed. The "word" gifts

97. Cicero, *Epistles to Friends* 13.19.1.
98. *Didache* 11.3–6; 12.1–5.

of equipping people with God's message (Eph. 4:11) are meant to equip *all* believers to serve and build up Christ's body with their gifts (4:12). During the outpouring of the Spirit at Asbury University in February 2023, the leaders kept emphasizing that there is no real hero, and there should be no celebrity, except Jesus (cf. 1 Cor. 3:4–9).

It is important for us to remember that gifts are just that: *gifts*. We may grow in them, but we did not earn them and we cannot boast in them (1 Cor. 4:7). Both Peter and Paul use *charisma* in connection with *charis*, **grace** (1 Pet. 4:10; see Rom. 12:6; cf. Eph. 4:7); God's generous benevolence not only rescues us but also equips us to be his agents in gifts for one another. God has graced each of us with different gifts, and therefore we can use these to serve one another. We must share these gifts, since God gave them to us for the church as a whole (Rom. 12:4–8; 1 Cor. 12:7; Eph. 4:11–12). **In its various forms** (4:10) highlights the idea that God uses different individuals in different ways, but it is the same God working through all of us (cf. 1 Cor. 12:4–6, 11).

In 4:10, the term for **stewards** (*oikonomos*) literally means "household managers." Most often these were slaves or freedpersons. This image fits with the image of the church as a divine house or household elsewhere in 1 Peter (2:5; 4:17). Paul likewise uses this language (1 Cor. 4:1–2; 9:17; Eph. 3:2; Col. 1:25); he and Peter might be drawing it from Jesus (Luke 12:42; 16:1).

In 4:11, Peter elaborates this notion of gifts (4:10), although he offers only two sorts of examples (unlike Paul's longer lists).[99] We may speak as those who communicate the oracles of God (the NIV's **very words of God** translates an expression that often refers to prophetic utterances). This may refer to the spiritual gift of prophecy, which Paul sometimes mentions toward the beginning of his lists of spiritual gifts (Rom. 12:6; 1 Cor. 12:28; Eph. 4:11). Alternatively, it may refer to all sorts of speaking (including teaching), suggesting that we should depend on God's grace for any speaking, as we would *if* we were prophesying (cf. Eph. 4:29). Scripture and ancient Jewish thought often linked the Spirit and prophecy (e.g., 2 Chron. 20:14–15; Neh. 9:30; Joel 2:28; Mic. 3:8).

In addition to prophetic speech, Peter encourages anyone who **serves** (*diakoneō*; cf. *diakonia* in Rom. 12:7; *diakonos* in Rom. 16:1; 1 Cor. 3:5; Eph. 3:7; 6:21). In this ministry, too, believers must depend on God's **strength**. (The mention of strength that God **provides** might also evoke the Spirit [cf. Gal. 3:5; Phil. 1:19; cf. perhaps spiritual gifts in Eph. 4:16; Col. 2:19].)

By acknowledging their dependence on God, believers credit God for what he accomplishes through them, bringing him honor and glory. Ancient

99. Paul Achtemeier even treats these as the two comprehensive categories of *charismata* (*1 Peter*, 298), but they are likelier simply prominent examples.

PENTECOSTAL INTEREST

Is the Gift of Prophecy for Today?

God worked through prophets throughout the Old Testament. Despite Moses's desire, however, not all God's people were prophets (Num. 11:29). Yet Joel prophesied that in the final era all God's people—male or female, slave or free, young or old—would prophesy (Joel 2:28–29 [MT, LXX 3:1–2]). At Pentecost, Peter says that the risen Jesus has poured out the promised Spirit (Acts 2:33), confirming the beginning of his messianic reign (2:34–36).

The outpoured Spirit characterizes these "last days" as the time both of all God's people prophesying (Acts 2:17–18) and of salvation through calling on Jesus's name (2:37–38). If God did not pour out the Spirit, Peter's argument for Jesus's exaltation collapses. If this is not the era of prophesying, it is not the era of salvation. If it was the "last days" in Acts 2, it now must be, if anything, "laster days" (pardon the neologism)—still the era of the Spirit and prophecy.

Denying that prophetic gifts remain today risks denying that we are in the age of the Spirit inaugurated by Jesus and celebrated throughout the New Testament. Moreover, while Scripture sometimes addresses local or cultural issues, God pouring out the Spirit of prophecy is a matter of practical theology. No text in the Bible distinguishes among gifts as if some (such as tongues) are merely temporary whereas others (such as teaching) are permanent (e.g., Rom. 12:6–8; 1 Cor. 12:8–10, 28–31; 14:6, 26). No text speaks of gifts passing in this age; they pass explicitly only at Jesus's return (1 Cor. 1:7; 13:8, 12). (Moreover, in 1 Cor. 13:8 prophecy is scheduled to pass when knowledge does; if prophecy has ceased, so has teaching!)

Those who deny that such gifts continue often condemn charismatics for practicing the gifts. Yet deniers of the gifts lack explicit biblical support and themselves contradict New Testament commands to seek gifts and not to forbid tongues (1 Cor. 12:31; 14:1, 39; 1 Thess. 5:19–20). They often worry that prophecy risks extrabiblical doctrine; yet most charismatics recognize that it is teaching, not prophecy, that is meant to provide doctrine. Meanwhile, the teaching that prophecy has ceased, since it is not found in the Bible, *is* an extrabiblical doctrine—the very sort of error that deniers of prophecy fear!

I would define "charismatic" as continuationism-in-practice. It is not enough for us to affirm the continuation of spiritual gifts if we neglect to use them to build up the body of Christ. We need to simply make sure to do this in orderly ways that honor the unity of Christ's body (1 Cor. 14:31, 40) and to evaluate prophecy (1 Cor. 14:29; 1 Thess. 5:20–22). Paul always addresses gifts in the context of Christ's body (Rom. 12:4–8; 1 Cor. 12:12–27; Eph. 4:11–12, 16).

We need to respect *all* the gifts, not just those celebrated in our own circles. Some circles emphasize teaching; others, evangelism; others, tongues; others, prophecy. The body of Christ is a whole body that needs all its members for optimum health. We can live without a hand or an eye, but ideally we would prefer to have them. Some kinds of churches amputate certain members of the body. Some other kinds of churches pile up the amputated members, emphasizing only their favorite gifts. Neither fits the ideal of wholeness for a body. We in different parts of Christ's body have much to learn from one another.

Mediterranean reciprocity and obligation ideals understood that recipients of **grace** (*charis*; 4:10) were to respond with gratitude (also called *charis*), honoring the giver.[100] Thus through these gifts **God may be praised**.

Suffering for Christ (4:12–19)

The term rendered as **fiery ordeal** (*pyrosis*; 4:12) can refer to the furnace used for testing and purifying gold (Prov. 27:21; cf. Wis. 3:6), relevant to the image of fiery testing in 1 Pet. 1:7. The image was very familiar from the Old Testament (Job 23:10; Ps. 66:10; Prov. 17:3; 27:21; Isa. 48:10; Ezek. 22:18, 20, 22; Dan. 11:35; 12:10; Zech. 13:9; Mal. 3:2). The *Didache*, in the late first or possibly early second century, applies it to the period of final tribulation and testing before Christ's return.[101] Peter expects gentiles to be "surprised" (*xenizō*) that Jesus's followers do not share their behavior (4:4), but he exhorts believers **not** to **be surprised** [*xenizō*] that they face testings (4:12).

Peter now gives us reasons to take courage when we are persecuted or mocked for Christ. Those whose suffering shares in Christ's **sufferings** can **rejoice** (4:13), because we will also share his glory (5:1; cf. Rom. 8:17; Phil. 3:10; 2 Tim. 2:12). Rejoicing in the face of suffering for Christ is a common early Christian theme (e.g., Luke 6:22–23; Acts 5:41; Rom. 5:3; James 1:2; cf. 1 Pet. 1:6–8) that reflects Jesus's teaching that we are blessed when mocked for

100. Harrison, *Language of Grace*; Barclay, *Paul and the Gift*.
101. *Didache* 16.5.

him (Matt. 5:11–12 // Luke 6:22–23; cf. 1 Pet. 4:14). When we suffer for Christ, Christ also identifies with us (Luke 10:16; Acts 9:4–5). When soldiers abused Dr. Helen Roseveare in Congo, she felt the Lord saying, "These are not your sufferings. They are not beating you. These are *my* sufferings. All I ask of you is the loan of your body." His words did not reduce the pain, she notes, but it gave it new meaning: "the inestimable privilege of sharing in some little way in the fellowship of his sufferings."[102]

Peter expects that we will **be overjoyed** (*charēte agalliōmenoi*) at Christ's future revelation (4:13), just as he earlier probably spoke of present "rejoicing with joy" (*agalliasthe chara*) while awaiting his future revelation (1:7–8). Jihadists have murdered thousands of Christians (as well as some moderate Muslims) in Nigeria in recent years. Yet ECWA, a Nigeria-based denomination with ten thousand churches, made their theme for 2018 "Joy in Suffering," using 1 Pet. 4:13. Elsewhere in Nigeria, one jihadist grew angry to find Christians singing and celebrating Jesus even though the jihadist had recently bombed their church. He decided that he could eliminate them only by infiltrating their ranks; once there, however, he was won over by their love and became a follower of Jesus.[103] John Sanqiang Cao, a missionary who spent seven years in a Chinese prison for sharing the gospel, noted that he had already expected persecution based on Jesus's teachings: "So when the day came, I had a great peace in my heart. I knew I would pay a price for my faith, so I felt very joyful."[104]

The best way to prepare for such greater hardships is to be faithful in the smaller ones. It was because Daniel and his three friends passed the test of

102. Roseveare, "Counting the Cost," 38–39.
103. Voice of the Martyrs, *I Am N*, 65–67.
104. Cao, "My Faith."

APPLICATION

Learning from the Persecuted Church

Romanian Lutheran pastor Richard Wurmbrand endured years of torture, drugging, isolation, near-starvation, and malnutrition-related disease for his faith.[a] He recounts how his communist torturers in Romania sometimes made him stand motionless for hours in a tight container surrounded by nails that would pierce him if he relaxed.[b]

His wife, Sabina, and other prisoners often suffered the same torture.[c] Sabina often was placed in crowded cells that sometimes held eighty persons, rendering movement nearly impossible.[d] Because of malnutrition she and many other prisoners succumbed to scurvy and other deficiency diseases; dysentery was also pervasive.[e] After someone mocked her for her faith, a guard entertained himself by tossing her into the Danube River. Rocks there broke two of her ribs and left much of one side of her body discolored, but the labor camp's overseers would not excuse her from work. Only God's healing intervention enabled her to continue.[f]

Richard Wurmbrand invited Western Christians to help the persecuted church by sharing their lives of sacrifice and joining them in praying for their persecutors' conversions.[g] He found the complacency of Western Christianity more shocking and painful than the persecutions he endured from open enemies of the cross.[h]

I spent three summers teaching in theological institutions in Nigeria's Middle Belt in the late 1990s, where I experienced astonishing hospitality from brothers and sisters in Christ. But jihadists had already begun murdering Christians as well as moderate Muslims. In 2012, Boko Haram demanded the removal of millions of Christians in the north.[i] From 2009 to early 2023, an international commission estimated the murder for religious reasons of more than 52,000 Nigerian Christians.[j] In 2023, more than four thousand Nigerian Christians died for their faith[k]—on average, ten a day, or one dying for their faith nearly every two hours. Global Christian Relief calculates that in 2024 that figure rose to nearly ten thousand.[l] At the time of this paragraph's writing, secular media in the United States have virtually ignored the crisis.

Organizations that help persecuted Christians include Global Christian Relief (https://globalchristianrelief.org/), Open Doors (https://www.opendoorsus.org/en-US/), and Voice of the Martyrs (https://www.persecution.com/).

a. R. Wurmbrand, *Tortured for Christ*, 51, 142; S. Wurmbrand, *The Pastor's Wife*, 296. Grounds for imprisonment were often fabricated (S. Wurmbrand, *The Pastor's Wife*, 309). This sidebar draws on material from Keener, *Suffering*, 76.

b. R. Wurmbrand, *Tortured for Christ*, 35.

c. S. Wurmbrand, *The Pastor's Wife*, 123, 146. She notes that this torture often was applied all night after a full day of labor.

d. S. Wurmbrand, *The Pastor's Wife*, 109.

e. S. Wurmbrand, *The Pastor's Wife*, 182, 199, 232.

f. S. Wurmbrand, *The Pastor's Wife*, 177–80.

g. R. Wurmbrand, *Tortured for Christ*, 147. He also invites us to feel their pain (153). Apologetics that answered hostile propaganda was also a major part of witness (150).

h. R. Wurmbrand, *Tortured for Christ*, 156.

i. Marshall, Gilbert, and Shea, *Persecuted*, 242, 286.

j. Cited in Global Christian Relief, "Persecution Reports: Nigeria," https://globalchristianrelief.org/christian-persecution/countries/nigeria/.

k. Chimtom, "Nigerian Christians."

l. Global Christian Relief, "The 2025 Global Christian Relief Red List," https://globalchristianrelief.org/gcr-red-list/.

the king's food (Dan. 1:8–14) that they were prepared for the tests of the fiery furnace (3:12–18) and the lions' den (6:10–13).

Declaring that those insulted for the **name of Christ . . . are blessed** (4:14) echoes Jesus's teaching ("Blessed are you when people insult you" [Matt. 5:11 // Luke 6:22]) and passion (Mark 15:32; Rom. 15:3). Believers are **blessed** not only because of future glory (4:13) but also because they already experience the **Spirit** who brings **glory**, **the Spirit of God** (4:14 NRSV). The Spirit provides a foretaste of future glory (Rom. 8:23; 1 Cor. 2:9–10; 2 Cor. 1:22; 5:5; Gal. 5:5; Eph. 1:13–14; cf. Heb. 6:4–5).

Unjust suffering invites God's presence and favor (1 Pet. 2:20). Thus, for example, after spending six months in prison for hosting a house church, Sister Tong explained that prison had been "a *wonderful* time" because she felt Jesus's presence with her there like never before.[105] Likewise, driven from his home for following Christ, Iraqi convert Zarguos spent six months sleeping in a cemetery. "It was a wonderful time for me," he explains. Noting God's special presence, he considered it "the best time of his life with God."[106]

That **the Spirit . . . of God rests on** us (4:14) may evoke the experience of the prophets (cf. 4:11; Num. 11:25–26; 2 Kings 2:15). The Spirit empowers some to prophesy (Num. 11:17, 25–26, 29; 24:2; 1 Sam. 10:6, 10; 19:20, 23; 1 Chron. 12:18; 2 Chron. 20:14), lead (Judg. 3:10; 6:34; 11:29; 1 Sam. 16:13), or even exhibit superhuman strength (Judg. 14:6, 19; 15:14). While in the Old Testament the Spirit sometimes rested on individuals temporarily (Num. 11:25–26), here the Spirit **rests on** believers continually, more like Num. 27:18; 2 Kings 2:15. Jewish people emphasized sanctifying "the Name" (i.e., God) and suffering for it; here the **name** is that of Jesus (4:14).

Chains, imprisonment, conviction, and the like were considered causes of great shame in antiquity; most people did not want to be associated with someone so punished.[107] One should not bring reproach on the name of Christ by suffering for real crimes (4:15); but if one suffers as a Christian, one should **not be ashamed** (4:16). Although we recognize that typically it is better not to suffer than to suffer, many ancient thinkers pointed out that it is also better to suffer for doing good than to suffer for doing bad.[108] The term translated as **any other kind of criminal** is simply the Greek word *kakopoios*, a "wrongdoer," and reminds readers to avoid giving any substance to the slanders against them (2:12, 14; cf. the verb *agathapoieō*, "do good," in 3:17). The meaning of the term translated

105. Nettleton, *When Faith Is Forbidden*, 117.

106. Nettleton, *When Faith Is Forbidden*, 253–54.

107. Rapske, *Paul in Roman Custody*, 288–91, esp. 293.

108. Thus emphasizing virtue (e.g., Xenophon, *Apology of Socrates* 28; Musonius Rufus, *Lectures* 9, p. 76.5–11; Pseudo-Crates, *Epistles* 16).

as **meddler** (*allotriepiskopos*) is debated, but here it might be a warning not to tell non-Christians how they should behave as if they were Christians (cf. Prov. 26:17; Matt. 7:6; 1 Cor. 5:9–12; 7:16).[109]

In the earliest period, Christians called themselves "saints," "brothers," "believers," "the way," or "disciples," several of these being terms that outsiders would not concede to them readily. Suffering **as a Christian** (4:16) uses what was probably then still a non-Christian description of Christians. The New Testament includes the title "Christian" only in 1 Peter and in the mouth of non-Christians in Acts 11:26 and 26:28, probably originally to mock Jesus's followers. It was outsiders in Antioch who first called believers "Christians" (Acts 11:26; 26:28). Opponents of Jesus's movement apparently mocked its members by using the language of Roman political parties: "the partisans of Christ" (i.e., of the Judean king), comparable to the pre-Christian Pompeians or Caesarians. They may have misunderstood Jesus's followers as thinking Jesus to be *politically* king of Judea. Understood literally, that charge would entail treason (Acts 17:7), but Antiochenes originally used the title "Christian" merely to make fun of them.

Perhaps in Rome, after debates about a messiah,[110] **Christian** came to be associated with *political* "meddling" (cf. 4:15). Apparently, by 64 CE, people in Rome called the disciples "Christians,"[111] and Roman governors continued to apply the term to the group in legal settings in the early second century.[112] By the second century, Christians themselves adopted the title. Related language for **ashamed** here appears in 2:6 and 3:16; in 2:6, it comes from LXX Isa. 28:16 (also a source for Paul's "unashamed" statements in Rom. 9:33; 10:11). Christians should not be ashamed of their faith (1 Pet. 4:16); those who trust in the rock will not be shamed in the end (2:6). When Christians are dishonored for Christ's **name** (including his reputation), God's Spirit, the Spirit of true glory and honor, rests on them (4:14).

Concern for honor and shame dominated ancient Mediterranean urban relationships, inevitably making the message of the cross appear as folly and weakness to a status-conscious culture (1 Cor. 1:18–23). The world's hostility could provide temptation to be ashamed (cf. 2 Tim. 1:8, 12, 16; 1 Pet. 4:16), but God's servants could trust that they would not be shamed eschatologically

109. Peter is addressing Christians as a small minority within society. In a context where Christians have more social power, such as in a democracy where they and those they influence constitute a majority, they are right to work for standards of justice that prevent some people from oppressing others. Deciding which issues merit vocal involvement remains a matter of debate; whereas we must oppose genocide and rape even in the face of disdain and injury (Gen. 19:9), Scripture does not urge us to supervise non-Christian adult consensual sexual practices (cf. 1 Cor. 5:9–13).

110. Suetonius, *Life of Claudius* 25.4.

111. Tacitus, *Annals* 15.44.

112. Pliny the Younger, *Epistles* 10.96.

(Rom. 5:5; 9:33; 10:11). If ancient Christians could take courage despite their culture's emphasis on honor and the potential for persecution, how much more should we, who often face less? **Praise God** (4:16) is literally, "Glorify God"; that is, honor him, and he will also ultimately honor you. If others ridicule you as a "Christian," Peter says, use this as an opportunity to honor God; in the end, God will remove the shame and vindicate his servants (4:13; cf. Mark 8:38).

Peter warns believers to be ready to suffer for being Christians (4:16) because the time had come for **judgment** to begin (4:17). Nero soon burned Christians alive to light his gardens at night. Soon after that, civil war and massive bloodshed rocked the empire. God can use the wicked to judge his own people (Isa. 10:5; Hab. 1:12), and he can use persecution to discipline and refine us (1 Pet. 5:6–10; Heb. 12:3–11), to make us stronger spiritually. Recognizing God as sovereign, the Old Testament understood many sufferings of the pious as divine discipline;[113] Jewish thought continued to develop this idea in the Second Temple period. Peter is aware of God's sovereignty over all times and seasons (1 Pet. 1:11; 5:6; cf. Dan. 2:21; 7:12; Acts 1:7; 1 Thess. 5:1).

Some see the judgment in 4:17 in terms of expected end-time sufferings before the Lord's coming.[114] Christians did expect an end-time period of suffering and apostasy (2 Thess. 2:3, 10–12; 1 Tim. 4:1; 2 Tim. 3:1; 2 Pet. 3:3; cf. Mark 13:9–13; 1 John 2:18), although viewing it as at least partly present already (e.g., Matt. 24:6–8; Rom. 8:22; 2 Thess. 1:4; 2:7; 1 Tim. 4:1–2; 2 Tim. 3:1–6; 1 John 2:18; Rev. 1:9; 12:1–6). Others believe that Peter envisions here the final judgment, beginning in a proleptic way. Either way, in the Old Testament, God sometimes was stricter with his own people first, since they knew better (Jer. 25:29; Amos 3:2). The Lord could begin judgment with his own house (**household** [4:17]), his own sanctuary (Ezek. 9:6; cf. Mal. 3:1–4). In 1 Peter, God's household is his spiritual house, the spiritual temple of Jesus's followers (2:5).

Peter reinforces the point of 4:17 with a verbatim quotation in 4:18 of the Greek version of Prov. 11:31 (which differs somewhat from the Hebrew). In the context in 1 Peter, the difficulty with being **saved** seems to be the suffering that they endure (4:16–17), which requires perseverance in the face of hardship (2:20; 5:8–10). If God's own people suffer now, how much more can we expect God to punish the wicked?

Suffering **according to God's will** in this context is suffering on account of one's devotion to Christ rather than for one's crimes or stupidity (4:15–16). Peter

113. See, e.g., LXX Deut. 8:5; Ps. 93:10–13 (ET 94:10–13); Prov. 3:11–12; Jer. 26:28 (ET 46:28).

114. Compare *Damascus Document*[a] (CD A) 4.12–13; *1QWar Scroll* (1QM) 15.1; *1QWords of Moses* (1Q22) 7–8; *1 Enoch* 91.7; *Jubilees* 23.13; *Sibylline Oracles* 3.213–15, 635–48, 652–56; 5.74; *Testament of Moses* 7–8; *4 Ezra* 6.24; 8.63–9.8; 13.30; 14.16–18; *2 Baruch* 26.1–29.3; *m. Sotah* 9.15; *Sipre Deuteronomy* 318.1.10.

emphasizes God's will (cf. 4:2), including in 3:17 and 4:19 (and probably 2:15). God is sovereign, a sovereignty displayed not only in him choosing us (1:1–2; 2:9) but also in our suffering.

God can use suffering in our lives, whether as discipline to transform us (4:17), for his honor through our witness (4:16), for testing that proves our faith (1:7), or for other reasons. Suffering thus does not mean that we are bad, or that one who suffers now is worse than someone who does not suffer now. Suffering according to God's will means that we can trust that God has a purpose in our suffering, and that our suffering has meaning, even if wicked people (rather than God) are the ones directly causing it. This does not mean that we should seek suffering; Peter is encouraging those who are in a situation of suffering that they have not chosen (for example, Satan tests Jesus, but Jesus does not test God by putting *himself* in danger; cf. Matt. 4:6–7 // Luke 4:9–12). We can trust ourselves in the hands of God, who is **faithful** and our **Creator**.

Servant Leaders and Mutuality (5:1–7)

In light of the suffering just elaborated, Peter now elaborates church leaders' responsibility for the welfare of the flock (5:1–4). Leaders are not mere time-keeping caretakers; they must equip God's people to *persevere* in hard times.

Peter rests the credibility of his appeal on his threefold role: **a fellow elder**, a sharer in coming **glory**, and, noted between those two, **a witness of Christ's sufferings** (5:1). The other two roles build rapport with his fellow elders, who will also share in glory at Christ's coming (5:5). Peter's authority is distinctive, however, especially as **a witness of Christ's sufferings**. This letter often focuses on suffering (2:19–20; 3:14, 17; 4:1, 13, 15, 19; 5:9–10), including that of Christ (1:11; 2:21, 23; 3:18; 4:1, 13). Although Peter did not witness Jesus's crucifixion (cf. Mark 14:72; 15:40–41; 16:7), he did experience enough of Jesus's passion (14:29, 33, 37, 54, 66–72), and was close enough to the original events and other witnesses, to be able to testify authoritatively about them (cf. Acts 1:22; 2:32; 3:15; 4:33; 5:32; 1 Cor. 15:5). Peter also witnessed a foretaste of Jesus's glory (Mark 9:1–2; 2 Pet. 1:16–18).

Elder was a widespread leadership title in the Old Testament and the contemporary world, recognized among early Christians long before this letter (e.g., Acts 11:30; 14:23; 15:2–6, 22–23; 20:17; 21:18), as was leadership generally (e.g., Rom. 12:8; 1 Cor. 12:28; Phil. 1:1; 1 Thess. 5:12; cf. Heb. 13:17). **Shepherd** (5:2) was a massively widespread image for leadership roles in antiquity (see comment on 2:25). All the New Testament depictions of church leadership predate the adoption of bishops over larger areas, which was apparently already widespread very early in the second century.

Ancient society expected younger persons to respect their elders and defer to them wherever possible. If Peter was roughly twenty when he began following Jesus (most disciples likely were teenagers, but Peter's marriage [Mark 1:30; cf. 1 Cor. 9:5] suggests that he was slightly older), and if he authored this letter shortly before the Neronian persecution, he would be in his mid-fifties by this point, which would make him an elder, though not aged.[115] Peter was clearly also an elder in terms of authority or witness.

The Old Testament often compared Israel to a **flock** and its leaders to **shepherds** (5:2; see comment on 2:25); in the New Testament, too, leaders must be compassionate shepherds who care for God's flock (John 21:16; Acts 20:28; 1 Cor. 9:7; Eph. 4:11; contrast Jude 12). **Watching over** (*episkopountes*; 5:2) is missing in some key early manuscripts but appears in other early manuscripts and may be original; it may evoke the title *episkopos*. It probably belongs to a period when "overseers" (*episkopoi*), "elders" (*presbyteroi* [cf. 5:1]) and "shepherds/pastors" (*poimēnes* [cf. 5:2–4]) designated mostly the same role (Acts 20:17, 28; Titus 1:5, 7), before the need for wider overseers in the early second century.

One may serve either as someone compelled or voluntarily (1 Cor. 9:16–18); Peter urges the importance of being **willing** (5:2) (for volunteers, see 1 Tim. 3:1). Nor should one do it for **dishonest** [lit., "shameful"] **gain**; one must be **eager to serve**. A shepherd whose heart was in serving the sheep would take better care of them than would another (cf. John 10:12–15).

Not lording it over (5:3) reflects Jesus's countercultural instruction for leadership: serving rather than overpowering or flaunting authority (Mark 10:42–45; cf. 2 Cor. 1:24; 4:5). In 5:3, **entrusted** (NASB: "assigned"; ASV: "charge allotted") means that those whom leaders shepherd belong to God's plan for them, not an accident; serving this flock is thus serving God. Instead of leading by fiat, the elders could lead as **examples** (5:3).

Like Peter (5:1), the elders he addresses can expect to share in glory when Christ appears. Peter identifies Christ as **the Chief Shepherd** (5:4), the leader (and in this case, the shepherd) over the other **shepherds** (5:2; see comment on 2:25).

Marble statue of the good shepherd carrying a lamb

115. The age of sixty could demarcate *presbyteroi* ("elders") in Philo, *Special Laws* 2.33.

The term here for **crown** (*stephanos*), when used in its literal sense, referred to a garland of leaves, often used as an award, most prominently the victor's wreath in athletic settings (though it was also used in military settings and for other honors or celebrations). Playing on this image, thinkers sometimes spoke of more worthy garlands, such as garlands of reputation or virtue. Early Jewish sources speak of such garlands and crowns for future rewards,[116] as for martyrs, for example (4 Macc. 17:15). Victory garlands were naturally associated with honor and **glory** (Job 19:9; Isa. 28:5; Sir. 1:11), but this is true in a special way in this passage because the garland is associated with the glory to be revealed at Christ's return (1 Pet. 5:1). Early diaspora Christians often used this garland image (e.g., Phil. 4:1; 1 Cor. 9:25; 1 Thess. 2:19; Rev. 2:10), whether for the reward whose content is life and immortality (2 Tim. 4:8; Rev. 2:10), righteousness or vindication (James 1:12), or glory, as here.

That the crown **will never fade** fits our promised inheritance (1:4) and our birth from the Lord's word (1:23–25). It contrasts with grass and flowers (1:24), as well as with the perishable wreaths awarded to physical athletes (1 Cor. 9:25).

In the same way (5:5) invites younger members to submit to elders the way that Peter has invited elders to humble themselves in 5:1–3; it also corresponds to how Peter introduces instructions to wives (3:1) and husbands (3:7), just as the New Testament addresses young men (Titus 2:6) among the different groups in Titus 2:2–10. This exhortation continues the motif of submission, or deference and respect, to those respected in society, as in 1 Pet. 2:13, 18; 3:1, 5, and the exhortation to humble-mindedness in 3:8–9. Although 5:1 addresses elders in their role as leaders, the idea here is comparative: those who are younger should defer with greater respect to those who are older.

Respect for the aged was a conventional value in ancient Mediterranean society, and people often associated age with wisdom and reserved the highest offices for the aged. In formal settings the eldest usually spoke first; young men rose before elders to offer their seats. Ultimately, however, Peter makes explicit in 5:5–6 that *all* believers should humble themselves. Peter's **all of you** (5:5b) means that both older (5:1–4) and younger (5:5a) must exercise **humility**.

Those who would one day don a wreath of honor (5:4) must now **clothe** themselves **with humility** (5:5b; cf. 3:8). Humbling ourselves frees us to depend on God's grace to exalt us (5:6). This idea revisits the motif of submission seen throughout the letter (2:13, 18; 3:1, 5), climaxing here with a Christian ideal of humility for all believers, ultimately (5:6) as submission to God. **Clothe yourselves** (5:5b) contrasts with what is "put off" in 2:1 and reflects an ancient idiom (e.g., Isa. 52:1; 61:10; Zech. 3:3–4), especially familiar from being clothed with

116. *1QRule of the Community* (1QS) 4.7; Wis. 5:16; *2 Baruch* 15.8.

the divine Spirit in the Greek version of the Old Testament (LXX Judg. 6:34; 1 Chron. 12:19 [ET 12:18]; 2 Chron. 24:20). To support the value of humbling themselves, Peter quotes Prov. 3:34 verbatim,[117] as he recently quoted Prov. 11:31 (4:18).

Despite their different objects, the use of **humble** language in these two adjacent verses (5:5–6) is no coincidence. One humbles oneself under others (5:5) not because one is inferior to them but because, by humbling oneself before others for the Lord's sake (cf. 2:13), one is humbling oneself before God, who is sovereign (5:6). Like nonretaliation, leaving one's honor with God recognizes whose honor really matters and expresses vulnerable trust in God.

Around the time of my doctoral work, I faced some false accusations.[118] Because I did not yet have means to completely prove my innocence, the pastor said that there must be some truth in the accusations or they would not have been offered. He thus restricted me from most ministry. I could look only to God to vindicate me and fulfill what he had called me to do. Thus, I embraced this passage, humbling myself under God's hand and waiting for him to lift me up if it was truly his will. After several years, God did vindicate me and lift me up, but that period of humbling was far better for me spiritually than I recognized at the time.

The grace that God gives to reward the humble in 5:5 (NIV's **favor** is *charis*, "grace") corresponds to God exalting the humble in 5:6. This fits the divine pattern of God exalting those who **humble** themselves (5:6), whether in the Old Testament (e.g., Pss. 18:27; 138:6; Isa. 2:11–12, 17; 57:15; Ezek. 21:26) or in early Christian texts (Luke 1:52; 14:11; 18:14; cf. Acts 7:9–10; 13:17; Phil. 2:8–9). Humbling oneself before God is equivalent to fearing him (cf. 1 Pet. 1:17; 2:17) and entrusting ourselves to God's hand. **In due time** allows for exaltations in the present, though its ultimate and certain fulfillment is when Jesus returns (5:4). James 4:6–10 covers the same material as 1 Pet. 5:5–9.

Because God promises ultimate exaltation (5:5–6), we can entrust our cares to him (5:7). In 5:7, Peter echoes Ps. 55:22 and possibly Wis. 12:13. The translation of *merimna* as **anxiety** risks different connotations in a day when people are medicated for anxiety disorders; the issue that Peter addresses is not problems of the nervous system, but rather mind-consuming worry. Jesus urges his followers to abandon worries or cares (Matt. 6:25, 27–28 // Luke 12:22, 25–26; Matt. 10:19 // Luke 12:11); Paul agrees with the principle (Phil. 4:6), although he freely applies related language to caring about one another's needs (1 Cor. 12:25; 2 Cor. 11:28; Phil. 2:20; cf. 1 Thess. 3:5).

117. Quoted also in James 4:6; *1 Clement* 30.2.

118. Detailed more fully in Keener and Keener, *Impossible Love*, 54–56, but not meriting the space for digression here.

General Exhortation (5:8–11)

In Greek, both **alert** and **of sober mind** (5:8) involve vigilance; for Christians this often means living in light of Jesus's future coming (1 Thess. 5:6). The devil is the **enemy** (*antidikos*; cf. a rough synonym, *echthros*, in Matt. 13:39; Luke 10:19), the ruler of those spirits against whom believers contend (Eph. 6:12). The Hebrew word *satan* means "adversary," fitting the depiction in 1 Pet. 5:8; the Greek word *diabolos* (**devil**), the term here, is the one that the standard Greek version of the OT always uses to translate *satan* (e.g., 1 Chron. 21:1; Job 1–2; Zech. 3:1–2). Used generically, the term also means "slanderer." Satan functions as accuser (Job 1:6–2:7; Zech. 3:1–2; Rev. 12:10), tempter (Luke 4:2; Matt. 4:3; 1 Thess. 3:5; cf. 1 Chron. 21:1), and deceiver (John 8:44).

Ancient writers often contrasted shepherds, who sought to preserve the sheep (cf. 5:2–4), with the latter's predators, of which lions were the most powerful. Scripture already applied this image to enemies (e.g., Pss. 7:2; 10:9; 17:12; 22:21). The translation **prowls around** suits a **lion** (the translation could otherwise be "walking around") and is suitable to the Satan in Job 1:7; 2:2. Ezekiel compares the false prophets of his day with greedy lions (Ezek. 22:25, 28), **like a roaring lion** devouring lives (22:25).

The admonition to **resist** (*anthistēmi*) the devil (5:9) also appears in James 4:7 (where the devil acts as tempter); here the devil persecutes, tempting for apostasy. Likewise, Eph. 6:13 uses this verb in connection with standing firm in resistance, in a context in which the battle is against spiritual powers (6:12). Similarly, Eph. 4:27 tells believers not to give place to the devil. Whereas we submit to human authorities (1 Pet. 2:13–3:7), one another (5:5), and certainly God (5:6), we should **resist** the spiritual power behind many worldly authorities (5:9).

"Spiritual warfare" does not always have to be spooky:

- In Eph. 4:27, we resist the devil by treating one another rightly (4:25–32).
- In Eph. 6:11, we resist the devil with righteousness, salvation, faith, truth, and the like (6:13–17).
- In James 4:7, we resist the devil by opposing the demonic wisdom of hostility and choosing God's wise way of peace (3:13–4:7).
- In 1 Pet. 5:9, we resist the devil by standing firm and not turning from the faith when tested (5:8–9).

The term in 5:9 rendered as **family of believers** (*adelphotēs*) appears elsewhere in the New Testament only at 2:17. **Throughout the world** includes their fellow believers in "Babylon" (5:13). Reminding hearers of others' sufferings was often used to comfort them. Our war is a corporate, not merely individual, one. All believers face temptation and attack (1 Cor. 10:13).

The God of all grace (5:10) consummates **grace** at our future full deliverance (1:10, 13; 3:7; cf. 5:12) and provides it in our suffering (2:19–20), serving (4:10), and submitting (5:5). We may take courage because God himself **called** us (cf. 1:15; 2:9, 21; 3:9; 5:10), here to share in **his eternal glory** (i.e., when we are glorified [5:1, 4]).

Such hope helps us endure testing. Psychologist and Holocaust survivor Viktor Frankl (1905–97) observed that, on average, those who lost hope died much faster in the concentration camps.[119] But our hope is more than wishful thinking; it is secured because Jesus has already risen and defeated death. As Jürgen Moltmann points out, we have not merely "hope," in the English term's sense of mere wishes, but *expectation* that rests on Christ's accomplished victory in history and unfailing promise.[120]

Peter's term in 5:10 for **make you steadfast** (*themelioō*) can apply to laying a foundation, relevant to the image of the church as a building (cf. the noun *themelios* in Rom. 15:20; 1 Cor. 3:10–12; Eph. 2:20), as in 2:5–6. The suffering for **a little while** in 5:10 and 1:6 is **a little** by God's standards rather than ours (Rev. 12:12; 17:10), but it does remind us that triumph will conclude our period of testing, which is of finite duration (cf. Wis. 3:5). What some Greeks called Asianic-type rhetoric (considered more suitable in Asia Minor than the Greek mainland) accumulated related terms (here, **make you strong, firm and steadfast**), but Old Testament prophetic poetry could do the same; for example, "I will strengthen you and help you and confirm you" (Isa. 41:10 AT), and "I will bring back the wandering and bind up the broken and strengthen the failing" (Ezek. 34:16 AT; cf. Eph. 1:19; 3:16; 6:10; Col. 1:11). (For more on Asianic rhetoric, see "Style and Polemic" in the introduction to 2 Peter.)

Epistolary Postscript/Closing (5:12–14)

Peter's closing consists of acknowledgments, greetings, and a final exhortation. **Silvanus** (NIV note; cf. 2 Cor. 1:19; 1 Thess. 1:1; 2 Thess. 1:1) is usually regarded as a Latinized version of the name "Silas" (Acts 15:22–18:5 passim), a traveling companion of Paul in Macedonia and Achaia. **Silvanus** apparently was a Roman citizen (Acts 16:37; suggested also by the name), a fairly rare privilege for those

119. See Frankl, *From Death-Camp to Existentialism*; Frankl, *Embracing Hope*. Frankl's existential courage differs from Christian expectation, but it shows the human need for meaning beyond our finite limitations.

120. During "Expectation and Human Flourishing," a special symposium sponsored by the Yale Center for Faith and Culture, June 22–23, 2015, at the Yale Club in New York City.

from the eastern empire, and it is thus likely that he was fairly well-educated. Just as early second-century tradition says that Peter depended on Mark (cf. 1 Pet. 5:13) for writing his memoirs about Jesus, here Peter might depend on Silvanus to compose this letter.

Peter says that he has **written** this letter **through Silvanus** (5:12). The expression "written through" was used for delivering letters, not just for composing them. Moreover, one normally listed coauthors near the beginning of a letter. Nevertheless, contrary to what some commentators have suggested, "written through" also applies to scribal help,[121] and assistance that did not make one a coauthor could be acknowledged in closing greetings (or not at all; Tertius the scribe inserts himself in Rom. 16:22 only because he is a Christian). The connection of **written** with **briefly, encouraging** probably does suggest a role in composition. Silvanus did participate somehow in composing some apostolic letters (see 1 Thess. 1:1; 2 Thess. 1:1), some with suggested stylistic connections to 1 Peter.

Peter's claim to write **briefly** may sound odd, since most ancient letters were shorter than one hundred words, but it was also a way of implying that he could have gone on much longer (cf. Heb. 13:22). **Stand fast** (*stēte*), rendering the final Greek word in 5:12, may recall "resist" (*antistēte*) in 5:9; we are to stand against the devil, which we do by standing firm in God's genuine grace.

Greetings from others (5:13) were common in letters by this period. Greetings most often appeared "before the farewell wish,"[122] which is close to where they appear here (5:13–14). Just as Peter highlights in 1:2 that his audience is "chosen" (like all believers [2:6, 9]), so near the end, in 5:13, he writes from another **chosen** church. This one is in **Babylon**, surely a symbolic name (just as "Sodom and Egypt" in Rev. 11:8 must be symbolic, perhaps representing the city of the world—i.e., the world system). The vast majority of ancient and modern interpreters understand this city as Rome. **Babylon** could stand for the diaspora world in which Peter's audience are resident aliens (1 Pet. 1:1; 2:11), like Judahites in Babylon of old; but for Peter's audience in Roman Asia Minor, that would also be a fitting description of the wider empire of Rome. By AD 70, Rome had even destroyed the Jerusalem temple just as Babylon had over half a millennium earlier. Even well before 70, however, many Jewish thinkers viewed Rome as one of the evil empires destined to succeed Babylon in Dan. 2:38–40; 7:17.

Mark (5:13) is presumably the same John Mark associated with Paul and the Jerusalem church elsewhere in the New Testament. He ministered in Rome

121. See examples in Keener, *1 Peter*, 393–402, drawing esp. on the work of Esteban Hidalgo.
122. Weima, *Neglected Endings*, 45.

in roughly this period (Col. 4:10; Philem. 24; cf. 2 Tim. 4:11). **My son** was an affectionate title for a younger mentee (1 Cor. 4:17; Phil. 2:22; 1 Tim. 1:2, 18; 5:1–2; 2 Tim. 2:1; Philem. 10). **Mark** was a common Roman name, but far less common in Judea, where Peter had flourished. The Latin praenomen "Marcus" is otherwise unknown in Judea, and it was uncommon enough among Jews that all New Testament references are probably to the same person.

Letter writers often sent greetings to others; in 5:14 Peter invites members of the entire community to **greet one another**. Kisses often expressed familial affection, appropriate to the community of believers as a spiritual family (2:17; 5:9); kisses were also used for many other acquaintances. Among family or peers, such kisses were often a light kiss on the lips. What Peter calls a **kiss of love**, Paul calls a "holy" or "sacred" kiss (Rom. 16:16; 1 Cor. 16:20; 2 Cor. 13:12; 1 Thess. 5:26). Concerned with abuses, later Christians eventually restricted its practice to members of one's own gender. It came to express Christian ideals of spiritual equality.

Peace was more than a greeting; it was a blessing, formally addressed to the recipient but implicitly functioning as a request that God would bless the person with well-being (cf. Num. 6:26; Matt. 10:13; Luke 10:5). Blessings often included, "Peace be on [so-and-so]." Like many letters, then, Peter's begins and ends with a blessing. Like the rest of this letter, Peter's conclusion breathes affectionate concern for the brothers and sisters elsewhere in the world. Peter expects them to carry on his legacy until Christ's return.

2 Peter

Introduction

To keep within space constraints, I cite only a fraction of my research here, but I include what I believe is most useful for following, preaching, and teaching the text. As noted in the introduction to 1 Peter, I supply my own translations for 2 Peter and Jude. My translation here leans more toward interpretive paraphrase (since this is a commentary) than I would actually encourage in a stand-alone Bible translation per se.

Inspiration, Authorship, and Date

The message of 2 Peter is consistent with the message of undisputed first-century apostolic works, one of the ancient church's criteria for canonicity. Spirit-filled believers today may also resonate with Calvin's idea that the Spirit bears witness to Scripture; many of us can attest hearing the Spirit through 2 Peter. The purpose of "canon" (lit., a "measuring stick") is to establish a minimum standard of texts on which the church agrees, by which we can evaluate all other claims to speak for God. As part of what has been accepted as the Christian canon for more than sixteen hundred years, 2 Peter can certainly serve this function.

Regarding authorship, most Petrine scholars today doubt that Peter wrote this letter, although some scholars (especially many evangelical scholars) demur or believe that it includes material that Peter authorized.[1] The differences between 1 Peter and 2 Peter are noticeable, though less dramatic than some contend,[2]

Scripture quotations in the commentary on 2 Peter are the author's own unless otherwise noted.

1. Even Luther regarded the letter's authorship as disputable.

2. For reuse of some of 1 Peter's specific language in 2 Peter, see Gilmour, *Significance of Parallels*, 91–95. Some even find similar scaling; see Barr, "Structure" (attributing the similarities to

and Jerome thought that they could be explained by the use of a different scribal assistant.[3]

Whereas Christians recognized 1 Peter as authentic quite soon after its composition, 2 Peter remained debated long after, so the external evidence for 2 Peter is much weaker than for 1 Peter. Disciples sometimes practiced writing essays in the names of their schools' founders and communicating what they held to be their ideas. Wanting to approve only the minimum of the most certain documents (following ancient expectations for evaluating which works belonged in the canon), had I been on the early church's canon committee (speaking now tongue-in-cheek), I might well have voted against 2 Peter. Happily for the church (and myself as a preacher), though, I was not, and 2 Peter is in our Bible.

It is important to remember that by ancient standards, significant content or authorization from an author might count as authenticity.[4] While scholars may debate the degree of memory of Peter's voice and rhetorical reframing, the author calls himself Peter. This commentary must follow suit, since the commentary is designed to explain the Spirit-inspired text as it stands.

Debated books that the church ultimately recognized as canonical, such as 2 Peter, have a stronger case than books that were not admitted to the canon, though some of those (such as *1 Clement* and the *Didache*) have much more merit than some others (such as *Shepherd of Hermas*).

One reason that the early church debated 2 Peter's canonicity later than most other New Testament books is its use of Jude. As F. F. Bruce notes, whoever directly pulled together the content of 2 Peter "incorporates much of Jude," except for Jude 1–2, 19–23.[5] Where they overlap, 2 Peter is more detailed; 2 Peter rearranges Jude's examples chronologically and softens them with reminders of grace. Peter also deletes Jude's extrabiblical stories and mentions Paul. Some even see 2 Peter as an updated "reissue" of Jude or propose that Jude functioned as Peter's secretary; or (as I think likelier) the author may have simply deemed it efficient to reuse the material, with overlap reused as with Ephesians and Colossians.[6] Matthew and Luke plainly use Mark. Similarly, 1 Pet. 5:5–9 uses the same material as James 4:6–10, whichever of the letters came first. Imitating a work

---

Silvanus). Scalometry examines lengths of sentences and other semantic units, recurrence of words and phrases, and so forth for testing authorship.

3. Jerome, *Epistles* 120.11.

4. Baum, "Content and Form," esp. 383–85; cf. Metzger, "Literary Forgeries," 22. For others upgrading the style of earlier works, see Larsen, *Gospels before the Book*, 114. For later writing of earlier memories, see Iamblichus, *Life of Pythagoras* 35.252–53.

5. Bruce, *Message of the New Testament*, 93.

6. For a reissue of Jude, see Sidebottom, *James, Jude, and 2 Peter*, 65–69, here esp. 69; for Jude as the secretary, see Robinson, *Redating the New Testament*, 193. Compare *Sibylline Oracles* 2.56–148, which borrows from *Pseudo-Phocylides*.

that hearers would recognize (*imitatio/mimēsis*) was also considered an expression of literary or rhetorical sophistication. My best guess (which could still be wrong) is that 2 Peter is an edited work, bringing together for contemporary needs early memories of Peter's apostolic teaching along with such memories of Jude, which may contain material used catechetically by Peter and/or his followers. Whether Peter instructed his editor(s) to incorporate it, or they wrote later and simply considered it a good idea, would be hard to resolve at this remove.

The date of the final version is uncertain, but it is probably (against some scholars) from the first century. Given the strongly Jewish material and eschatological orientation, 2 Peter predates the second-century apostolic fathers. Against earlier academic claims that it polemicizes against second-century Gnosticism, the letter best fits in a first-century Hellenistic Jewish setting.[7] An allusion to 2 Peter's wording appears already in *Barnabas* 15.4, suggesting wide circulation by the time that work was composed (cf. also *2 Clement* 16.3). Whether it dates earlier than about AD 67 depends on whether Peter authorized the current version of the letter directly or it incorporated material only after his death.

Style and Polemic

The editor(s) contextualizes Peter's message in so-called Asianic rhetoric—that is, grander and more bombastic, with lavish description and redundancies as opposed to being concise. The letter abounds in rare words, marking its high style. If Peter writes to Asia Minor, this style may be contextualized as Asianic (note likewise Ephesians).[8] Second Peter shares some vocabulary with 1 Peter, and with some of the other so-called General Epistles it displays grammatical features more complex than is typical in much of the New Testament. The greater complexity reflects forethought appropriate to more literary letters, prepared with special care possibly (and in the case of 1–2 Peter and Jude, likely) with the aid of advanced assistants (like Cicero's secretary Tiro).

The target of Peter's polemic, like that of Jude, need not be limited to a specific known group (suggestions for one or the other include Carpocratians, Gnostics generally, and more plausibly teachers that shared some features with Epicureans).

7. For a first-century date, see Bauckham, *Jude, 2 Peter*, 157–58; Thiede, "Pagan Reader of 2 Peter."

8. Many others rejected Asianic style, esp. when Attic style was dominant; see Cicero, *Best Kind of Orators* 3.8; *Orator* 3.11.43; *Brutus* 8.27; Dionysius of Halicarnassus, *Ancient Orators* 1.1; cf. Dionysius of Halicarnassus, *Isocrates* 2; Longinus, *Sublime* 3.2. For a mediating style, see Cicero, *Orator* 6.21; Dionysius of Halicarnassus, *Demosthenes* 15; Quintilian, *Institutes of Oratory* 12.10.18; Aulus Gellius, *Attic Nights* 6.14. Asianic style suggests also a date before the dominance of the Second Sophistic (though even then some demurred from pure Atticism) (Pliny the Younger, *Epistles* 7.12.2–4; 9.26.1–12), except when composing epideictic (see Fronto, *Marcus Caesar* 3.16.1). For variation within an author, see Suetonius, *Rhetoricians* 6.

A more general reconstruction is sufficient. The gentile world did not share biblical sexual ethics emphasized by Jews and Christians; gentiles also largely rejected their apocalyptic eschatology. It is hardly surprising that some "progressive" voices in the church would challenge the "old-fashioned" Judean convictions of the earliest generation in light of cultural mores in which they felt more comfortable.

In antiquity, witty insults were part of good oratorical skill. When I was in high school, the rhetorical level of demeaning wit rarely exceeded, "Your mother!" to which the customary response was, "No, *your* mother!" Ancients, however, perfected the art of ridicule in more sophisticated manners. Thus, for example, one orator denounces an opponent by charging that his parents did a disservice to the Roman state by having him as a son. Polemic among different Jewish groups charged one another with apostasy and promised eternal damnation.[9]

Some contend that 2 Peter's polemic disqualifies it from speaking for God. Certainly, modern political divisiveness (at least in the United States at the time of writing) warns us that stereotyping polarizes, inhibits dialogue, and debases discourse. Oppressors often stereotype the oppressed. Instead of evaluating ancient sources by modern rhetorical conventions, however, it seems less anachronistic to understand them in light of the pervasive polemical language used by most social groups in antiquity.[10] From the standpoint of Peter (or earlier prophets; or the Dead Sea Scrolls; or Jesus, e.g., in Mark 12:38–40), those misleading and exploiting God's people are the (theological and moral) oppressors, meriting what we might call a sharp postcolonial critique.

My translation does not aim for close word correspondence as much as to communicate the meaning simply. I have thus changed many participles to main verbs and passive to active forms. I have also tried to use wording that differs from major translations, where possible, not to demean those translations but to offer alternatives to what is familiar in order to provoke fresh engagement with the passages.

Outline

1. God's blessings (1:1–4)
2. How to ensure perseverance (1:5–11)
3. Peter's reminder (1:12–15)
4. The transfiguration confirms Scripture (1:16–21)

9. For example, *1QHodayot*[a] (1QH[a]) 10.24; see Johnson, "Anti-Jewish Slander." For executions, see 3 Macc. 7:14–15 (though this is novelistic). For Old Testament and Jewish background, see I. Marshall, *Power of God*, 29–50.

10. Note Andrew Mbuvi's warning against reading Jude too much in light of "our modern sensitivity to political correctness" (while also rightly recognizing the dangers of oppressors stereotyping people) (*Jude and 2 Peter*, 65). Compare other appropriations to protect the global church: Moses, *Contending for the Faith*, ix; e.g., from imported, unbiblical US prosperity doctrine, Amoafo, *Stand Up for the Gospel*, 49–54; touching a wide range of issues, Tamfu, *2 Peter and Jude*; Uytanlet, *2 Peter and Jude*.

5. Beware of the false teachers (2:1–3)
6. Biblical precedent for God judging the wicked (2:4–10a)
7. The wicked's moral stupidity (2:10b–19)
8. Apostates are worse off (2:20–22)
9. The promise of his coming (3:1–10)
10. Live in light of his coming (3:11–18)

Recommended Resources

Amoafo, Emmanuel Kwasi. *Stand Up for the Gospel: Getting the Church Back on Track.* Oasis, 2022.

Bauckham, Richard. *Jude, 2 Peter*. Word Biblical Commentary 50. Word, 1983.

Frey, Jörg. *The Letter of Jude and the Second Letter of Peter: A Theological Commentary.* Translated by Kathleen Ess. Baylor University Press, 2018.

Green, Gene L. *Jude and 2 Peter*. Baker Exegetical Commentary on the New Testament. Baker Academic, 2008.

Mbuvi, Andrew M. *Jude and 2 Peter*. New Covenant Commentary Series. Cascade Books, 2015.

Reese, Ruth Anne. *2 Peter & Jude*. Two Horizons New Testament Commentary. Eerdmans, 2007.

Tamfu, Dieudonné. *2 Peter and Jude*. Africa Bible Commentary Series. HippoBooks, 2018.

Thornhill, A. Chadwick. *2 Peter.* New Cambridge Bible Commentary. Cambridge University Press, forthcoming. (Thornhill's work was published too late for me to engage here.)

God's Blessings (1:1–4)

The opening of this epistle, like good ancient openings generally, builds friendly rapport and introduces various motifs to be revisited in the course of the discourse.[11] Although Peter does not revisit every point, those that he does revisit include the following:

A *slave* of Christ (1:1)	*Slaves* of corruption (2:19)
Christ's *righteousness* (1:1)	Noah preached *righteousness* (2:5); some turn from the path of *righteousness* (2:21); *righteousness* inhabits the new creation (3:13)
Our God *and Savior Jesus Christ* (1:1)	*Our* Lord *and Savior Jesus Christ* (1:11; 2:20; 3:18)
Knowing God and Jesus (1:2)	*Knowing* God and/or Jesus (1:3, 8; 3:18); *knowledge* (about the faith?) (1:5–6); some abandon their *knowing* of Jesus and his way (2:20–21)

11. Many commentators find parallels with ancient decrees, but analogies are hardly limited to such decrees.

Godliness (1:3)	Godliness (1:6–7; 3:11); godly persons (2:9); the ungodly (2:5–6; 3:7)
God's *promises* (1:4)	The *promise* of Christ's coming (3:4, 9) and the righteous new creation (3:13); false teachers' false *promises* (2:19)
The divine *nature* (1:4)	The false teachers' bestial *nature* (2:12)
Believers have *escaped* corruption (1:4)	Some who *escape* may relapse (2:18, 20)
The *world* is a place of corruption (1:4)	God destroyed the *world* of Noah's day (2:5; 3:6); some who escaped the *world's* defilements may revert (2:20)
Lust (illicit passion) causes the world's corruption (1:4)	False teachers play on people's defiling, fleshly *lust* (2:10, 18); end-time mockers follow their *lusts* (3:3)
Believers have escaped *corruption* (1:4)	The false teachers reap *corruption* (destruction) (2:12); they are its slaves (2:19)

Here and elsewhere, Peter sharply demarcates his audience from the false teachers and their followers, reinforcing their distinct social identities.

> [1:1]**From: Simeon Peter, slave and apostle of Jesus Christ.**
> **To: Those who've received a faith worth the same as ours, by the righteousness of our God and Savior Jesus Christ.**

The Gospels give Peter's original name as Simon. "Simon" was a Greek name that had become the most popular Judean and Galilean name because of Sim(e)on Maccabee (1 Macc. 2:65) and because it closely resembles the patriarchal name **Simeon** (see Gen. 29:33). Texts emphasizing Peter's Jewish identity occasionally therefore preferred to call him **Simeon** (Acts 15:14).

The **slave** of a person of high status, such as Caesar, could wield enormous power and status. In the Old Testament, Moses and the prophets were slaves of YHWH. An **apostle** is a commissioned agent; as **slave and apostle** of the Lord of the universe, Peter holds a prestigious role indeed, recognized among those who honor Jesus (cf. 3:2; Rom. 1:1). By contrast, the false teachers are slaves of corruption (2:19).

In 1:1, the word *lanchanō*, which most translations render as **received** (NASB, NIV, NJB, NRSV) or "obtained" (Douay-Rheims, ESV, KJV), usually means "obtain by lot or divine gift" (e.g., Wis. 8:19). One might render it as "gifted" (appropriately, NET: "granted") or "chosen"; because apportioned lots in the Old Testament often have to do with inheritance in the land, "inherited" (cf. BBE: "have a part") might give the sense.[12]

12. For detail on the character of lots in antiquity, see Keener, *Acts*, 1:776–79.

The term translated as **righteousness** (*dikaiosynē*) typically means "justice," or "rightness" by God's standards (2 Pet. 2:5, 21; 3:13). The Greek translation of the Old Testament often speaks of God's righteousness in terms of his covenant faithfulness to vindicate his people, here naturally applied to the work of Christ. Scripture often speaks of God as the **Savior** (e.g., Isa. 43:3; 45:15; 49:26; 60:16); there is no savior except him, the righteous God (Isa. 43:11; 45:21; Hosea 13:4).

Peter here calls Jesus **God**. In Greek, we normally expect two nouns in the same case introduced by a single definite article to refer to the same entity; thus the translation here: **our God and Savior Jesus Christ** (rather than "our God" being distinct from "our Savior Jesus Christ"). Old Testament prophets often spoke of a coming Christ (Davidic king), sometimes identifying him as God coming to his people (Isa. 9:6–7; cf. Jer. 23:5–6). Peter's point was not novel. Paul often applies Old Testament passages about God to Jesus (Rom. 10:9–13, using Joel 2:32; 1 Cor. 8:6, using Deut. 6:4; Phil. 2:10, using Isa. 45:23; 1 Thess. 3:13, using Zech. 14:5). Some other passages also apply to Jesus the Old Testament divine title **God** (Rom. 9:5; Titus 2:13; John 1:1, 18; 20:28), though more commonly they apply to him the Old Testament divine title "Lord."

Treating his audience as fellow believers rather than inferiors, Peter addresses them as those who share **a faith worth the same as ours**. The term emphasizes the value and/or honor (the expression can refer to either or both) of their faith, which is also the apostolic faith of Peter and his colleagues. In a culture that prioritized honor, Peter places himself on the same level with his audience. Just as Jesus, secure in his identity, humbled himself rather than asserting his prerogatives (Phil. 2:6–8), so, too, we can afford to humble ourselves rather than having to always assert our role to others.

> **1:2 May God cause his grace and peace to abound to you in knowing God and our Lord Jesus.**

On this greeting, see comment on identical wording in 1 Pet. 1:2. Here, too, Peter parallels **God** and the **Lord** (cf. Deut. 6:4; 1 Cor. 8:6), the latter specifying Jesus; blessings to hearers normally invoked divine persons, here again indicating Jesus as divine (see comment on 2 Pet. 1:1). Peter here specifies the blessing of **knowing** God and Jesus, an issue of "knowledge" that he will revisit (with the same noun *epignōsis*) in 1:3, 8; 2:20 (cf. *nosis* in 1:5, 6; 3:18, although Peter uses this latter noun in a somewhat weaker way; for the verb *epiginōsko*, 2:21; for the verb *ginōskō*, 3:3).

Knowing Christ frames 1:3–8; no status is greater than this. By apostasy, however, one could turn away from knowing Christ (2:20–21). In Scripture, knowing Christ involves several dimensions. There is a moral/justice dimension to knowing God (Jer. 22:16); merely knowing *about* God's requirements is not enough (Jer. 2:8). Those who keep God's covenant know him (Jer. 24:7; Hosea 2:20), so knowing him characterizes all heirs of the new covenant (Jer. 31:34). Knowing God further implies a dimension of personal relationship with him (see Hosea 2:20; John 10:3–4, 14–15) by the Spirit (John 15:15; 16:13–15; Eph. 1:17); knowing him relationally forever is what eternal life is all about (John 17:3).[13]

> **1:3His divine power has gifted us with everything [needed] for life and reverence [or, "godliness"]. He has done so through our knowing the one who called us to his own glory and virtue.**

Divine power is what enables us to conduct ourselves in God's ways.[14] Second Peter often speaks of **reverence** (*eusebeia*) or "piety," "godliness," "duty" (1:3, 6, 7; 3:11), or of a "reverent" (*eusebēs*, "godly, pious") person (2:9). The term applies here to respecting deity—in Old Testament language, fearing the Lord. Ancient honorary inscriptions underline how highly the Greco-Roman world appreciated the virtue of such *eusebeia*. As God "called" Abraham and Israel (Isa. 48:12; 51:2; Heb. 11:8), so has he **called** us (see 1 Pet. 1:15; 2:9, 21; 3:9; 5:10). Translations often say that he "called us *by* his own glory and virtue," but the dative nouns could also be translated "called us *for/to* his own glory and virtue." The translation **to** makes sense because God conforms us to his divine nature (1:4). Ancient sources often praise both **glory** and **virtue**, sometimes together. **Glory** can mean "honor."

Virtue translates a basic, generic Greek term for "virtue" (*aretē*), which was a frequent topic for intellectual discourse.[15] Many intellectuals, including Stoics, regarded it as the chief goal.[16] The first-century Jewish philosopher Philo uses the term nearly a thousand times, and the first-century Jewish historian Josephus uses it nearly three hundred times. Earlier, *Letter of Aristeas* 272 defines *aretē* as "the fulfillment of good works."

> **1:4Through these he has gifted us with his precious and great promises. That is so that through these promises you may become sharers in the divine nature, escaping the corruption that is in the world by illicit desire.**

13. See discussion in Keener, *Gift and Giver*, 17–35.

14. For the idea, see Gal. 5:22–23; Eph. 3:16–17; Col. 1:11; for the wording, cf. *Letter of Aristeas* 252 (part of Pseudo-Aristeas's style [157, 236]).

15. For example, Dio Chrysostom, *Orations* 69.

16. Diogenes Laertius, *Eminent Philosophers* 6.9.104; 7.1.30; Arius Didymus, *Epitome* 2.7.6e, p. 40.11–15, 26–32. See further discussion in Keener, *Mind of the Spirit*, 227.

Grammatically, the antecedent of **through these** in 1:4 is potentially ambiguous. Does it apply to "power," "life," "godliness," "knowing," "glory," or "virtue" (1:3)? Since it is plural, it cannot refer to merely a single noun but presumably applies to all of the above, to the most direct agents of "power and knowing," or to the final pair, "glory" and "virtue." Verses 3 and 4 are parallel, both using the verb that I have translated as **gifted** (*dōreomai*), which appears only one more time in the New Testament. In 1:3, God's "power has gifted us with everything [needed] for life and reverence"; in 1:4, God **has gifted us with his precious and great promises** that enable us to **become sharers in the divine nature**. In both of these parallel lines, our holy lives are the fruit of God's work in us. It is his "divine" power (1:3) that enables us to share in his **divine** nature (1:4) (both using *theios*, which, like *dōreomai* above, appears in only one other New Testament passage).

God's **promises** in the Old Testament frequently involved inheriting the land, a promise that early Jewish tradition extended to the entire earth.[17] Peter includes in the **promises** the new creation (3:13), a foretaste of which believers experience in our present new-creation life (cf. 2 Cor. 5:17; Gal. 6:15). God's **promises** (in the Old Testament prophets and through Jesus and the apostles) of a future world (cf. 3:4, 9, 13) invite us to abandon this-worldly desires—one reason that scoffers deny such promises (3:3–4).

Ancient thinkers often spoke about sharing the divine mind.[18] Moreover, for Plato and his followers, the ideal is to become like God, including immortality.[19] For many gentiles, some kinship with deity is believed to be innate, especially through reason.[20] By contrast, Scripture teaches that the transformation comes from God, as his gift through Christ. Greek-speaking Jewish sources earlier than and contemporary with 2 Peter use such language in ways similar to 2 Peter, acknowledging one God and the possibility of sharing his immortality and divine character.[21]

Sharing the **divine nature** does not suggest becoming equal with God in rank or authority but rather entails becoming like God in character. This is a key passage for the Eastern Orthodox teaching of *theosis*, or divinization. I like to avoid that language (even Peter does not use it, though it was available in his day) because of some errors that I have encountered (such as an extreme charismatic teaching of "Manifested Sons").[22] Nevertheless, Orthodox Christians, following

17. For example, *1 Enoch* 5.7; *Jubilees* 22.14; 32.19; Rom. 4:13.

18. See discussion in Keener, *Mind of the Spirit*, 127–32.

19. Plato, *Laws* 4.716CD; Maximus of Tyre, *Orations* 26.9.

20. Pindar, *Nemean Odes* 6.4–5; Longinus, *Sublime* 1.2; Musonius Rufus, *Lectures* 17, p. 108.8–22; Dio Chrysostom, *Orations* 12.29; Maximus of Tyre, *Orations* 6.4; 33.7; Menander Rhetor, *Treatises* 2.9, 414.21–22.

21. For example, Wis. 2:23; 4 Macc. 18:3; *Pseudo-Phocylides* 104; Philo, *Allegorical Interpretation* 3.44; *Worse Attacks the Better* 86; *Preliminary Studies* 84.

22. Noted briefly in Keener, *Spirit Hermeneutics*, 122, 380n41, 382n11.

in the footsteps of leading trinitarian advocate Athanasius, do not mean that we literally become new members of the Trinity. Orthodox *theosis* is instead transformation into God's likeness, which is an emphatically biblical notion.

Paul can speak of this transformation in terms of the fruit of God's Spirit working in us (Gal. 5:22–23). The idea of transformation through vision of the divine was readily intelligible to Greeks, although the New Testament grounds the idea of transformation through seeing God in Moses's experience with God in the Old Testament. Beholding God's glory temporarily transformed Moses externally (Exod. 34:29–35). We are transformed into Christ's image spiritually as we contemplate his glory (cf. 2 Cor. 3:18; 1 John 3:6), and we will be transformed fully when we see him as he is (Rom. 8:29–30; Phil. 3:21; 1 John 3:2). In the language of 1 Pet. 1:3, 23, we have been born from God's Spirit; like begets like, and so we reflect his character (so also John 3:5–6; Gal. 4:29; 1 John 2:29; 3:9; 4:7; 5:18). We may need to renew our minds (Rom. 6:11; 12:2) to agree with the identity that God has given us in Christ; neuroplasticity allows for such transformed recognition of our identity. As God's Spirit within us changes us, we increasingly reflect the moral character of God.[23]

The present **world** is subject to **corruption**, decay. Even without knowledge of entropy in physics, ancients recognized that because matter is always changing, it is subject to decay[24]—contrary to whatever shares the **divine nature**. They believed that decay characterized the earthly rather than heavenly realm.[25] Some gentiles argued that pursuing reason enables **escaping** perishable connections[26]—though again in the New Testament such escape comes only through Christ (Rom. 1:22; 8:5–7; 12:2). Jesus's followers become immortal and imperishable not by escaping all physicality (we anticipate resurrection of the body to immortality [Rom. 8:11; 1 Cor. 6:13–14; 15:35–44]) but by escaping the power of sin (2 Pet. 1:4; also 1 Cor. 15:53–57).

Peter later returns to the subject of the wicked's destruction (2:12, 19) and the destruction of the **world** (by the flood [2:5; 3:6]); in contrast to God's promise, their "promise" of freedom is empty (2:19). Whatever is based on mortal flesh will perish (1 Cor. 15:42, 50; Gal. 6:8).

23. On *theosis*, see esp. Gorman, *Inhabiting*; on transformation, see, e.g., Keener, *Mind*; Keener, "Transformation"; Keener, "Transformed Thinking"; on the fruit of the Spirit, Keener, "Comparison of Fruit."

24. Emphasized esp. in the Platonic tradition, such as Philo, *Special Laws* 3.178; Plutarch, *Isis and Osiris* 78, *Moralia* 382F; *E at Delphi* 18, *Moralia* 392C; Porphyry, *To Marcella* 33.516; Iamblichus, *On the Soul* 8.43, §456. Second Peter recognizes matter's perishability, but does not share what came to be a common Platonic antimaterial agenda; rather, human sin corrupted God's good creation (Gen. 3:17; Rom. 8:20–21; *4 Ezra* 9.19–20).

25. Cicero, *Republic* 6.17.17; Plutarch, *Isis and Osiris* 78, *Moralia* 382F.

26. Cicero, *Laws* 1.23.60.

Many ancient thinkers regarded as dangerous *epithymia*, here translated as **illicit desire**;[27] although for many thinkers the problem was desire in general, the New Testament calls us away from its illicit form, desiring what God has forbidden, such as what belongs to someone else (e.g., Rom. 1:24; 6:12; 7:7; Eph. 2:3; 1 Pet. 1:14; 2:11; 4:2–3). Such **illicit desire** from the flesh characterizes the false teachers (2:10, 18; 3:3).

How to Ensure Perseverance (1:5–11)

> **1:5 So for this very reason,**
> **by your trust in God zealously[28] supply all virtue,**
> **and by your virtue, knowledge,**
> **6 and by your knowledge, self-control,**
> **and by your self-control, endurance,**
> **and by your endurance, reverence for God,**
> **7 and by your reverence for God, brotherly love,**
> **and by your brotherly love, the ultimate form of love.**
>
> **8 For if these [virtues] belong to you and are increasing, they don't make you useless or fruitless for [or, "in"] knowing our Lord Jesus Christ.**

The **very reason** might refer to God's provision of everything needed for life and godliness (1:3), or perhaps concerns the danger of destruction (1:4). Because God has supplied what is needed, the virtues in 1:5–7 are available so believers can add each of them.

Ancient writers and speakers often listed virtues, sometimes offering virtue lists and vice lists side by side (e.g., Gal. 5:19–23).[29] Ancient hearers were familiar with the sort of progression of elements found in 1:5–7. This rhetorical format is called *climax*, *sorites*, or (in Latin) *gradatio*.[30] Early Christians sometimes applied this form to encourage perseverance despite challenges, as here (Rom. 5:3–5; 8:29–30; James 1:2–4). Peter's parallel Greek structure here also fits other elite rhetorical preferences, and most virtue categories in the chain were widely

27. For example, Xenophon, *Apology of Socrates* 16; Maximus of Tyre, *Orations* 24.4; Lucian, *Nigrinus* 16.

28. Literally, "exerting all diligence." Virtues grow "by study and practice" (Xenophon, *Memorabilia* 2.6.39).

29. See documentation in Keener, *Galatians*, 508.

30. See *Rhetorica ad Herennium* 4.25.34–35; Demetrius, *Style* 5.270; Rowe, "Style," 130; Anderson, *Greek Rhetorical Terms*, 57–58; Aune, *Literature and Rhetoric*, 446. For examples, see Demosthenes, *Against Conon* 19; Maximus of Tyre, *Orations* 16.3; Porphyry, *To Marcella* 14.242–46; Wis. 6:17–20; *m. Sotah* 9.15; *Sipre Deuteronomy* 161.1.3.

valued in ancient Mediterranean thought. Peter frames them, however, with the supreme Christian virtues of Godward trust and love.

Peter begins with **trust in God** (1:5); God has already supplied us with all we need for life and virtue (1:3–4), so we cultivate the other virtues the same way we experienced new life in Christ to begin with: by *trust* in what God has done for us in Christ (1:5; cf. Rom. 6:11).[31] On **virtue** (*aretē*; 1:5), see comment on 1:3. Virtue enables **knowledge** (1:5–6; here *gnōsis*, perhaps in a generic sense of knowledge about God and his ways [cf. Prov. 1:7]). Philosophers often considered vice the result of ignorance; biblically, however, reverence for God is a foundation for welcoming right knowledge about God (Ps. 111:10; Prov. 1:7; 9:10). Correct knowledge does help empower **self-control** (*enkrateia*; 1:6). The Greek term *enkrateia* denotes restraining the passions or baser emotions.[32] Self-control enables one to endure, and endurance (cf. Rom. 5:3–4) leads to honoring God (2 Pet. 1:6–7).

For **brotherly love** (*philadelphia*), see comment on 1 Pet. 1:22. Fitting the primacy of love in 1 Cor. 13, Gal. 5:22, and 1 Pet. 1:22; 4:8, the climactic virtue here is **the ultimate form of love** (I render *agapē* ["love"] thus here only to distinguish it from *philadelphia* in the context). Although love was a common Jewish virtue and one later first-century sage treated it as the highest virtue,[33] the one ancient movement that consistently ranked love above all else was Jesus's movement. This is because that is where Jesus, the movement's author, ranked it (Mark 12:30–31; see comment on 1 Pet. 1:22).

That these virtues should be **increasing** reminds us that those who are not growing (3:18) risk declining (Heb. 6:1–8; cf. 3:13; 10:25). Those who fail to cultivate virtues (sowing to the Spirit and thus bearing the Spirit's fruit [Gal. 5:22–23; 6:8]) become fruitless for **knowing our Lord Jesus Christ**. For the image of fruitlessness, see comment on Jude 12.

> **1:9For the one to whom such virtues are not present is blind or eye-diseased, because [or, "in that"] they have forgotten that God purified them from their former sins. 10Therefore, my brothers and sisters, be even more zealous to make certain your calling and chosenness! For so long as you do these things I've mentioned, you'll never stumble. 11For**

31. See Keener, *Mind of the Spirit*, 31–54.

32. See Isocrates, *To Demonicus* 21, *Oration 1*; Xenophon, *Economics* 7.27; *Hellenica* 4.8.22. See further comment in Keener, *Galatians*, 523.

33. For example, *Jubilees* 36.4, 8; *m. Avot* 1.12; as the highest virtue, *Sipra Qedoshim* pq. 4.200.3.7; *Genesis Rabbah* 24.7.

in this way God[34] will richly supply you with the entrance into the eternal kingdom of our Lord and Savior Jesus Christ.

Eye-diseased (*myopazō*), translating a rare Greek term, implies squinting as one is going blind from untreatable ophthalmia; here it applies figuratively to being virtually blind, at least regarding the long-range future.[35] If instead of having gratitude, some **have forgotten** what God has done, they risk reverting to the old life (see 2:20–22). The Greek Old Testament uses this term for **purified** (*katharismos*) to refer to making people or things ritually acceptable, often by sacrificial blood (Exod. 29:36; 30:10); Jesus accomplished this for us (Heb. 1:3) at the ultimate cost to himself (Heb. 9:14; 1 John 1:7). God himself has made us the firstfruits of his new creation, sharers in his divine character (2 Pet. 1:3–4), so we can live new and transformed lives; but if we refuse to trust the reality of what he has given us, we can eventually walk away from the very trust in him by which we were saved. To **have forgotten** runs counter to maintaining the *knowledge* of Jesus (1:2–3, 8); better not to have *known* him to begin with than to turn away (2:20–21). Because those who **have forgotten** risk damnation, Peter insists on *reminding* them (1:12–13, 15).

Because we are so accustomed to the language of **brothers and sisters**, rendering the expression instead "my family" might communicate the force even better (cf. Mark 3:35). In a similar way, ancient writers could compare intimate friends to brothers;[36] Jewish people could address fellow Jews as brothers.[37] Meeting together in homes would have further reinforced early Christians' sense of family.

Some people turn away from faith, but choices that we make now can help ensure our perseverance later. Peter earlier urged supplying virtue "zealously" (1:5); now he urges them to be even **more zealous** (1:10; cf. Heb. 6:11); soon he adds his own zeal to prepare them for the future (1:15), and later he reminds them again to be zealous (3:14). Just as God made his prophetic message "more certain" (*bebaioteron*; 1:19), so they should make their own calling more sure or **certain** (*bebaios*; 1:10). Similarly, after another list of proper virtues, the psalmist declares that one who does these things will never be shaken (Ps. 15:5c).

God graciously calls us to eternal life, but some people who emphasize such **calling and chosenness** might wonder how they can be sure that they are chosen. Peter is clear about our way of confirming it: if we continue in the virtues

34. Supplying the subject for what I presume to be a divine passive.

35. For untreatable ophthalmia here, see G. Green, *Jude and 2 Peter*, 198. For discussion of spiritual blindness in ancient sources, see Keener, *Acts*, 2:1641–42; 4:3520–22.

36. For example, *Ahiqar* 49, col. 4; Euripides, *Iphigenia at Tauris* 497–98; Cicero, *Epistles to Friends* 13.1.5; Plutarch, *Many Friends* 2, *Moralia* 93E; Pliny the Younger, *Epistles* 7.23.1.

37. For example, Tob. 5:10; 7:3; 2 Macc. 1:1; *1QRule of the Community* (1QS) 6.22; *1QRule of the Congregation* (1QSa) 1.18; *1QWar Scroll* (1QM) 13.1; 15.4. See further Keener, *Acts*, 2:1663–64.

he mentions, we will **never stumble** (i.e., fall away from the faith).[38] And God himself has enabled us to fulfill these virtues (1:3–4)!

That **God will richly supply** [*epichorēgeō*] **you** complements believers' own zeal to "supply" (*epichorēgeō*) virtue in 1:5. If we do our part by simply continuing and growing in the faith, God will also supply our **entrance** (*eisodos*) into his kingdom forever. (The "entrance" [*eisodos*] is the goal of the "way" [*hodos*] of truth and righteousness in 2:2, 21, but may also play on Peter's impending "exodus" [*exodos*]—i.e., death—in 1:15.) Because Jesus, the king, has already come yet will come again, the divine **kingdom**, or God's reign, is already at work in the present, yet will be consummated in the future. Peter refers here to its future consummation. In contrast to false teachers who deny future judgment and thus live immorally (3:3), we live in holiness because we trust God's promise (3:11, 13–14).

This **kingdom** is **eternal**. God reigns forever (Exod. 15:18; Ps. 146:10; Dan. 4:34; 6:26; Mic. 4:7), and he promised that David's descendants would reign forever (2 Sam. 7:13, 16; 1 Chron. 17:14; 22:10; 28:7), a reign that would be uninterrupted once the ultimate king came (Isa. 9:7; Dan. 7:14, 18).

Lord and Savior is a divine title in the Greek Old Testament and some other Jewish sources (e.g., *Psalms of Solomon* 8.33), and it is a favorite Petrine title for Jesus (2 Pet. 2:20; 3:2, 18). Peter also speaks often of simply "our Lord Jesus Christ" (2 Pet. 1:8, 14, 16). The consistent **our** in the formulation places Peter and his audience on the same level as servants before the Lord; Peter is also a slave of Christ (1:1).

Peter's Reminder (1:12–15)

> **1:12 This is why I'll always be ready to remind you about these things, even though you already know them and have been established in the truth that is with you. 13 While I'm still in this tent, I consider it appropriate[39] to stir your memory. 14 I need to do this because I'm aware that the removal of my tent will happen soon, just as our Lord Jesus Christ showed me. 15 And I'll also be zealous so that after my death you'll always remember these matters.**

Because *forgetting* that God has made us new, and so neglecting to live a virtuous life, leads to apostasy (1:10; 2:20–22), Peter is zealous **to remind** his audience

38. The image of stumbling or falling can refer to apostasy (Mark 9:42–47), although the fall is not necessarily irreversible (cf. Mark 14:27); it applies to unbelieving Jewish people in Rom. 11:11; 1 Pet. 2:8. It already applies to sin in Sir. 9:5; 23:8; 32:15.

39. Here, "appropriate" translates *dikaios*. For this potential nuance of *dikaios*, see, e.g., Phil. 1:7; Josephus, *Jewish Antiquities* 3.250; 4.149, 178; perhaps 2 Thess. 1:6.

(1:12–15; 3:1). Framing an exhortation as a reminder acknowledges that one's audience is already familiar with the truth it conveys. It thus reduces the risk of resistance or criticism for sounding too elementary (Rom. 15:15).[40] Moralists often coupled their exhortation with assurance that they believed that their hearers were already on the right path (Rom. 15:14; Heb. 6:9). That the truth **is with you** [*pareimi*; NIV: "you now have") contrasts with those who lack virtues (in 1:9, negating *pareimi*). The reminder is important because even though they **have been established** (*stērizō*), false teaching could cause them to fall from their being established (3:17, using the cognate noun *stērigmos*).

For now, Peter remains in his **tent** (1:13–14), speaking of his mortal body, which will soon be removed (1:14; cf. Wis. 9:15; 2 Cor. 5:1, 4). Possibly, the metaphor also evokes Peter's proposal of building tabernacles on the Mount of Transfiguration (Mark 9:5), an incident recalled further in this context (2 Pet. 1:16–18). That Jesus **showed** Peter about his death evokes the experience recounted in John 21:18;[41] because the transfiguration prefigured Jesus's future coming, Jesus's promise in Mark 9:1 did not preclude the subsequent death of the three disciples present (John 21:23). Peter failed to follow to the cross the first time (Mark 14:66–72), but tradition recounts that he eventually did so, probably crucified upside down.[42]

Peter's **death** here is literally his exodus (*exodos*; see comment on *eisodos* in 1:11), or departure, a term used for Jesus's death and exaltation in the transfiguration context in Luke 9:31.[43]

The Transfiguration Confirms Scripture (1:16–21)

> **[1:16]For we didn't follow simply artfully designed myths when we made known to you the power and coming of our Lord Jesus Christ. Instead, we were eyewitnesses of his majesty. [17]For he received honor and glory**

40. See Cicero, *Epistles to Friends* 13.75.1; Dio Chrysostom, *Orations* 17.5; Pliny the Younger, *Epistles* 8.24.1, 10. Not only testaments (e.g., Tob. 4:19) but moral exhortation in general included many invitations to "remember" (e.g., Isocrates, *To Demonicus* 21, *Oration* 1; Philodemus, *Frank Criticism* col. 14b; Epictetus, *Discourses* 4.13.23; *m. Avot* 3.8).

41. On which, see Keener, "Youthful Vigor."

42. See *1 Clement* 5.5; *Acts of Peter*; Tertullian, *Scorpion's Sting* 15; Eusebius, *Ecclesiastical History* 2.25.5; 3.1. Many scholars see 2 Peter, particularly 1:12–15, as a testament, but merely preparing hearers to carry on after one's death does not automatically constitute a testament. Predicting one's death was not limited to testaments (e.g., *Jubilees* 35.6; Mark 8:31). More generally, the passage fits the genre of a departure speech (cf., e.g., Menander Rhetor, *Treatises* 2.15, 430.9–434.9). It might also constitute a rhetorical *narratio*, if it provides the letter's occasion (1:16–18 is less occasional but also continues the narrative). For an embedded epistolary testament, see *2 Baruch* 78.5; 84.1–10.

43. The term applies to death in Sir. 38:23; Wis. 3:2; 7:6; Moses's death in Josephus, *Jewish Antiquities* 4.189.

from God the Father when such a voice was conveyed to him by the Majestic Glory: "This is my beloved Son! I am so pleased with him." [18]Indeed, we ourselves heard this voice conveyed from heaven when we were with him on the holy mountain. [19]And we have the prophetic message more certain. You do well to heed that message. It's like a lamp shining in a dark place, until the day dawns and the morning star rises in your hearts.

Peter refers here to his experience on the Mount of Transfiguration (the **mountain** in v. 18), shared with two other apostolic witnesses (hence **we**). In the New Testament, only 2 Peter employs the verb *exakoloutheō* (translated here as **follow**, but the form differs from the simple *akoloutheō* that appears elsewhere in the New Testament), and 2 Peter does so always to refer to following something negative (1:16; 2:2, 15).[44] The transfiguration revealed Jesus's **power** (cf. Mark 9:1) and foreshadowed his future **coming** (cf. Mark 8:38). (The language of "coming" often applied to the arrival of a ruler, dignitary, or deity.) Ancient thinkers often contrasted **myths** with genuine historical information,[45] and early Christians warned against trusting myths instead of truth (1 Tim. 1:4; 4:7; 2 Tim. 4:4; Titus 1:14). In antiquity, as today, **eyewitnesses** close to the actual events normally were considered the most reliable source of historical information.[46] The term **majesty** (*megaleiotēs*) refers to grandeur or magnificence and could apply to a deity (Acts 19:27), including God,[47] as in 2 Pet. 1:17.

The **voice** came at the transfiguration (Mark 9:7), and Peter's **conveyed** (*pherō*) or "carried" (in 1:17–18) corresponds also to how the Spirit "moved" (the same Greek term) prophets to prophesy (1:21). The heavenly voice, like

44. It appears negatively more often than not in the LXX, as in Job 31:9; Isa. 56:11; Amos 2:4; Sir. 5:2. For following myths, see also Josephus, *Jewish Antiquities* 1.22.

45. For example, Herodotus, *Histories* 2.23.1; 2.45.1; Justin, *Epitome* 11.3.11; Diodorus Siculus, *Library of History* 1.2.2; esp. Polybius, *Roman Republic* 34.4.2–3. Although *mythos* had a neutral sense (Aelius Theon, *Progymnasmata* 3.2; *Sibylline Oracles* 1.33), it sometimes was negative (Plato, *Republic* 2.377C–383C; Philostratus, *Lives of the Sophists* 2.1.554; *Letter of Aristeas* 137, 322). Jewish thinkers distinguished their Scriptures from myth (*Letter of Aristeas* 168; Philo, *Creation* 2, 157; Josephus, *Jewish Antiquities* 1.15).

46. See Byrskog, *Story as History*; Bauckham, *Jesus and the Eyewitnesses*. While *epopteia* appears in the mystery cults, the term *epoptēs* ("eyewitness") used for an initiate was hardly limited to such associations (see, e.g., Josephus, *Against Apion* 2.187), and Jewish people praised God himself as the witness (2 Macc. 7:35; 3 Macc. 2:21; *Letter of Aristeas* 16), as did some gentiles (Apollonius Rhodius, *Argonautica* 2.1123; Callimachus, *Aetia* 3.85.15; Cornutus, *Greek Theology* 9, §9.20; Porphyry, *To Marcella* 12.205–6). God sees without being seen (Plutarch, *Isis and Osiris* 75, *Moralia* 381B; Targum Pseudo-Jonathan on Gen. 16:13) and is the "all-seeing" (Aeschylus, *Eumenides* 1045; *Suppliant Women* 139; Xenophon, *Cyropaedia* 8.7.22).

47. 1 Esd. 4:40; Luke 9:43; Aristobulus 10:17 (*OTP* = Greek text 2:18); Josephus, *Jewish Antiquities* 1.24; 8.111; *Against Apion* 2.168.

the biblical prophets, thus speaks God's message. **This is** (as opposed to "you are") fits the Markan transfiguration (Mark 9:7) better than the baptism (Mark 1:11), though in Matthew it fits either one (Matt. 3:17; 17:5). **So pleased** appears in the voice at Jesus's baptism (Mark 1:11); it appears explicitly in the transfiguration parallel only in Matthew's version (Matt. 17:5). The transfiguration adds to the baptismal voice "Heed him" (Mark 9:7), missing here; Peter himself was present only at the transfiguration, not the baptism (though he would have learned about it; Peter's wording might be Mark's source even for the baptism).

God earlier declared the Davidic ruler's sonship (Ps. 2:6–7). Gospels scholars often find in the wording of the heavenly voice allusions to the exalted Davidic son in Ps. 2:7, the beloved sacrificial son in Gen. 22:2 (in the context of a heavenly voice [22:11–12]), and/or the God-pleasing servant in Isa. 42:1 (because of the association with the Spirit).

Although my translation often changes the passive voice to active forms for simpler English intelligibility, I retain the passive **was conveyed** in 1:17, since Peter seems at pains to provide a circumlocution in calling God the **Majestic Glory** (although Peter does not insist on circumlocutions even in this sentence; the familiar Jewish title **Father** indicates his providential care and immanence). **Glory** was a suitable circumlocution for God[48] and appropriate to the transfiguration context (cf. Luke 9:26, 31–32; also the background in Exod. 33:18–22; 34:29–35).

That the **voice** (1:17–18) is **from heaven** (1:18) fits the transfiguration, though the Synoptic Gospels associate it more explicitly with the voice at Jesus's baptism (Matt. 3:17; Mark 1:11; Luke 3:22). A heavenly voice also appears at times in earlier Scripture (Gen. 21:17; 22:11; Dan. 4:31).[49]

The holy mountain usually was a title for Zion (e.g., Pss. 3:4; 48:1), the holy mountain where God confirmed the sonship of the Davidic royal line (Ps. 2:6–7).[50] Peter here instead describes the unnamed **mountain** (most often thought to be Tabor or especially Hermon) as **holy** because Jesus revealed his glory there, just as God revealed his glory on Sinai.

Grammatically, 2 Peter 1:19 could mean that **the prophetic message** in Scripture is more certain than the transfiguration, but this makes little sense

48. *1 Enoch* 14.20; 102.3; *1QWar Scroll* (1QM) 10.10; frequent in Aramaic paraphrases of Scripture; in later rabbis, see Kadushin, *Rabbinic Mind*, 223–29; Abelson, *Immanence of God*, 98–134.

49. For further treatment of the heavenly voice in Jewish tradition, see discussion in Keener, *Acts*, 2:1634–35.

50. Gentiles also had various sacred mountains (e.g., Justin, *Epitome* 12.7.7; Dio Chrysostom, *Orations* 1.67; Macrobius, *Saturnalia* 1.18.3), but Old Testament usage is pervasive, singular, and dominant (e.g., Pss. 15:1; 43:3; 99:9; Isa. 11:9; 27:13; 56:7; Ezek. 20:40; Dan. 9:16; Joel 2:1; 3:17; Zeph. 3:11; Zech. 8:3).

of the context. Instead, it probably means that the voice at the transfiguration confirmed **the prophetic message**. In turn, one might argue that **the prophetic message** refers to the content of the voice on the mountain; but a heavenly voice was not ordinarily called prophecy. More likely, it could mean particular allusions in the voice at the transfiguration (cf. Gen. 22:2; Ps. 2:7; Isa. 42:1). Most likely of all, however, because it would be more obvious to most hearers than particular allusions, it refers to everything in Scripture (cf. 2 Pet. 1:20–21, noting every "prophecy in Scripture").

Peter provides three expressions of light. The first, **a lamp**, provides light in the dark and refers to the present period of awaiting Christ's return (cf. Luke 12:35). **The day** presumably is the day of judgment (2:9; 3:7), the day of the Lord (3:10, 12; cf. 3:18). The Greek term *phōsphoros*, "light-bearing," conjoined with **rises** (*anatellō*) could apply to the sun,[51] which makes more sense here, but in the strong majority of ancient instances it refers instead to **the morning star** (the planet Venus), which was supposed to herald the dawn.[52] Either way, **the morning star**, like **the day**, is eschatological, fulfilled at the coming of Jesus (cf. Rom. 13:12–13; 1 Thess. 5:2–5), who is the bright morning star in Rev. 22:16 (cf. Rev. 2:28; Luke 1:78–79).[53]

We currently have **the prophetic message**; we may not always understand all of it in this age, but when we know as we are known, our knowing of God will be perfect (1 Cor. 13:9, 12). This means that until Jesus returns, Scripture offers our fullest access to hearing God. We thus neglect it to our peril. Sadly, however, even many sermons today engage audiences on other levels (trying to compete with popular social media) yet fail to teach Scripture. Rising biblical illiteracy in the church renders us vulnerable to dangerous errors like those in Peter's day (cf. "every wind of teaching" [Eph. 4:14]). Insofar as the daylight is eschatological, the full glory of the coming day is not limited to our **hearts**, though it includes them; Peter specifies our hearts, however, because they are what are in need here (cf. 2 Cor. 4:6). Our **hearts** are also where we can treasure God's voice in Scripture until that day.

51. See Philo, *Drunkenness* 44; cf. stars in *Creation* 29, 53; *Dreams* 1.214; *Life of Moses* 1.120; 2.102. The verb applies to the sun in 26 percent of LXX uses, 25 percent of Josephus's uses, 49 percent of Philo's uses, and 55 percent of New Testament uses. Pausanias, *Description of Greece* 4.31.10 applies it to Artemis (cf. Strabo, *Geography* 3.1.9). Like the sun, the morning star signifies light (Sir. 50:6–7) and the coming of day (Catullus, *Carmina* 62.34–35), though the morning star falls short of full light of day (Maximus of Tyre, *Orations* 11.1). It was identified also as the evening star (Pliny the Elder, *Natural History* 2.6.36; Diogenes Laertius, *Eminent Philosophers* 8.1.14). Some suggest that 2 Peter reverses the temporal order for rhetorical effect.

52. BDAG 1073; LSJ 1968.

53. For "star" as a messianic title, see Num. 24:17; *Damascus Document*[a] (CD) 7.18–19; *1QWar Scroll* (1QM) 11.6–8; as an eschatological harbinger, *Sibylline Oracles* 5.155–61. For prophets or Scripture as light, see, e.g., Ps. 119:105, 130; *Sibylline Oracles* 5.238–39; *4 Ezra* 12.42.

> [1:20]**Above all, recognize that no prophecy in Scripture came about from [a prophet's] personal interpretation.** [21]**This is clear because human will never brought about [true] prophecy. Instead, people moved by the Holy Spirit spoke from God.**

Scholars diverge as to whether Peter denies polyvalent interpretations of prophecy[54] or simply the prophet's own error. Because he refers to prophecies **in Scripture**—those accepted as canonical—he probably indicates the prophet's own interpretation (fitting this context). Still, so limiting the meaning of the prophecy would also limit the authority of other interpretations to those that cohere with its message.[55]

Prophecy involves an element of cognition (1 Cor. 14:2–3, 14), and God used the distinctive style of different prophets (e.g., "son of man" is his special nickname for Ezekiel). But genuine prophecy is a matter of inspiration and does not originate from human reasoning, even if it may sometimes make use of it at an inspired level.[56] The Greek verb *pherō* appears twice in 1:21: human will did not "move" (**never brought about**) prophecy forth; rather, the Holy Spirit **moved** people to speak from God (cf. Rom. 1:2; 2 Tim. 3:16).

In modern times, popular "prophecy teachers" have been taking verses out of context to predict (usually inaccurately) the future for well over a century.[57] There is a place for "futurists," those who observe trends and offer probable diagnoses and wise planning for the future (e.g., you're wise not to buy beachfront property if the sea level is expected to rise a couple feet). The Spirit can work through this as through other modes of discourse, but futurism by itself is not prophecy. Educated guesses have value (certainly more than uneducated ones), but they are not prophecy. Genuine prophecy is supposed to communicate just what God is saying.

Just as God's Spirit moved true biblical prophets (1:20–21), so in biblical times false prophets arose, similar to the false teachers of Peter's era (2:1). By disregarding prophecies of a future coming (3:3–4), these false teachers surely also deny the common refrain of biblical prophets that the day of the Lord (3:10,

54. For example, Rome's Sibylline Books could be interpreted so as to justify almost any decision. See, e.g., Cicero, *For Rabirius Postumus* 2.4.

55. See Keener, *Spirit Hermeneutics*, 99–151.

56. This contrasts with, e.g., figuring out divinatory signs, a use of the same term, *epilysis* ("interpretation"), in the Greek version of *Jubilees* 11.8. For prophesying under divine compulsion, see, e.g., Jer. 6:11; 20:9; Mic. 3:8; in a more ecstatic sense, Virgil, *Aeneid* 6.77–102; Plutarch, *Oracles at Delphi* 21, *Moralia* 404E; *Sibylline Oracles* 3.1–7, 295–99, 489–91; 12.295–96; Josephus, *Jewish Antiquities* 4.118. For the sense here, cf. Philo, *Special Laws* 1.65; 4.49; Justin Martyr, *First Apology* 36; *Numbers Rabbah* 18.12.

57. See Kyle, *Last Days*; Wilson, *Armageddon Now!*

12) is near (Isa. 13:6; Ezek. 30:3; Joel 1:15; 2:1; 3:14; Obad. 15; Zeph. 1:7, 14). It had not fully materialized despite eight centuries of prophecy, yet it always remained imminent, even if not immediate. We need to continue to live in light of Jesus's coming, meanwhile remaining vigilant to test all prophecies by Scripture, God's confirmed message.

Beware of the False Teachers (2:1–3)

> **2:1But false prophets also arose among the people, just as there will also be false teachers among you. They will sneak in their divisive movements that lead to destruction. They do this by denying the Master who bought them, thereby bringing on themselves swift destruction. 2Many will follow their unrestrained license. People will slander the way of truth because of them. 3In their greed they'll exploit you with their made-up ideas! God has not forgotten their long-awaited condemnation or slept through their appointed destruction.**

Just as Scripture provides the message of true prophets (1:20–21), it also recounts the activity of **false prophets** (2:1). Jesus warned against false prophets (Matt. 7:15; Mark 13:22; Luke 6:26) and false prophesying (Matt. 7:22). Such warnings also appear widely in early Christianity (2 Pet. 2:1; Rev. 2:14, 20; *Didache* 11.5–10; 16.3), for *many* false prophets exist (1 John 4:1). Anticharismatic movements today throw out the baby with the bathwater, but it is incumbent on charismatics to guard carefully against false claims to revelation, especially those that misrepresent Jesus and undermine biblical ethics. Deuteronomy 13 and 18 warn against false prophets; Peter's Greek term, *pseudoprophētēs* (2:1), appears already in the Greek version of Zech. 13:2 and especially that of Jeremiah (6:13; 26:7, 8, 11, 16; 27:9; 28:1; 29:1, 8 [LXX 6:13; 33:7, 8, 11, 16; 34:9; 35:1; 36:1, 8]). Jewish tradition often treated Balaam (2 Pet. 2:15) as the prototype for false prophets.[58]

Peter does not deny the possibility of prophets (true or false) in his own day; he is not contrasting teaching with prophecy but rather is focusing on the primary mode of error that his audience faces. They face teaching error more than prophesying error, but Peter regards both as dangerous. That Peter uses future tenses in introducing false teachers may show that he expects more to come, as some commentators suggest, but Peter is also addressing a present situation already in their midst (e.g., 2:17–19; 3:5). The correspondence between false prophets and false teachers in 2:1 should give pause to those strictest with the

58. For example, *4QList of False Prophets ar* (4Q339); *Sipre Deuteronomy* 357.18.2.

prophetic gift today: we should require absolute infallibility of neither teachers nor prophets (neither of whose pronouncements are meant to be added to Scripture), but we should require significant accountability for both. A single misinterpretation does not make a pastor a false teacher; regularly teaching error or teaching egregious error makes one a false teacher. Likewise, a mistake in prophetic discernment merits apologies but does not make one a false prophet in the biblical sense (1 Sam. 16:6; 2 Sam. 7:3); leading people in rebellion against the Lord (Deut. 13:2, 6–7; 18:20)[59] and against central affirmations such as Jesus's lordship and atoning death (2 Pet. 2:1) marks false prophets. Both moral (Jer. 23:14; Lam. 4:13; Matt. 7:15–23; 2 Pet. 2:2–3) and theological (Deut. 13:2; 18:20; 1 John 4:1–6) tests for prophets are important.

That they **sneak in** their divisions (cf. Jude 4) makes them less than obvious, but they create their own **divisive movements** (*hairesis*; lit., "sect," from which we get the word "heresy"). Peter twice associates them with **destruction**, a future fate that they themselves deny (3:3–4). **Denying** Jesus merits being denied before God (Matt. 10:33 // Luke 12:9; 2 Tim. 2:12); people can deny him by their deeds (1 Tim. 5:8; Titus 1:16) or by disbelieving God's power while pretending to be religious (2 Tim. 3:5). The warning here carries over from Jude 4, but Peter would be aware that repentance for such a denial remains possible (cf. Mark 14:66–72; 16:7).

The term for **Master** (*despotēs*) can apply to a slaveholder (1 Pet. 2:18), to God (Acts 4:24; Rev. 6:10),[60] and, as likely here, to Jesus (Jude 4). Traditional cultures could relate to an understanding of chiefs, kings, and other sorts of authority, which were sometimes benevolent and sometimes tyrannical. In the United States, our trajectory since the American Revolution has been to value independence. Positively, this trajectory has helped the vital cause of individual human rights (such as opposing slavery and discrimination). Negatively, it gives us fewer analogies to understand loyal obedience to superiors—and sometimes even less sympathy for *other* individuals' human rights. Positively, it births an entrepreneurial, pioneering spirit through which Spirit-filled believers begin new churches and organizations; negatively, it sometimes weakens cooperation and unity. Military service; respect for benevolent employers, parents, or church leaders; and other analogies might help us regain some sense of a **Master** (though even some of these become more like peer relationships). Yet we also experience perversions of authority in church, society, or even family that can also make leadership harder to trust. Beyond analogies, as we submit to Scripture

59. The Hebrew term *zid*, translated as "presume" (NIV) or "presumptuously" (NASB) in Deut. 18:20 (cf. *zadon* in 18:22), normally means "insolently" or "rebelliously," rather than referring to a mere miscalculation (see, e.g., Exod. 18:11; Deut. 1:43; 17:13).

60. See also Wis. 8:3; *Testament of Abraham* 1.12, 25 A; *Testament of Job* 38.1–2; for Zeus among gentiles, *I. Eph.* 1240.1; Longus, *Daphnis and Chloe* 4.21.

and are led by the Spirit, we can begin to understand Jesus as our trustworthy **Master** in the best and truest sense by our relationship with him.

We would rightly belong to the Lord by virtue of creation, but here we belong to this master because he has **bought** us, freeing us from the corruption to which we had foolishly sold ourselves (2 Pet. 2:19). Jesus **bought** us with the ultimate price (Acts 20:28; 1 Cor. 6:20; 7:23; 1 Pet. 1:18–19; Rev. 5:9; 14:3–4); this is the language of redemption, of freeing someone (normally by paying a price for them [e.g., Gal. 3:13; Eph. 1:7]). God redeemed Israel from slavery in the exodus (Deut. 7:8; 13:5; 24:18) and redeemed us from slavery to sin (Rom. 3:23–24; Col. 1:14; Titus 2:14). By continuing to live in sin, however, the false teachers deny Jesus's redemption from it. Ancient thinkers recognized the irony of abusing the rhetoric of freedom (really, license) to enslave people to passion.[61] One who frees us from an older master by purchasing us becomes our new master. Under Roman law, a freedperson still owed allegiance to their most recent master; ingratitude for freedom constituted grounds for their reenslavement.[62] Despising the Lord who bought us by his own blood is the ultimate ingratitude. These false teachers, however, proceed one step further: They go on to exploit others whom he **bought** (2:3)!

Many **follow** (2:2) false teachers who in turn follow the way of Balaam (to destruction [2:15]; see comment on 1:16). *Aselgeia*, the term I rendered as **unrestrained license** (2:2), means "dissolute," "wild," "without moral restraints"; Peter applies it also to Sodom (2 Pet. 2:7; it appears also in 2:18; 1 Pet. 4:3; Jude 4). Scripture designates as false prophets not only those who speak falsehood but also those who disobey God's true teachings (Jer. 23:11, 14; Matt. 7:15–23).

Slander (2:2) translates the Greek term *blasphēmeō*, "speak with hostility against" (2 Pet. 2:10, 12; also 1 Pet. 4:4; Jude 8, 10), or "blaspheme" (when against God). **The way of truth**[63] is also the way of righteousness (2:21; cf. Prov. 8:20; 12:28; 16:31; Matt. 21:32). Ancient wisdom spoke of two ways: a righteous way leading to life and a wicked way leading to death (e.g., Deut. 30:15, 19; Ps. 1:6; Prov. 12:28; Jer. 21:8; Matt. 7:13–14).[64]

61. For example, Livy, *History of Rome* 5.6.17; 27.31.6; Dio Chrysostom, *Orations* 14.3–6, 18; see further Keener, *1 Peter*, 172. For falsehood enslaving, see Arrian, *Anabasis* 3.11.2; Seneca, *To Lucilius* 8.7; 27.4; Plutarch, *Lectures* 1, *Moralia* 37E; *Superstition* 5, *Moralia* 167B. Enslavement to passion was an even more common idea; see, e.g., Xenophon, *Memorabilia* 1.3.8, 11; 1.5.1, 5; 4.5.3, 5; Sophocles, *Antigone* 756; Cicero, *Friendship* 22.82; *Duties* 1.29.102; 1.38.136; 2.5.18; Seneca, *To Lucilius* 14.1; 39.6; 47.17; 110.9–10; 116.1.

62. In some other ancient societies, compare, e.g., Valerius Maximus, *Deeds and Sayings* 2.6.6–7a.

63. Compare *1QRule of the Community* (1QS) 8.13; *4QEnoch^{g} ar* (4Q212) f1.4.22; *4 Ezra* 5.1.

64. See also Seneca, *To Lucilius*. 8.3; 27.4; *4 Ezra* 7.3–16, 60–61; 8.1–3; *Testament of Abraham* 11.2 A; *Testament of Asher* 1.3, 5; *2 Enoch* 30.15; *m. Avot* 2.9; *Didache* 1.1–6.2; *Barnabas* 18.1–21.9.

When leaders are corrupted by money, sex, or power, they bring reproach not only on themselves but also on their movements.[65] Stereotypes of greedy preachers today play on the minority of ministers who are flamboyantly rich, who commit financial or sexual misconduct, and/or who abuse authority over others. Pastors most in the limelight are often most at risk. Pride may tempt them more often (cf. Prov. 27:21); when we are in front of people, they can be attracted to our persona, which we (or they) may wrongly assume is attraction to our person (a vulnerability especially for those with emotionally deprived backgrounds). (The equivalent danger in counseling is transference and countertransference.) This is one reason why it is important to welcome peer relationships with colleagues who are not afraid to tell us the truth—encouraging at times but also ready to set us straight if we let status go to our heads (Prov. 27:6). Pride does make way for a fall (Prov. 11:2; 16:18; 29:23). Also at risk are those drained by ministry without sufficient time alone with God to be refreshed with God's perspective and their calling.

Billy Graham offers a good example of a minister who bent over backwards to make sure that no one could accuse his ministry of corruption in money or sex.[66] Violations of some cultural values turn people from the gospel, especially those looking for excuses anyway (1 Tim. 5:14–15; 6:1; Titus 2:5). Sex and money scandals are particularly dangerous (e.g., 1 Sam. 2:12–17, 22, 24) because they display failure to practice what we claim to believe; the devil is sure to target leaders where they are most vulnerable (cf. Luke 22:31).

Greed (2:3) characterizes the wicked (2:14), not God's faithful servants (2 Cor. 12:17–18; 1 Thess. 2:5). People in antiquity were already concerned about greedy prophets and sages.[67] The term translated as **exploit** (*emporeuomai*) can simply mean "do business," but using God's people as a business (cf. John 2:16), for personal gain, is exploitation (cf. 2 Cor. 2:17; 4:2). Motive makes a difference:[68] Everyone needs to make a living (cf. 1 Cor. 9:7–14; 1 Tim. 5:17–18), but the motive of serving God's people differs from using them for **greed**. Their **greed** (2:3) offers a tragic contrast with the Master who bought us (2:1). **Made-up ideas** or "deceptive words" (NRSV), "fabricated stories" (NIV), are humanly

65. In antiquity, see, e.g., Plutarch, *Lectures* 12, *Moralia* 43F; Lucian, *Runaways* 21.

66. Still, we have to contextualize the principle. As I learned the hard way, today's environment offers different challenges, in which the "Billy Graham rule" sometimes gets charged with sexism. The principle of always trying to have two or three witnesses remains valid.

67. For prophets, see Jer. 8:10; Ezek. 22:25; Mic. 3:5, 11; *Didache* 11.5, 9; Sophocles, *Antigone* 1061; for sages, Lucian, *Runaways* 4, 20; *Fisherman* 42; *Timon* 54–57; see Malherbe, "Gentle as a Nurse."

68. In antiquity, too, prosecutors had to offer credible motives (e.g., Cicero, *For Sextus Roscius* 22.61–62). In the second century, Lucian mocks gullible Christians' vulnerability to exploitation (Lucian, *Passing of Peregrinus* 13).

contrived teachings (1:16) in contrast to true messages from God (1:21). They use the Bible to make up their teachings (3:16; see comment there).

In the New Testament, only 2 Peter uses the term rendered as **long-awaited** (*ekpalai*; 2:3), referring to something from long before (potentially as early as creation [3:5]). **Condemnation** (*krima*; 2:3) is judgment or a decree of judgment (also Jude 4). Peter returns here to the issue of their future **destruction**, already mentioned twice in 2:1 and reiterated in 3:7, 16. Just because their judgment has not come yet is no reason to think that God is looking the other way; the one who keeps his people will not slumber (Ps. 121:3–4).

Biblical Precedent for God Judging the Wicked (2:4–10a)

> **2:4For[69] God did not spare the angels who sinned; instead, he cast them into hell in chains[70] in[71] darkness, handing them over to be reserved for the judgment. 5Nor did God spare the ancient world. Instead, he protected Noah, the eighth, a herald of righteousness, when he brought on the world of the impious a flood. 6God likewise condemned the cities of Sodom and Gomorrah, turning them to ashes. Thus he made an example of them for what awaits the impious! 7Likewise, God rescued righteous Lot, who was oppressed by the unrestrained conduct of lawless[72] people. 8That righteous man was oppressed in that, while he lived among those lawless people, the lawless actions he saw and heard day after day tortured his righteous soul. 9These examples make clear that the Lord knows how to rescue reverent people from testing but to reserve unrighteous people for punishment on the day of judgment. 10aThis is especially true for those who go after the flesh in its impure passion and despise authority.**

The wicked (2:1–3) will face judgment (2:4–10). In 2:4–10a—one long sentence in Greek—Peter elaborates on his point with examples from Scripture as it was understood by his generation's audience. (Orators often elaborated points with

69. I omit Peter's "if" (*ei*) in 2:4 to shorten the long sentence that runs from 2:4–10a, compensating in my translation of 2:10a.

70. Manuscripts of 2 Peter vary between reading "chains" (from *seira*) and "pits" (from *siros*), but because Jude 5 (on which Peter draws) speaks of chains under darkness, "pits" was likely a later attempt to make more sense of the phrase (cf. Rev. 20:1–2).

71. Most translations render the genitive "of" (which is a safe way to translate it). Because a genitive just establishes relationship between two nouns, and because Peter evidently has in view Jude 5, I render it here as "in."

72. Here, *athesmos* is not the usual term for "lawless" (*adikos*, found in 2:9; esp. *anomos*, in 2:8), but that may be the closest sense of the term here.

examples.) Peter borrows two examples from Jude 6–7, omitting Israel (Jude 5) and adding Noah (cf. 1 Pet. 3:20).

2 Peter 2:4–6	Jude 6–7
Angels sinned (v. 4).	Angels abandoned their assigned sphere (v. 6).
God reserved those angels chained in darkness for judgment (v. 4).	God reserved those angels chained in darkness for judgment (v. 6).
God condemned Sodom and Gomorrah (v. 6).	God condemned Sodom and Gomorrah (v. 7).
God burned them with fire (v. 6).	God consigned them to eternal fire (v. 7).
God displayed them as an example (v. 6).	God displayed them as an example (v. 7).

Whereas the examples in Jude 5–7 function primarily as warnings against apostasy, Peter balances examples of judgment (2:4–6) with examples of preservation (2:5–8). Possibly against the false teachers' eschatological skepticism (3:3–4), Peter emphasizes that God is able to protect the righteous even as he judges the wicked (2:9). God keeps the wicked for judgment (2:4, 9) but preserves the righteous from it (2:5).

The angels who sinned (2:4) appear before mention of Noah (2:5), fitting their respective locations in Gen. 6; in Peter's day, most interpreters viewed the sons of God mating with human women (Gen. 6:1–4) as fallen angels (see discussion at 1 Pet. 3:19–22). Because they act from a position of superior power and influence, angels who sinned with women are analogous to the greedy teachers who exploit their followers (2 Pet. 2:1).

Cast . . . into hell (*tartaroō*) plays on ancient language for what we call hell. Jewish people expected the wicked to burn in Gehinnom (see Matt. 10:28 // Luke 12:5; Mark 9:43–47). The Jewish *Sibylline Oracles* also speak of Gehenna as a place "of terrible, raging, undying fire" (1.103; cf. 2.288–89, 305) or "immeasurable darkness" (2.292).[73] The Greek equivalent of Gehinnom, though reserved only for the most harshly damned, was Tartarus,[74] which Greek-speaking Jews used to translate the idea.[75] In Greek mythology, many of the Titans, the race of

73. For fire and eternal judgment, see also *1 Enoch* 91.9; *1QRule of the Community* (1QS) 2.7–8; persecutors in 4 Macc. 9:9; 12:12; 13:15; for Pharisees affirming eternal suffering, see Josephus, *Jewish War* 2.163; *Jewish Antiquities* 18.14. Some envisioned a temporary hell until destruction (*1QRule of the Community* [1QS] 4.13–14; *t. Sanhedrin* 13.3–4); later rabbis varied in their views.

74. For example, Plato, *Phaedo* 113E–114B; Virgil, *Aeneid* 6.621; Tibullus, *Elegies* 1.73–80; Seneca, *Hercules* 749–59; Lucian, *Funerals* 8. Some texts apply the term more generically to the realm of the dead (Statius, *Silvae* 5.1.206; 5.5.78; Silius Italicus, *Punica* 6.40).

75. *Sibylline Oracles* 1.101–3; 2.291, 302–3; 4.186; 5.178; cf. Philo, *Rewards and Punishments* 152; *Embassy to Gaius* 49, 103; Josephus, *Against Apion* 2.240; Pseudo-Philo, *Biblical Antiquities* 60.3; 2 Pet. 2:4; *1 Enoch* 20.2 Gk.

PENTECOSTAL INTEREST

The Fate of the Lost

Early in the 1980s, it appeared to me that sooner or later our culture would move churches that lacked a firm commitment to Scripture to reject at least two issues: the sinfulness of same-sex intercourse and the lostness of those without Christ. Because I had both friends who were gay or lesbian and unconverted family members, these two issues disturbed me as well. Indeed, they still tear at my heart. The second issue is the one raised by the present text.

All people do justly merit punishment. People lack gratitude for God's many gifts around us (not least our own existence), and we wrong (at least in our hearts) others made in God's image. We thereby sin against an infinitely holy God and alienate ourselves from him. Despite this, God paid an infinite price to make available to us restoration to himself. Tragically, collective sinful resistance against that good news in many spheres and the frequent sinful failure of God's human agents minimize many people's access to that news.

Thinkers have tried in various ways to reconcile the notion of eternal lostness with God's love. Obviously, God's justice and the horrible depth of human depravity are major factors. Many, however, also have appealed to God's gift of choice to humanity, a point highlighted graphically in C. S. Lewis's *The Great Divorce*, which experiments with a sort of purgatorial imagery without actually claiming to be perfect theologically.[a]

In 1989, when I was working on my PhD, a bright undergraduate from one of the campus's ministry groups could not reconcile the idea of God being loving with that of God bringing judgment. I explained that God sends judgments to get humanity's attention and turn us from the ultimate judgment—from God eternally handing us over to our choice of our alienation from him (see, e.g., Amos 4:6, 8–11; Rev. 9:20–21; 16:9, 11). God's judgments in this world are therefore mercy, because ultimately there is no real life apart from God (cf. Jer. 2:13; Hosea 13:9; John 17:3).

The student then conceded that God could use judgments as discipline in this life but protested the idea of hell. "And if you persuade me that there's such a thing as hell," she warned, "I just won't believe in God at all." I surely could understand her sentiments, as I have my own theological and especially emotional struggles with the idea. But I told her a story. My first wife had left me for her friend's husband two years earlier. To reduce her shame in case she returned, I had kept it a secret as long as possible, but by now everyone knew. My wife was pressing for divorce so she could marry the man for whom she left me, who had now secured his divorce too. I was fighting the divorce in the hope and prayer that she would change her mind.

"The pain of her rejection hurts me so much," I explained. (Not least because of such pain, it took fifteen years after she left before I remarried.) "On the days that I have hope that she might return, it is worth all the pain. Yet on the days that my hope fails, I just want to let the divorce go through so I can put an end to the pain." The kind-hearted student nodded sympathetically.

"A God of infinite love has infinite pain at our rejection of him," I continued. "So great was such love and pain that God chose the pain of his own Son being nailed to the cross to restore us to himself. If, despite that pain, we continue to spurn his love, eventually the time comes when God declares, 'Enough! I divorce you.' That's what hell is like." The student did not answer, but I could tell that she was thinking. The idea of being cut off from God's saving love forever is awful; it indicts, however, not God's love but the depth of human depravity.

a. Lewis, *The Great Divorce*. For my own argument more extensively, see Keener and Usry, *Defending Black Faith*, 108–35; for the illustration here, 130.

gods before the reigning ones, were consigned to Tartarus;[76] in Jewish thought, such pagan gods are demons (Deut. 32:17; Ps. 106:37; Bar. 4:7; *1 Enoch* 19.1; 1 Cor. 10:20; Rev. 9:20). Legends held that God kept the fallen angels chained in darkness, awaiting their fuller damnation at the final judgment (see comment on Jude 6).

Just as God **did not spare the angels** (2:4), neither did he **spare** the antediluvian world (2:5). If God did not spare angels or the world, certainly no one else should presume on his mercy without repentance (cf. Rom. 11:21; 2 Cor. 13:2)! While Enoch was seventh from Adam (Jude 14), **eighth** here must refer to the eight saved in the flood, referred to in 1 Pet. 3:20, a letter apparently known to 2 Peter's audience (2 Pet. 3:1).

As a **herald of righteousness** (2:5), Noah might prefigure Christ,[77] who later proclaimed judgment to the fallen angels (1 Pet. 3:19). Scripture does not describe Noah preaching to his contemporaries, but Jewish tradition does.[78] God

76. Homer, *Iliad* 8.13, 481; Hesiod, *Theogony* 717–19; Plato, *Republic* 10.616.1; Cornutus, *Greek Theology* 7, §7.20–21; Menander Rhetor, *Treatises* 2.17, 438.30–439.1; *Sibylline Oracles* 1.307–23; 2.231. As the rightful abode of demons, see Pseudo-Philo, *Biblical Antiquities* 60.3 (most manuscripts).

77. So also Justin Martyr, *Dialogue with Trypho* 138.

78. *Sibylline Oracles* 1.129, 168; Josephus, *Jewish Antiquities* 1.74; *b. Sanhedrin* 108a.

protected Noah and his family, as he is also able to preserve us (Jude 1, 24), and as we are called to keep ourselves (2 Pet. 3:17; Jude 21). God keeps the fallen angels and their followers for future judgment (2 Pet. 2:4; Jude 6, 13) but keeps us from the judgment. The **flood** (*kataklysmos*; also in LXX Gen. 6:17; 7:6–10, 17; Sir. 44:17–18) prefigures the future day of judgment (2 Pet. 3:6), as also in Jesus's teaching (Matt. 24:38–39 // Luke 17:27). Of the New Testament's other two uses of the word *epagō* (**brought on**, applicable to the flood in LXX Gen. 6:17), one applies to the false teachers bringing judgment on themselves (2 Pet. 2:1); again, Peter is using the flood to foreshadow future judgment. **Impious** (*asebēs*) means "disrespectful" (including "neglectful") of deity (see comment on Jude 4, 15).

Orators often cited examples (Gk. *hypodeigmata*, Lat. *exempla*); New Testament writers often used Old Testament events as examples (e.g., 1 Cor. 10:1–11). Peter explicitly follows that practice with an **example** (*hypodeigma*) in 2:6. The law (Deut. 29:23; 32:32), prophets (Isa. 1:9–10; 3:9; 13:19; Jer. 23:14; Amos 4:11; Zeph. 2:9), Jesus (Matt. 11:24 // Luke 10:12), and his followers (Rev. 11:8) used Sodom as a model of depravity and destruction (see fuller discussion at Jude 7). Jewish tradition naturally often treated together the flood (2 Pet. 2:5) and Sodom (2:6) as examples of judgment;[79] so did Jesus, who treats these events as foreshadowing the day of judgment (Luke 17:26–29, 32).

Just as God protected Noah when he destroyed the impious world (2 Pet. 2:5), he also **rescued** Lot (2:7) when he destroyed Sodom and Gomorrah (2:6); this rescue becomes a preeminent example of Peter's point in the paragraph: God knows how to **rescue** the pious (2:9). In 2:7, Peter also revisits the **unrestrained** character of the wicked (2:2, 18; cf. Jude 4). Their evil **conduct** (cf. 1 Pet. 1:18) contrasts with the godly conduct that Peter urges (2 Pet. 3:11; cf. 1 Pet. 1:15; 2:12; 3:1–2, 16).

How was **Lot . . . oppressed** (v. 7)? Certainly, Lot's neighbors' attempted rape of him when he was trying to protect his guests (Gen. 19:9) counts as oppression, but this onetime experience was not **day after day** (although that expression may go with **while he lived among those lawless people**). This event may have climaxed earlier offenses. More critically, the explanation that follows in 2 Pet. 2:8 shows that the oppression also included the suffering of having to endure behavior that he hated (cf. Pss. 26:5; 31:6; 101:3; 120:6–7). It also included their

79. For example, *m. Sanhedrin* 10.3; *t. Sanhedrin* 13:6, 8; *Mekilta Bahodesh* 10.20–23 (Lauterbach, *Mekhilta de-Rabbi Ishmael* 2:278); *Sipre Deuteronomy* 43.3.2, 5; 310.2.1. Other peoples also recounted the flood (e.g., Diodorus Siculus, *Library of History* 1.10.4; Dio Chrysostom, *Orations* 36.49; Josephus, *Jewish Antiquities* 1.93–94; *Against Apion* 1.130–31); some associated it with Phrygia (*Sibylline Oracles* 1.196, 261–62; 7.13). Genesis itself certainly connects Gen. 9:21–27 and 19:31–38.

attitudes toward him and his family as immigrants (Gen. 19:9); they brought up this status when he protested their plan to gang rape guests, and they accused him of judging them (Gen. 19:9)—just as the unjust often do today when we challenge their acts of injustice.

While Peter calls Lot **righteous** three times (linking him with Noah, herald of righteousness [cf. Gen. 6:9; 7:1; 18:23–28]), in Genesis the surrounding values helped reshape those of Lot and his family. He was more righteous than his neighbors, but by itself this is not saying much! While honoring hospitality, he offered his daughters in lieu of the guests (Gen. 19:8). Why not offer himself (especially in view of their expressed same-sex interest)? Perhaps he was trying to shame his neighbors, whom he thought would not actually rape his own daughters, given their same-sex interest and especially given that they knew that his daughters were engaged to local Sodomites. Still, he does effectively place himself at greatest immediate risk (Gen. 19:9) and is comparatively righteous (contrast Judg. 19:25). Sodom's culture also impacts his family: His wife values too much what she left behind (Gen. 19:26; cf. Luke 17:31–32); his daughters get him drunk to commit incest with him (Gen. 19:31–36).[80] Although God was sovereignly involved in the choice (Gen. 13:9–12; cf. 36:6–8), Lot's choice of more fertile land in Gen. 13:10–11 failed to take account of the kind of neighbors he was choosing. This, too, can be a lesson for us (cf. Ps. 84:10); we and our families risk being affected by peer pressure and debased standards (unless we deliberately serve in such places for committed mission).

The **reverent** (2:9) are those who practice "piety" (*eusebeia*), respect for deity (1:3, 6–7); future judgment provides an incentive for this behavior (3:11). The opposite of such reverence is "impiety" (*asebeia*), the conduct of the impious or irreverent (2:5–6; 3:7; Jude 4, 15). Verse 9 contrasts the **reverent** more generally with the **unrighteous** or "unjust," cognate language to which recurs in 2:13, 15. The **reverent** may face **testing** (2:9; cf. 1 Pet. 1:6; 4:12), but the Lord will **rescue** them, whether in the short (Pss. 33:19; 34:7, 17; Matt. 6:13) or (as perhaps emphasized here) long term.[81] Just as God reserves the fallen angels for judgment (2 Pet. 2:4; Jude 6), so does he **reserve** for it **unrighteous people** (2 Pet. 2:9, 17; Jude 13), while preserving the righteous (Jude 1, 21).

80. The perspective of Genesis rejects the elder daughter's reasoning (Gen. 19:31), using the story to explain the sinful ancestry of Moab (meaning, "from a father") and Ammon (cf. Deut. 2:9, 19). Note also the partial parallelism with Gen. 9:21–25. Some postbiblical traditions, however, highlight the righteous aspects of his behavior (e.g., *1QGenesis Apocryphon* [1Q20] 20.22–23; Wis. 10:6; Josephus, *Jewish Antiquities* 1.200; *1 Clement* 11.1; contrast some later rabbis, e.g., *Sipre Deuteronomy* 43.3.6; *Genesis Rabbah* 50.4).

81. The distinction between temptation and sin, in Christian terms, exercised ancient philosophy and church fathers influenced by it. See Sorabji, *Emotion*, 2–11, 73–75, 118–19, 372–84, 417.

Grammar alone does not resolve whether **punishment** belongs with **reserve** (ESV, NASB, NRSV; in which case they may experience punishment in the waiting period; cf. the darkness in 2:17) or with **the day of judgment** (KJV, NET, NIV, NJB; cf. 2:1).[82] Theologically, many would allow for either option (cf. Luke 16:23, 28). Peter envisions **the day of judgment** in terms of fiery destruction

82. For torment of the wicked in the intermediate state, see *4 Ezra* 7.76–87, 93; *2 Baruch* 36.11.

BIBLICAL BACKGROUND

Flesh[a]

Neoplatonic and Gnostic dualism absorbed by later Christianity denied that the body was good, and some scholars today, reacting against this wrong conception, argue that the New Testament use of "flesh" (*sarx*) bears little relation to *sōma*, "body." This reaction sometimes goes too far. For example, the NIV note on "flesh" (*sarx*) in 2 Pet. 2:10 (and its inconsistent translation of *sarx* in many places, such as Jude 7–8), treating it as "sinful nature," plays into some inappropriate ideas of two natures struggling within the believer.

"Flesh" remains connected with the body in normal first-century usage. The Old Testament already contrasted humanity as embodied creatures (*sarx*) with God's Spirit (LXX Gen. 6:3; cf. 1 Pet. 3:18; 4:6; *1QRule of the Community* [1QS] 4.21). The Old Testament employed the equivalent Hebrew term *basar* for humans (or other animals) in their limited creatureliness, including their mortality (also, e.g., Sir. 28:5; *Jubilees* 5.2). *Basar* and its Greek translation *sarx* did not present the body as inherently evil, but as embodied "human weakness" *sarx* was vulnerable. By Peter's day, some Jews employed *basar* for human weakness in its susceptibility to sin.[b] Today we may think of it this way: God gave us bodily desires to be used rightly (e.g., sexual passion for marriage and procreation), but he also gave us minds to know right from wrong and use our bodies for good. Humanity allowed desires to corrupt our thinking, but God's Spirit transforms and empowers us to choose rightly (cf. Jude 19–20). "Flesh" is not meant to lead human life; rather, it is meant to be the arena in which we live in obedience to God.

a. I borrow these comments on flesh from Keener, *Romans*, 95–97. For fuller discussion, see Keener, *Mind of the Spirit*, 101–5.

b. *1QRule of the Community* (1QS) 4.20–21; 9.9; 11.9, 12.

(3:7); **the day of judgment** (also Matt. 10:15; 11:22, 24; 12:36; Rom. 2:16; Jude 6) is the day of the Lord and his wrath against evil (Isa. 13:13; Zeph. 1:15, 18; 2:2–3; Rom. 2:5; Rev. 6:17). On that day, the unrighteous will go to eternal **punishment** (cf. Matt. 25:46).

God designed bodily desires, **passion** (2:10a), for honorable purposes. For example, he designed sexual **passion** for the propagation of life; but he also provided moral instruction so we know to reserve intercourse for marriage. Those ruled by fleshly **passion** follow no higher rule, like animals (2:12, 16, 22; Jude 10), so their passion is **impure** (2 Pet. 2:10a, 18; note especially "defile the flesh" in Jude 8, which Peter paraphrases).[83]

83. Peter's term here for "impure" (*miasmos*) can include moral pollution (Cornutus, *Greek Theology* 9, §11.1–3).

APPLICATION

Sexual Morality[a]

Some modern readers hear the biblical tradition's emphasis on sexual restraint as if it were designed to inhibit pleasure rather than to establish wholeness in relationships. This was certainly the case among many ascetics of late antiquity, including some philosophers and Christian monks; but it is not the point of the New Testament or of most other first-century Jews. Much of Western culture, overreacting against late antiquity's tradition repressing sexuality, has come to value casual sex with anyone as a form of recreation.

Yet by rejecting any restraints (and practical observations formed by many societies throughout human history), our world underestimates how deeply sexuality inheres in our humanity (Gen. 1:27). As with other animals, our sexual drives serve a procreative function for the species as a whole; but for humans, sexuality is also distinctively relational. For example, most female mammals are "in heat" only rarely, and females in few other species experience orgasm. Unlike most other animals, humans are able to mate face-to-face, and perhaps most significantly, romantically in the context of a relationship. Sexual intimacy is difficult to separate from emotional intimacy, and such intimacy flourishes in the context of vulnerability and trust, hence commitment. Counselors today must address the lives broken by betrayal and exploitation, where intercourse is often a self-gratifying act isolated from a person or a relationship.

Israelites, like most other societies, sought to protect their children's innocence against sexual predators. They also took sexual acts (and the possibility of consequent pregnancy and the conception of more humans in God's image) more seriously than modern Western society does. In a society where men controlled most wealth, they demanded that a man who risked getting a woman pregnant be committed to and provide for her (cf. Deut. 22:29); in this perspective, a prostitute sold herself cheaply, but casual sex was cheaper still (Deut. 22:21). By contrast, valuing one's neighbor as oneself demanded reserving one's deepest gift of intimacy for a partner who ideally would offer one nothing less than their own life. The gender-based double standard for sexuality (challenged in Gen. 38–39) and polygamy severely limited the fulfillment of this ideal. Nevertheless, permanent, mutual commitment remained the ideal to which God's plan pointed (Gen. 1:27–28; 2:24). To use another person's sexuality for one's own pleasure without genuinely committing oneself to that person was exploitive.

Today, as in antiquity, many people (most often men) exploit others' sexuality. Deceived by promises of education or legitimate jobs, thousands of girls from Bangladesh and Thailand are lured annually into an involuntary sex trade, a modern form of slave prostitution. In the West, thousands of runaway teenagers end up as prostitutes to find places to sleep at night. My wife recounts horrifying accounts of men, often relatives and neighbors, raping young girls in her native Central Africa, a tragedy exacerbated further by recent wars there that she witnessed. One of humanity's most precious gifts is also most easily abused by others who value momentary gratification over another human being's personhood.

a. I borrow this material from Keener, *1 and 2 Corinthians*, 60–61 (© Craig S. Keener 2005, reproduced with permission of the Licensor through PLSclear). There I follow esp. insights in Yancey, *Rumors of Another World*.

Since Peter here paraphrases some material in Jude, that the unrighteous **despise authority** (2:10a) takes for granted that this rejection of authority includes disrespect for angels (Jude 8–9), as becomes clear in 2 Pet. 2:10b–11. It could refer to despising Jesus's lordship (1:2; cf. *Didache* 4.1), but the only other New Testament uses of this term for **authority** (*kyriotēs*) refer to angelic powers, perhaps equivalent to the Jewish tradition of angels of nations, angels over various spheres (Eph. 1:21; Col. 1:16; cf. Dan. 10:13, 20–21). These powers stood behind earthly authorities. For that matter, Peter would also reject speaking disrespectfully against human authorities (cf. 1 Tim. 2:1–2; Titus 3:1–2; 1 Pet. 2:13–14), an activity that, unfortunately, many US citizens practice even against officials they help elect. By contrast, ancient Christian martyrs usually practiced respectful civil disobedience regarding their faith, not arrogant denunciation.

The Wicked's Moral Stupidity (2:10b–19)

> **2:10bThese people are reckless, self-willed, speaking with hostility against glorious ones without trembling. 11Yet angels who are stronger and more powerful don't raise against them a hostile decree of judgment before the Lord. 12But these people are like reasonless beasts, born as mere products of nature to be captured and killed. They speak with hostility against things they don't understand, and they will be destroyed just like those aforementioned beasts. 13Their reward for harming others is being harmed themselves.**
>
> **They consider daytime luxury banqueting as pleasure. They are stains and blemishes, in their deceptions luxury-banqueting when they feast together with you. 14Their eyes are completely full of an adulteress! They never take a break from sin! They entice unstable people. They have hearts developed by exercise in greed. Such accursed children!**
> **15Leaving the straight path, they wandered away, following instead the path of Balaam son of Beor, who loved the wages of wrongdoing. 16He got a reproof for his transgression. Speaking with a human voice, an [otherwise] speechless donkey intervened in the prophet's insanity!**

Although 2:10–18 is not the only section in which Peter draws on Jude to make his point, the concentration of references here allows for particularly vivid illustration:

2 Peter 2:10–18	Jude 8–13, 16
Flesh in its impure (*miasmos*) passion (2:10a)	Defile (*miainō*) the flesh (8)
Despise authority (2:10a)	Reject authority (8)
Slandering (angelic) glorious ones (2:10b)	Slandering (angelic) glorious ones (8)
Without trembling (2:10b)	Without fear (12)
Powerful angels do not slander glorious ones (2:11)	Michael did not slander the devil (9)
Slander what they do not understand (2:12)	Slander what they do not understand (10)
Like reasonless animals following instinct (2:12; cf. 2:16, 22)	Like reasonless animals following instinct (10)
They will be destroyed (*phtheirō*) (2:12)	They will be destroyed (*phtheirō*) (10)
Stains as they feast with you (2:13)	Stains (or, reefs) as they feast with you (12)

2 Peter 2:10–18	Jude 8–13, 16
Pursuing Balaam's error for money (2:15; cf. 2:13)	Pursuing Balaam's error for money (11)
Waterless springs (2:17)	Waterless clouds (12)
Mists driven by a windstorm (2:17)	Clouds carried by wind (12)
Deep darkness is reserved for them (2:17)	Gloom of darkness is reserved for them (13)
Boastful speech (2:18)	Boastful speech (16)

When used positively, *tolmētēs* (2:10b) designates an adventurous person, but here it refers to someone **reckless**, daring, unconcerned with the consequences of their actions (as in Sir. 8:15; 19:2–3).[84] The term translated as **self-willed** (*authadēs*; also in Titus 1:7; LXX Prov. 21:24) suggests insolence, stubborn and resistant, and again sometimes connotes recklessness (LXX Gen. 49:3, 7). Because of Peter's next verse, and because his language takes for granted Jude 8 (and probably his audience's familiarity with it), **speaking with hostility against glorious ones** involves dishonoring angelic powers, probably those with authority over various spheres (as in the "authority" in 2:10a). That they act **without trembling** underlines their foolish daring—that is, their being **reckless** and **self-willed**.

These **reckless** people speak against angelic powers even though angels themselves do not do so (2:11).[85] As Dieudonné Tamfu points out in this connection, "Only fools rush in where angels fear to tread."[86] These angels are **more powerful**, perhaps meaning more than the angelic powers addressed but likelier meaning (and certainly true concerning) **more powerful** than the **reckless** people. (The use of the cognate *blasphēmos* [**hostile**] in 2:11 reinforces the connection with *blasphēmeō* [**speaking with hostility**] in 2:10.) Again, Peter takes for granted Jude 8–9, where Michael addresses the devil without slandering him. Rather than risking giving credence to a noncanonical source, however, Peter omits Jude's reference to a particular extrabiblical story; Zech. 3:1–2 would be sufficient to make Peter's point.

In contrast to **angels**, which are more powerful than humans yet refuse to slander (2:11), and certainly in contrast to anyone sharing the divine nature

84. See also Josephus, *Jewish War* 3.475; *Jewish Antiquities* 20.199. For haughty speech, see Ps. 12:3–4; Prov. 21:24.

85. Some associate these angelic powers with eschatological judgment (cf. Zech. 14:5; Matt. 24:31), given the mockers' aversion to eschatology (2 Pet. 3:3–4). Yet they also seem to have a problem with authority more generally.

86. Tamfu, *2 Peter and Jude*, 57.

(1:3–4), these people belong on the other end of the spectrum: They act **like** animals (2:12).[87] (Peter comes short of fully *identifying* them with beasts; **like** signals merely comparison.) They are like **reasonless** [*alogos*] **beasts** (2:12), or like doomed Balaam, whose "speechless" (*aphōnos*) donkey acted smarter than he (2:16). Thinkers often compared those they considered irrational to beasts.[88]

Being merely **products of nature** (*physikos*; a downgrade from Jude 19's *psychikos*), they act by instinct rather than reason (*physikos* refers to what is inborn, so in their case instinct). Denying that animals had reason, most philosophers of the period denied that animals had rights. Many humans hunted such reasonless beasts, or watched captured beasts be killed for sport in the arena. (Peter is making an analogy, not a comment on ethical treatment of animals; under Nero, Christians too were killed for public entertainment.) Just as some humans kill reasonless beasts, so these aggressive humans are reasonless compared to the higher level of being they oppose, and so will face destruction (perhaps sometimes at the hands of those angels).

Harmed (2:13) translates *adikeō*, meaning "wrong, treat unjustly"; I render the verb with "harm," as in the NIV, to retain the connection between **harming** (*adikia*) and **being harmed** (*adikeō*). **Reward** translates *misthos*, meaning "pay, wages," quickly illustrated by Balaam's pursuit of **wages** (*misthos*) of **wrongdoing** (*adikia*) (2:15; cf. Jude 11). Ancient moralists condemned the seeking of **pleasure**, especially immoderately.[89] Like beasts that care about nothing of higher value than enjoying food, they indulge in **daytime** banqueting, even though the Greco-Roman world normally reserved banquets for evening, after a decent day of some productive activity.[90] **Stains** and **blemishes** ruin something pure (cf. Eph. 5:27); the Greek version of the Old Testament regularly uses this

87. Many counted humans midway between gods and animals (Sallust, *War with Catiline* 1.2; Cornutus, *Greek Theology* 16, §20.18–20; Musonius Rufus, *Lectures* 18A, p. 112.24–25; Pseudo-Crates, *Epistles* 11; Maximus of Tyre, *Orations* 6.1; 33.7) or between angels and beasts (*Sipre Deuteronomy* 306.28.2).

88. Pervasively: Xenophon, *Memorabilia* 1.2.30; *Rhetorica ad Alexandrum* pref. 1420ab.4–5; Polybius, *Roman Republic* 1.80.10; Philodemus, *Death* 35.14–15; *Frank Criticism* frg. 52.2–3; Seneca, *To Lucilius* 103.2; Musonius Rufus, *Lectures* 10, p. 78.27–28; 14, p. 92.21; 18A, p. 112.31; 18B, p. 116.14; Epictetus, *Discourses* 1.3.7, 9; 2.9.3, 5; 4.1.127; 4.5.21; Dio Chrysostom, *Orations* 8.14, 21; 32.26; 77/78.29; Plutarch, *Demosthenes* 26.4; *Bride and Groom* 7, *Moralia* 139B; *Reply to Colotes* 2, *Moralia* 1108D; Pseudo-Diogenes, *Epistles* 28; Hierocles, *Elements of Ethics* 3.45–50; 11.15–16; 4 Macc. 12:13; Philo, *Rewards and Punishments* 88; cf. Ps. 73:22; Dan. 4:32–33 (MT 4:29–30). Irrational animals act according to their nature, by instinct, but humans must exercise reason and volition (Cicero, *Duties* 1.4.11; Arius Didymus, *Epitome* 2.7.8, pp. 50.32–52.4).

89. For example, Cicero, *Ends* 2.12.35–2.13.43; Seneca, *To Lucilius* 59.1; *Dialogues* 7.11.1; Musonius Rufus, *Lectures* 8, p. 62.16; Epictetus, *Discourses* 3.12.7; *Letter of Aristeas* 277. See discussion in Keener, *Mind of the Spirit*, 20–21, 77, 104.

90. See, e.g., Dionysius of Halicarnassus, *Demosthenes* 12; Seneca the Elder, *Controversiae* 2.6.9; Dio Chrysostom, *Orations* 8.13; Tacitus, *Germania* 22.

terminology for **blemishes** to characterize people or offerings too imperfect to offer to God (e.g., Lev. 21:17–23; 22:20–25). Sometimes sages applied the term figuratively to moral faults (e.g., Sir. 20:24; 33:23; 47:20).[91] (For deception in a banquet setting, cf. perhaps Prov. 23:1–3.) Peter urges his audience, by contrast, to be unstained and unblemished (3:14).

Pagan banquets often catered to sexual passion as well as gluttony and drunkenness (cf. 2:14). Pagan practice sometimes connected food and sex (cf. 1 Cor. 6:13; 10:6–8). At Greek (as opposed to Roman) male banquets of the period, prostitutes might be the only women present, but this was obviously not the case at Christian gatherings around the Lord's Supper. Gentiles often were ready to accommodate male sexual passion, and love charms were prominent in ancient magic. Jewish thinkers condemned desiring women's beauty in ways that risked sexual sin,[92] though in ancient Middle Eastern fashion some blamed the women for not covering up more fully.[93] Some warned against "eyes of fornication"—that is, looking for opportunity for intercourse (cf. 2 Pet. 2:14).[94] One pre-Christian work complains about the wicked whose "eyes are on every woman indiscriminately" (*Psalms of Solomon* 4.4 [trans. *OTP* 2:655]).

Possibly based on Exod. 20:17 // Deut. 5:21 ("You shall not covet your neighbor's wife"), Jesus warns against desiring a woman's sexuality (Matt. 5:28, using the LXX word for "coveting" a neighbor's wife). This means not simply noticing beauty but imbibing it for the goal of imagining or ultimately engaging in sexual activity. Perhaps partly because many in antiquity thought that eyes projected light rather than merely received it, **eyes . . . completely full of an adulteress** probably means that they are utterly focused on someone they might expect to sleep with.

Whether it is the sinners or (likelier) their eyes that **never take a break** from sin, the point is the same. They **entice** (*deleazō*) hearers by appealing to their fleshly desires (cf. 2:18, repeating the same term). That they **entice** or "lure"

91. Later, *Testament of Asher* 2.6; also intelligible among gentiles, e.g., Dionysius of Halicarnassus, *Roman Antiquities* 4.24.6; Apuleius, *Florida* 9.3; Macrobius, *Saturnalia* 2.2.8.

92. For example, Job 31:1, 9; Sir. 9:8; 23:5; 41:21; Sus. 8; *1QRule of the Community* (1QS) 4.10; *Sibylline Oracles* 4.33–34; *Testament of Issachar* 4.4; *Testament of Reuben* 4.1, 8; 6.1–3; *Testament of Judah* 17.1; *m. Niddah* 2.1. See fuller discussion in Keener, *Matthew*, 186–88.

93. On the danger of women inviting lust, see Sir. 25:21; 26:9; *Psalms of Solomon* 16.7–8; *Testament of Reuben* 3.11–12; 5.1–5; 6.1; Josephus, *Jewish War* 2.121; *Jewish Antiquities* 7.130; for typical expectation for head coverings, see Sus. 32; *m. Bava Qamma* 8.6; *m. Ketubbot* 7.6; *Sipre Numbers* 11.2.1–3.

94. *1QRule of the Community* (1QS) 1.6; *Damascus Document*[a] (CD) 2.16; *11QTemple*[a] (11Q19) 59.14; *1QPesher to Habakkuk* (1QpHab) 5.7; cf. Num. 15:39 (MT, LXX, and *4QInstruction*[c] [4Q417] f1.1.27); *Testament of Issachar* 7.2; cf. the effect of wine in *Testament of Judah* 14.1. Gentiles would also find "adulterous eyes" intelligible (Cicero, *Against Catiline* 1.6.13; Valerius Maximus, *Deeds and Sayings* 2.1.5; Philostratus, *Lives of the Sophists* 1.20.513), even in an oft-cited ancient pun of the shameless having prostitutes in their eyes (Plutarch, *Compliancy* 1, *Moralia* 528E; Longinus, *Sublime* 4.5).

them need not be limited to sexual seduction, but in this context (**eyes . . . completely full of an adulteress**) probably includes it. The **unstable** (*astēriktos*) people here are vulnerable like those in 3:16 (again, *astēriktos*); they are those not "established" (*stērizō*) in the truth (1:12); believers must thus avoid falling from their "commitment" (*stērigmos*; 3:17). Whereas one normally thinks of training (**developed by exercise**) as self-discipline for a positive objective, these have trained themselves only in **greed**. Mention of **greed** recalls Peter's description of these exploiters in 2:3; the idea might include sexual as well as pecuniary desire (as suggested by context in Eph. 4:19; 5:3; Col. 3:5). **Accursed children** is literally "children of a curse," a Semitic idiom for those who merit a curse (cf., e.g., "children of wrath" in Eph. 2:3; though for children being cursed, cf. Gen. 9:25; 49:7; Sir. 3:9).

The straight path [*hodos*] (2:15) is the "way" (*hodos*) of truth (2:2) and righteousness (2:21). A straight path is a better one logistically (Ps. 107:7) and is the Lord's way (Isa. 40:3; Hosea 14:9; Acts 13:10); the Greek version of Proverbs warns against leaving the straight "paths" (*hodos*; Prov. 2:13). (On the two ways, see comment on 2:3.) That they **wandered** (*planaō*; cf. Jude 13) fits their "error" (*plane*; 2 Pet. 2:18; 3:17; Jude 11).

The **path of Balaam** (2:15) is also the path of Cain (Jude 11), contrasting with the **straight path**. **Balaam** was **son of Beor** (eleven times in the LXX), not "Bosor" (a place name in the LXX), an unusual transliteration but one that does not change the meaning.[95] The monetary **reward** (*misthos*), or "wages, pay" (recalling 2:13), that Balaam could get for doing wrong initially eluded him (Num. 24:11) until he was able to find a way to bring a curse on Israel (Deut. 31:16). Clearly, he wanted not what God desired but rather to circumvent God's desire for the sake of King Balak's promised reward. Only bringing Israel to sin could turn God's blessing of them into a curse. Likewise, the false teachers whom Peter denounces lead God's people into sin. Balaam's **path** also plays on the path where the Lord's angel initially met Balaam to kill him (Num. 22:23, 31–32), a story to which Peter quickly turns. (On Balaam further, see comment on Jude 11.) The term rendered here as **wrongdoing** (*adikia*) is the same term used for doing "harm" in 2:13.

Balaam indulged his greed (2:15) by accompanying Balak's messengers (Num. 22:21) despite divine displeasure (22:12, despite 22:20). His donkey, however, saw the Lord's angel standing in the way, ready to slay Balaam, and so refused to go forward (22:23–27). When God miraculously enabled the donkey to vocalize her protest (22:28), Balaam engages in argument with her without stopping to wonder how his donkey is speaking (22:29). Contrary to ancient stereotypes of

95. For a survey of attempted explanations, see G. Green, *Jude and 2 Peter*, 289–90.

Rembrandt / public domain / Wikimedia Commons

Rembrandt's envisioning of Balaam striking his donkey

donkeys, they are neither stupid nor stubborn; but whereas horses bolt when they are afraid, donkeys freeze.[96] One thing they normally do not do, however, is talk!

In the **reproof** or rebuke for wrong, Peter plays on Balaam's **transgression** (*paranomia*) and his **insanity** (*paraphronia*). The verb for the donkey **speaking** (*phthengomai*) recurs for the false teachers speaking in empty pride in 2:18.[97] Its **voice** contrasts with the heavenly voice vouchsafed to Peter and his colleagues (1:17–18). Although Balaam prophesied true oracles, this **prophet's** greed (2:15) aligns him with the false prophets (2:1; cf. 2:3) and contrasts with true prophets (3:2). In this case, the donkey acts smarter than Balaam, and Balaam acts like one of the "reasonless beasts" doomed to perish in 2:12.[98]

> **2:17 These people are waterless springs and mists driven by a windstorm. God has reserved gloomy darkness for them. 18 This is what they deserve, because by speaking empty boasts they entice people. They entice them by appealing to their fleshly desires with the possibility for unrestrained license. Their victims are those who barely escape those who live in error. 19 The false teachers promise their victims freedom, even though they themselves are slaves of corruption! For a person is a slave to whatever subdues them.**

In 2:17, the errorists are **waterless**—hence useless—**springs**. Like **mists**, they obscure vision without providing water to drink. Most people in antiquity lacked access to running water, and many had to walk miles to obtain water. More obscuring than **mists**, however, is the **gloomy darkness** that awaits the agitators, a fate shared with the fallen angels (2:4; Jude 6).

In 2:18, I render *gar* ("for") as **this is what they deserve** because the conjunction predicates the fate in 2:17 on the errorists' behavior described in 2:18. **Empty** (I render the genitive noun here adjectivally) here refers to what is vain, futile, and worthless. Even in the honor-conscious Greco-Roman world, people considered **boasts** (also in Jude 16) obnoxious unless properly justified;[99] *empty* boasts were always obnoxious (e.g., Prov. 27:2).

96. See discussion in Keener, "Donkey Colt." For beasts shaming humans to change conduct, see Musonius Rufus, *Lectures* 7, p. 58.16. Animals spoke in the mythical pagan Golden Age (Babrius, *Fables*, prologue 5–7; Iamblichus, *Life of Pythagoras* 30.178), but by this period animal speech functioned as an omen (Livy, *History of Rome* 41.13.2; 43.13.3; Valerius Maximus, *Deeds and Sayings* 1.6.5; Appian, *Civil War* 4.1.4).

97. In biblical Greek, a cognate verb also applies at times to putatively inspired speech (LXX 1 Chron. 25:1; Ezek. 13:9; Mic. 5:11 [ET 5:12]; Acts 2:4), which would be ironic in a sentence calling Balaam a prophet; but the connection is not clear.

98. Jewish ethics expected God to judge people according to their crime; this judgment could include sending reasonless beasts to judge those who worshiped reasonless beasts (Wis. 11:15).

99. See Forbes, "Self-Praise."

Entice (2:18) revisits the errorists' "enticing" unstable people in 2:14. The **fleshly desires** involve bodily passions (as in 2:10; on the **desires**, see also 1:4; 3:3); instead of controlling them productively (such as sex in marriage or eating for health), the errorists offer their hearers the opportunity to indulge physical pleasures without restraint. Like the residents of Sodom (2:7), they value and even promote **unrestrained license**, as already noted in 2:2.

The particular term for **escape** (*apopheugō*; 2:18) appears in the New Testament only in 2 Peter, where it refers to escaping the corruption that is in the world (1:4; 2:20). Interpretations differ as to whether the victims **barely escape** the errorists, yet do escape (cf. ESV; NASB; NET note; Jude 23), or whether they have just recently escaped (cf. BBE; NET; NIV; NRSV; possibly NJB) and hence are vulnerable to being lured back. In view of 2:20, the latter interpretation seems likelier in this case. The term rendered as **error** (*planē*; also 3:17; Jude 11) fits "going astray" (*planaō*) in 2:15.

Most philosophic schools promised **freedom** (2:19) for those who followed their particular ideology. The errorists' false **promise** that enslaves people to **corruption** (2:19) contrasts with God's true promises that liberate us (1:4) and will be consummated in the future (3:4, 9, 13). Whereas Peter is an honorable slave of Christ (1:1), the false teachers are **slaves of corruption**. The idea of **corruption** (*phthora*) relates not only to moral depravity (cf. NIV; the relation to lust in 1:4) but also to consequent mortality (translated as "killed" and "destroyed" in 2:12; see also Rom. 8:21; 1 Cor. 15:42, 50; Gal. 6:8; Col. 2:22).

As conquerors often enslaved prisoners, whatever **subdues** one enslaves one (2:19; cf. John 8:34; Rom. 6:16); and these who were once liberated from corruption by Christ are now subdued by it again (2:20).

Apostates Are Worse Off (2:20–22)

> **2:20 This observation applies here: If they escaped the world's defile-
> ments by coming to know our[100] Lord and Savior Jesus Christ but get
> caught up in them again and so are subdued, they end up worse off
> than the way they were before! 21 For it would have been better for
> them not to have come to know the way of righteousness than to have
> known it and to turn from the holy command entrusted to them. 22 The
> true proverb came to pass in them: "A dog goes back to its vomit";
> and: "After washing itself, a female pig [goes back] to rolling around in
> the mud."**

100. The textual variant "the" does not affect the sense, given Peter's usage elsewhere.

Various lines of Jewish tradition concerned themselves not only with ritual but also with moral purity, the latter being the focus in the New Testament, including **defilements** (*miasma*) in 2:20. (I render the genitive cognate noun *miasmos* adjectivally in 2:10 as "impure.") It is **coming to know . . . Jesus** that sets us free, transforming us to be like him (see 1:3, 8; cf. 2 Cor. 3:18). Returning to **the world's defilements** after being freed from them in Christ, however, leaves apostates **worse off than the way they were before**.

Ancient speakers often chose to reinforce a point by elaborating it in different words. If someone who turns from Christ is **worse off than the way they were before** (2:20), then they would have been better off not coming to know the truth to begin with (2:21; maybe echoing Jesus [cf. Matt. 12:45 // Luke 11:26]). Knowing **Jesus Christ** (2 Pet. 2:20) and knowing **the way of righteousness** (2:21) refer to the same experience, as does embracing **the holy command** (2:21). Although **the holy command** is a suitable title for the law (Rom. 7:12), Peter likely refers to Jesus's message (the "command" of Jesus in 2 Pet. 3:2). That the **command** was **entrusted** [*paradidōmi*] **to them** means it was handed down to them (as in Jude 3), probably ultimately going back to the message of Jesus himself (the verb *paradidōmi* often applies to handing on teachings, as in Rom. 6:17; 1 Cor. 11:2, 23; 15:3).

The first proverb in 2:22 is from Scripture, though (as is common in allusions dependent on memory) in different words. Proverbs 26:11 declares, "Like a dog that returns to its vomit, so is a fool who repeats his folly" (the Greek version elaborates further regarding sin); the second apparently reflects a saying from the legend of *Ahiqar* (cf. Syriac 8.18; esp. Arabic 8.15): "Having just bathed, a pig wallows in slime."

In addition to living in gentile households, dogs were known to live in the streets and consume carrion. They were associated with anger,[101] filth,[102] sexual immorality,[103] uncleanness,[104] lack of bowel control,[105] and attachment to dung and sniffing other dogs' butts.[106] Both Greek and Jewish sources use "dog" as an insult,[107] both for males and females, sometimes with connotations

101. Callimachus, *Minor Poems* 380.

102. Lucian, *Ignorant Book-Collector* 5 cites a proverb: "What has a dog to do with a bath?" (trans. A. M. Harmon, LCL 3:183). The "vomit" in 2 Pet. 2:22 reflects Prov. 26:11, but some gentiles used canine vomit for alleged (external) cures (Pliny the Elder, *Natural History* 30.31.105).

103. Theophrastus, *Characters* 28.3; Plutarch, *Bride and Groom* 7, *Moralia* 139B; *y. Ta'anit* 1.6, §8; *Genesis Rabbah* 36:7; Rev. 22:15.

104. Martial, *Epigrams* 1.83.

105. Phaedrus, *Fables* 4.19.

106. Phaedrus, *Fables* 1.27.10–11; 4.19.

107. For example, Homer, *Iliad* 8.527; 9.373; 11.362; 20.449; 22.345; *Odyssey* 17.248; 22.35; Martial, *Epigrams* 1.83; Plutarch, *Exile* 7, *Moralia* 601DE; 1 Sam. 17:43; Prov. 26:11; Philo, *Giants* 35; *Mekilta Kaspa* 2.23–26; *y. Ta'anit* 1.6, §8; *Pesiqta of Rab Kahana* 7.6; *Genesis Rabbah* 36.7; *Song of Songs Rabbah* 2.13, §4; *Pesiqta Rabbati* 15.14/15.

PENTECOSTAL INTEREST

Apostasy and Perseverance

It is difficult to see how those who affirm "once saved, always saved" without perseverance can accommodate 2 Pet. 2:20–22. If a person is "worse off than" before knowing Christ, they are not in Christ so long as they remain in this condition. I know close friends with whom I used to pray, study Scripture, or go out sharing our faith on the streets who subsequently converted to other religions or left all religion and have not even claimed to be Christian for years. While I would wish that they would still count as saved, I also would wish that the world's hungry would be fed. Wishful thinking is not, however, a sound basis for our faith or practice. How many people will be lost because they were falsely taught that, having prayed a prayer or been baptized, they will be saved no matter their subsequent choices? Salvation belongs to those who remain Jesus's people (Mark 4:16–17; 9:42–43; John 8:31; 15:6; Rom. 11:22; 1 Cor. 15:2; 1 Thess. 3:5; Rev. 3:5).[a]

Arminians believe that a person can experience salvation yet fall away and be lost. Calvinists believe that a person can appear to experience salvation, but if they do not persevere, they are lost. The Calvinist approach focuses on God's perspective; if a person does not persevere, obviously they will not ultimately belong to Christ. That makes good sense theologically (cf. Rom. 8:29–30; 1 John 2:19). Since we do not know the future, I believe that the Arminian approach, dealing with human experience, is more relevant in typical pastoral practice (Acts 14:22; 2 Cor. 13:5; Gal. 5:4; Col. 1:23a; 1 Tim. 4:16; Heb. 3:14; 4:1).[b] Arminians, however, sometimes err in the other direction, fearing for their salvation. We are secure in Christ; one falls away from Christ not by accident but by turning from him. One does not drop in and out of grace; we declare our allegiance to Christ, and we maintain our status so long as we maintain our allegiance.

a. For apostasy, see also Matt. 24:10; 2 Thess. 2:3; 1 Tim. 4:1; perhaps 1 Tim. 5:15; 2 Tim. 4:3–4; Titus 1:11; in the New Testament generally, see I. Marshall, *Power of God*; Oropeza, *Apostasy*; Shank, *Life in the Son*.

b. I also believe that those who fall away can be restored (cf. Matt. 18:12–14; Gal. 4:19; James 5:19–20; 1 John 5:16–17), Peter being a conspicuous case in point (Luke 22:32). I understand passages that warn of the impossibility of such restoration to refer not to those who wish to return to the faith but to those who continue to refuse that option, perhaps too hardened by that point to consider it (Heb. 2:1–3; 3:12; 6:1–6; 10:26–31; 12:15–29).

for sexual promiscuity similar to some canine insults today.[108] Pork was a favorite food in the northern Mediterranean world, so most people were also aware of pigs' habits, including their wallowing in mud. But gentiles also knew that Jews avoided pork.[109] Pigs had a reputation for wallowing in filth,[110] lacking appreciation of value (Prov. 11:22; Matt. 7:6), gluttony,[111] and lack of sexual control.[112] Jewish texts generally regard dogs as unclean and scavengers[113] alongside pigs.[114]

What the two proverbs have in common is "reasonless beasts" (2:12): Acting on their passions, the false teachers and their followers care nothing for purity or the new life once entrusted to them. The **washing** happened when they first came to Christ (1 Cor. 6:11; Titus 3:5; Heb. 10:22), but these people have forgotten their purification from their former sins (2 Pet. 1:9).

The Promise of His Coming (3:1–10)

> **3:1 Loved ones, this is now the second letter I'm writing you. In both these letters my purpose is to wake up your sincere mind by reminders [of what you already know]. 2 My reminders are so you'll call to mind the things foretold by the holy prophets and the command of the Lord and Savior through your apostles.**

Naturally, a writer would sometimes refer to a previous letter to the same recipient(s).[115] Some suggest that the **second letter** (3:1) refers back to an earlier portion of 2 Peter, originally circulated independently (cf. 1:12–15). Most scholars, by contrast, argue plausibly that the **second letter** refers to 1 Peter as the first, especially if 1 Peter was widely circulated by the time 2 Peter was composed or arranged. That we know of no other first-century letters attributed to Peter raises the probability, though does not prove, that 1 Peter is in view here.

108. Aelian, *Nature of Animals* 7.19; cf. Deut. 23:18.

109. For example, Juvenal, *Satires* 6.160.

110. Aristophanes, *Peace* 24; Oppian, *Halieutica* 3.439–40; Musonius Rufus, *Lectures* 12, p. 86.29; *b. Berakhot* 25a; *b. Qiddushin* 49b; 2 Pet. 2:22.

111. Xenophon, *Memorablia* 1.3.7; Horace, *Epodes* 1.2.25–26 (also linking them with dogs); Musonius Rufus, *Lectures* 18B, p. 116.4, 14; Dio Chrysostom, *Orations* 8.14; Heraclitus, *Homeric Problems* 72.2–3.

112. Xenophon, *Memorabilia* 1.2.30; Horace, *Epodes* 1.2.25–26; Macrobius, *Saturnalia* 2.8.15.

113. For example, *b. Sanhedrin* 108b, bar.; *b. Shabbat* 121b, 128a.

114. Some texts link dogs and swine, known to inhabit unclean surroundings (e.g., Aristophanes, *Peace* 24; Horace, *Epodes* 1.2.25–26; Musonius Rufus, *Lectures* 18B, p. 116.14; Matt. 7:6; 2 Pet. 2:22; see also Davies and Allison, *Matthew*, 1:677).

115. For example, Pliny the Younger, *Epistles* 4.25.1; Symmachus, *Epistles* 1.80; 1 Cor. 5:9; 2 Cor. 2:3–4.

Still, the topics are quite different, and 1 Peter does not play on reminders; the audience could be different.

For **reminders** (3:1–2) and their rhetorical-pedagogic function, see comment on 1:12–15, which has a concentration of memory language.[116] The term translated as **sincere** (*eilikrinēs*) implies "without hidden motives or pretense,"[117] here perhaps suggesting lack of agendas that would prevent receiving the truth (cf. NIV: "to stimulate you to wholesome thinking").

The particular content of the **reminders** is elaborated in 3:2: the message of the **prophets** and of Jesus via the **apostles**, perhaps shorthand for the Old Testament message and the apostolic message that for us is exemplified in the New Testament (cf. Eph. 2:20, though that passage might refer to Christian prophets, as in 4:11). Second Peter associates the prophetic message with Scripture in 1:20–21 and already recognizes apostolic writings (a sort of proto–New Testament) as among inspired writings (3:16). The passage invites Christians today to immerse ourselves afresh in Scripture. The term that I translated **foretold** (*prolegō*; also Jude 17) can mean simply "say beforehand," but it is applied elsewhere to Old Testament prophetic warnings (Acts 1:16; Heb. 4:7), apostolic warnings of coming affliction (1 Thess. 3:4; cf. 4:6), and, perhaps most relevantly here, Jesus's warning of false prophets (Matt. 24:25; Mark 13:23).

The "Holy" Spirit (1:21) inspired **holy** prophets (3:2) with the "holy" command (2:21), which now includes the command from Jesus. The **command** of Jesus (3:2) probably refers to all his teaching, including about being ridiculed and even persecuted for our faith (3:3; Matt. 5:11 // Luke 6:22; Mark 13:9–13; John 16:1–4) and the cosmic impact of Jesus's return (2 Pet. 3:4–12; Mark 13:24–27), although the most specific command of Jesus often cited is his command to love (Mark 12:31; John 13:34; 15:12; Rom. 13:9; Gal. 5:13–14; 6:2; James 2:8). The phrase **your apostles** might refer to those who established their circle of churches (1 Cor. 9:2) or that apostles belonged to the mission (1 Cor. 3:22).

> **3:3 Above all, recognize that in the last days mockers will come, mocking while pursuing their own desires. 4 They mock, "Where's the promise that he's coming? For ever since the ancestors died, everything keeps going on just like it has since the beginning of creation!" 5 They think that because they willfully neglect the truth that the heavens existed long ago and the land formed out of water and through water by God's word. 6 Through them the world of that time perished, flooded with**

116. Letters could also recall past instruction, as in P.Mich. 202.3 (Hansen, *Abraham in Galatians*, 28).

117. BDAG 282.

water. [7]But by that same word the present heavens and the earth are stored up for fire, reserved for the day of judgment and of the destruction of impious people.

As in 1:20, Peter exhorts them to **above all, recognize** (3:3). **Mocking while pursuing their own desires** is a slight paraphrase of Jude 18. Peter here revisits his earlier comments about the errorists: They pursue their passions (2:10) and entice others by appealing to their passions (2:18); hence they are subject to the world's corruption (1:4). They live for present impulses like beasts (2:12), without contemplating an eternal future, and mock those who live for the promised world to come.[118] **Mocking while pursuing** is literally "mocking, pursuing," but I infer that **pursuing their own desires** is the motive to which Peter attributes their **mocking**.

Although sometimes used more favorably (2 Kings 2:14; Isa. 63:15; Jer. 2:8), **where's** evokes a common way for those who defy God to challenge him or his agents (2 Kings 18:34; Pss. 42:3, 10; 79:10; 115:2; Jer. 17:15; Joel 2:17; Mic. 7:10; Mal. 2:17). On the principle of analogy, the mockers appeal to historic precedent against a radical change in the future. They do not trust the words of earlier prophets or Jesus's apostles about a future day of judgment. For seven or eight centuries prophets had been warning that the day of judgment was coming soon (e.g., Isa. 13:6; Ezek. 30:3; Rev. 1:3; 22:7, 12, 20), and it had not yet happened. "Alas, for the day! For the day of YHWH is near! . . . For the day of YHWH comes, for it is near! . . . For the day of YHWH is near in the valley of judgment!" (Joel 1:15; 2:1; 3:14 AT; cf. Obad. 15; Zeph. 1:14).

Yet prophets continued proclaiming imminence rather than stopping after a century or two precisely because they understood it not as entailing immediacy but as demanding continued readiness. The mockers misunderstand the genre of the rhetoric spoken. From an eternal vantage point, *all* human lifetimes appear fleeting (e.g., Pss. 39:5, 11; 90:3–4 [echoed in 2 Pet. 3:8]; 144:4). The point of such announcements was not to predict a time frame for the end but to underline an unpredictability that requires continued vigilance.[119] Meanwhile,

118. Compare later Macarius Magnes, *Apocriticus* 4.1–7 (the end has not come), 24 (resurrection contradicts historical precedent). Many thought that denying the afterlife (hence judgment), as in Epicureanism, promoted immorality (e.g., Plutarch, *Pleasant Life Impossible* 23, *Moralia* 1103D). Many Jews likewise doubted the morality of those who denied the afterlife (Wis. 2:1–24; *b. Rosh Hashanah* 17a; Targum Neofiti 1 on Gen. 4:8; Targum Pseudo-Jonathan on Gen. 25:32); later the Qur'an also attributes its denial to the same cause (6.29; cf. 17.10; 23.35, 37, 82; 34.3). Other thinkers insisted that religion was needed for public morality, even if it was untrue (Polybius, *Roman Republic* 6.56.7–15; Proclus, *Poetics* 5, K51.11–14).

119. See Witherington, *End of the World*. In a similar vein, a rabbi urged disciples to repent a day before their death; and since they could not know when that would be, they should always be

many foreshadowings of the end provide nearer warnings (e.g., Matt. 12:28 // Luke 11:20; Mark 1:15; 2 Thess. 2:7; 1 John 2:18; Rev. 2:16). The very delay about which mockers complain is God's mercy to allow them opportunity for repentance (2 Pet. 3:9, 15)!

Peter also offers biblical precedent for radical, unexpected change (2 Pet. 3:5–7), God's different time reckoning (3:8), and key factors in the supposed

repentant (*Ecclesiastes Rabbah* 9:8, §1). Bede, commenting on 1 Pet. 4:7, writes, "So that no one might deceive himself in thinking that the future judgement . . . is far off, he advisedly warns that, although the time of the arrival of the final judgment is indefinite, yet it is definitely clear to all that they are unable to continue for long in this mortal life" (*Catholic Epistles*, 109).

PENTECOSTAL INTEREST

Jesus's Future Coming

Early Pentecostalism emerged in a period of radical eschatological hope. Although most early Pentecostals reflected the views dominant at their time, many differed on details. Many believed that their experience reflected a latter rain, restoring what the church had lost (citing Joel 2:23); others recognized more continuity with earlier outpourings of the Spirit in history yet emphasized that these experiences provided a foretaste of the coming kingdom. Most lived in light of their expectation of Christ's imminent return and their belief that their empowerment by the Spirit was eschatologically significant and the trust that it equipped them for the eschatological mission to the nations.

Influenced by the scholarly recognition that Jesus inaugurated the kingdom at his first coming but will consummate it at the second, many charismatics today (e.g., the Vineyard movement) welcome signs and wonders as a foretaste of the kingdom. In this way, too, people of the Spirit continue to live in light of kingdom expectation.

Some circles, however, have come to avoid preaching about Jesus's return, disillusioned or confused by failed promises of prophecy teachers who spoke so loudly in the 1970s and often do so today. We do not need to have all the details figured out, however, to yearn for and preach and teach about our Lord's return. Most New Testament passages about his return invite us to live lives consecrated to God and lives of hope in light of eternity. Charts and speculations confuse matters, but early Pentecostals (following the lead of others) were right to maintain the centrality of the teaching that Jesus is our coming king.

delay (God's mercy and human intransigence [3:9, 15]). Those who doubt a future climax to history read history the wrong way: God has been giving foretastes (within Scripture itself, notably partial restoration from exile, "already but not yet" in Jesus's ministry, and the destruction of the temple in AD 70), which guarantee the future fullness.

Last days paraphrases "the final time" in Jude 18 with a more familiar phrase. The phrase "last days" appears often in the prophets and early Jewish sources.[120] It begins with the Messiah's first coming (Heb. 1:2; 1 Pet. 1:20) and includes the present period (Acts 2:17–18; 1 Tim. 4:1–3; 2 Tim. 3:1–6).[121] (Contrast the more decisive "last day" for the resurrection and judgment [John 6:39–40, 44, 54; 11:24; 12:48].) One characteristic often assigned to this period is rebellion against God (1 Tim. 4:1; 2 Tim. 3:1–5), including an antichrist figure or figures (1 John 2:18). Ironically, end-time mockers mock the idea of an end time.

Peter speaks of Jesus's first **coming** in 1:16, but here in 3:4 he speaks of his second **coming**, which coincides with the coming of God's day of judgment (3:12), though most mockers apparently believe in neither (3:4). The **ancestors** may refer to the patriarchs.[122] In the Greek text, **died** is literally "fell asleep," but sleep had long been a conventional euphemism for death.[123] The mockers expect the future to be no different from the present, reasoning that the present is just like the past. Many people today think the same way; both ancient Epicureans and modern deists deny that any deity is involved in human affairs. Peter responds by pointing out that the past is *not* always like the present (3:5–6).

The term translated as **stored up** (*thēsaurizō*; also the cognate noun *thēsauros*) applies to "treasuring up" blessings in heaven (Matt. 6:19–21 // Luke 12:33–34; Mark 10:21; cf. Tob. 12:8–9; Sir. 29:11–12) or wrath in the judgment (Rom. 2:5; James 5:3).

The mockers **neglect** the truth (3:5),[124] but Peter exhorts his hearers *not* to "neglect" it (3:8). In 3:5 I translate the Greek term *gē* as **land** because of its

120. For example, Isa. 2:2; Jer. 23:20; 49:39; Ezek. 38:16; Hosea 3:5; Mic. 4:1; *1 Enoch* 27.2; 108.1; *11QMelchizedek* (11Q13) 2.4; *4 Ezra* 7.84, 95.

121. The delay of the end caused Qumran sectarians to recognize the period of last days as longer than first anticipated (*1QPesher to Habakkuk* [1QpHab] 7.7–13); compare the concern about the delay that can already be seen in Hab. 2:3.

122. The death of "the ancestors" could refer to earlier Israelite history (Zech. 1:6; John 6:58; 8:52; Acts 7:15), but gentiles also spoke of their ancestors (e.g., Herodotus, *Histories* 4.127.2; Cornutus, *Greek Theology* 9, §9.15).

123. For example, Dan. 12:2; 2 Macc. 12:45; Sophocles, *Oedipus at Colonus* 1578; Callimachus, *Epigrams* 11, 18; Plutarch, *Condolence to Apollonius* 12, *Moralia* 107D; *CIJ* 1.8, §3; 1.12, §17. For further discussion, see Keener, *Acts*, 2:1462–63.

124. Language that ancients sometimes used to respond to critics (Heraclitus, *Homeric Problems* 40.2).

relation to **water**, but in 3:7 I translate it as **earth** (which it also means) because it contrasts with **heavens**; together they constitute creation as it was understood. While some in antiquity insisted that the universe had always existed,[125] the mockers here appear more like early modern deists: They affirm **the beginning of creation** but doubt God's subsequent involvement (such as miracles or judgments). The influential first-century Jewish philosopher Philo affirmed creation, against Aristotle, but with him (if the disputed *Eternity of the World* is authentic) may have affirmed the universe's subsequent eternality; yet his Platonic philosophic tradition regarded only what was unchanging, such as (supposedly) the heavens, as eternal.[126] For Peter, only God and what he preserves are eternal (cf. Ps. 102:23–28; 1 John 2:17).

What God gave on earth in creation, he took back through the flood (3:6; cf. 2:5), restoring primeval chaos; *kataklysmos*, the cognate noun for **flooded** (*kataklyzō*), appears in Matt. 24:38–39 // Luke 17:27 and in Gen. 6:17; 7:6–17. For **the world**'s perishability, see 1:4. God does not want anyone to "perish" (3:9), but precedent demonstrates that the unrepentant do "perish" anyway (3:6).

The object **them** in **through them** (3:6) is not completely clear; one might take it as "through God's word," given the recurrent role of his word in 3:7a, although the likeliest reading in Greek here is plural. Most ancient thinkers regarded **water** (3:5–6), like **fire** (3:7), as one of the four primeval elements (cf. 3:10, 12).[127] Peter's mention of God forming **land . . . out of water** reflects the primeval role of water in Gen. 1:2 and the gathering of lower waters to reveal dry ground (1:9–10). What God gave through water, he could also remove by the flood, pouring out the upper waters and transgressing the boundaries of the lower ones (7:11).[128] After the flood, a sort of new creation emerged,[129] although sin already latent in humanity quickly corrupted it again (9:21–22). Jewish thinkers naturally used cataclysm by the flood to prefigure end-time cataclysm (as apparently in *1 Enoch*).

125. Especially Aristotle, *Heavens* 1.3, 270a.13–14; 1.10–12, 279b4–283b22; later Sallustius, *Gods and the Universe* §§7, 13, 17. Reporting varied views, see Seneca, *Natural Questions* 3.22.1; Hippolytus, *Refutation of Heresies* 1.9. Philo averred that such a denial undermines piety (*Creation* 9–11).

126. For affirmations of the cosmos's or at least the heavens' eternality, see Lucretius, *Nature of Things* 1.958–1115; Cicero, *Tusculan Disputations* 1.23.54; Plotinus, *Enneads* 2.1.1. For Philo's views, see Wolfson, *Philo*, 1:180, 301–4.

127. Thales viewed water as the cosmos's "generative principle" (Vitruvius, *Architecture* 8.pref.1; Hippolytus, *Refutation of Heresies* 1.1; cf. *Pesiqta Rabbati* 21.21), but others differed (e.g., Heraclitus viewed the principle as fire).

128. At least in Revelation, waters assume a new format in the new creation (Rev. 21:1; 22:1–2; contrast 21:8), perhaps because they are unmentioned in Isa. 65:17; 66:22.

129. Note Gen. 5:29; 8:21; parallelism between Gen. 1:26–30 and 9:1–3, 6–7; see also *Sibylline Oracles* 1.195; Philo, *Life of Moses* 2.64.

God's word formed the land (3:5), and **that same word** also reserves the present creation for fiery destruction (3:7). Peter was not the only Jewish thinker to recognize that God's promise to exempt the world from future destruction by water (Gen. 9:11; cf. 8:21) would not exempt it from fire.[130] The *nyn* ("now," **present**) in 3:7 contrasts with the *tote* ("then," **of that time**) in 3:6. Impious angels and people are elsewhere **reserved** for judgment (see 2:4, 9, 17); here corrupted creation, too, must be purified by fire.[131]

People could use water for ritual purification, but they could also use fire (see Num. 31:23; cf. Matt. 3:11 // Luke 3:16; see also 1 Pet. 1:7). God would burn the damaged old creation (2 Pet. 3:10, 12) to purify it from corruption to birth the wholly righteous new creation (3:13).

The day of judgment (3:7; also 2:9; cf. 2:4) is a familiar expression.[132] Peter uses in a parallel eschatological manner the phrase **day . . . of the destruction**,[133] which in the LXX referred to times of disaster (Deut. 32:35; Job 21:30; Jer. 18:17; Obad. 12–13). Peter elsewhere addresses the **destruction** (*apōleia*) of the impious (2 Pet. 2:1, 3; 3:16); I rendered the cognate verb *apollymi* as "perish" in 3:6, 9.

> **3:8But don't neglect this one point, loved ones: With the Lord, a single day is like a thousand years, and a thousand years are like a single day. 9The Lord isn't being slow in fulfilling his promise, as some are counting slowness. Instead, the Lord is being patient toward you, because he doesn't want anyone to perish, but everyone to turn from sin to God. 10But the day of the Lord will come like a thief, in which the heavens will pass away with a rushing sound and the elements will be destroyed through burning, and the earth and the works in it will be found.**

Peter appeals to the difference in God's time in Ps. 90:4, in which a thousand years are like a day to him.[134] The point of Ps. 90:4 is that human life is transitory, unlike God's eternality.[135] God watches over all creation each day, with far greater

130. Josephus, *Jewish Antiquities* 1.70–71; *Life of Adam and Eve* 49.3; *t. Ta'anit* 2.13.

131. For the flood as purification, see Philo, *Life of Moses* 2.64.

132. LXX Isa. 34:8; Jdt. 16:17; *1 Enoch* 10.6, 12; 22.11, 13; 27.3–4; 98.10; 99.15; 100.4; 104.5; *Psalms of Solomon* 15.12; Matt. 10:15; 11:22, 24; 12:36.

133. Compare *1 Enoch* 98.10; 99.4.

134. See also *Jubilees* 4.30; *2 Baruch* 17.1; 48.12–13; for six millennial periods, *b. Avodah Zarah* 9a; *b. Sanhedrin* 97a. Greeks sometimes spoke of differences between divine and human time (Pseudo-Apollodorus, *Bibliotheca* 3.4.2; Iamblichus, *Life of Pythagoras* 28.155).

135. If the sweeping away in Ps. 90:5 evokes a flood (so NASB), it fits comparison with the flood in 2 Pet. 3:6; but cognates can refer to any sort of storm (e.g., Isa. 4:6; 25:4; 28:2; 30:30), and the LXX lacks an analogous term.

attention to detail than humans could display even in a millennium; and for the creator of time and space, who is necessarily beyond both, no finite period of time is long (3:8). God can thus afford to be **patient** to fulfill his objective of more and more people coming to repentance (3:9).[136]

The **promise** that the Lord is not **being slow** about (3:9) is the promise of his coming (3:4) and the consequent new creation (3:13). The **some** who **are counting slowness** are the skeptics in 3:3–4 who scoff at the promise because it has been taking so long to happen (counting from Isa. 65, already nearly eight centuries by Peter's day). It is effectively God's mercy that they protest; God is "slow to anger" (Exod. 34:6; Num. 14:18; Neh. 9:17; Ps. 145:8; Joel 2:13). The term for the Lord **being patient** (*makrothymeō*) can connote putting up with or bearing something patiently. The Lord's patience is salvation (3:15); that is, it is allowing more people to be saved (cf. 1 Pet. 3:20). Peter will soon attribute this view also to Paul. For Paul speaking of God's patience bringing salvation (3:15), Peter might think of Rom. 2:4; 9:22; 11:11, 25–26, 30–32, God's plan that allows for both Jews and gentiles to come to Christ.

That the Lord wants all to be saved (3:9) but that not all will be saved (e.g., 2:1, 3; 3:7; cf. Ezek. 18:23; 33:13) shows that people's impiety is their own choice, not God's fault. God's ideal will is for everyone's salvation, but he also wills to limit that ideal by allowing people's rebellious choices in this age.[137] Tragically, then, many will be lost (Matt. 7:13 // Luke 13:24); Scripture does not support universalism.[138]

Though the Lord is **patient** for the sake of more coming to faith (3:9), he will come, overtaking the mockers (3:3–4) unprepared for his coming (cf. 1 Thess. 5:2–4). He will come **like a thief** (3:10): suddenly, unexpectedly, and dangerously for those unprepared for it. One may be well-armed, but if one is asleep, one may still be overtaken by a thief (as I learned from an account about the teller's friend in Nigeria). Jesus already spoke of coming like a thief (Matt. 24:43 // Luke 12:39; later, Rev. 3:3; 16:15). Applying Jesus coming as a thief to the **day of the Lord** (3:10; also 1 Thess. 5:2; cf. the "day" of Jesus's coming in Matt. 24:42)

136. On God's patience to bring salvation, see *Letter of Aristeas* 188; Wis. 11:23–26; Rom. 2:4; *4 Ezra* 7.74; *2 Baruch* 24.2; *Sipre Deuteronomy* 43.14.1; *y. Ta'anit* 2.1, §11; *Pesiqta of Rab Kahana* 7.10. But death and the day of judgment are too late for repentance (*1 Enoch* 60.5; *4 Ezra* 7.82; *2 Baruch* 85.12; *Ecclesiastes Rabbah* 7.15, §1). On the timing of the end as contingent on repentance, see *Sipre Deuteronomy* 43.16.3; *y. Ta'anit* 1.1, §7; *Testament of Dan* 6.4; possibly *Jubilees* 23.26–27; *Testament of Moses* 1.18; on obedience, *b. Bava Batra* 10a; *Exodus Rabbah* 25.12; *Deuteronomy Rabbah* 6.7; *Song of Songs Rabbah* 2.5, §3; 5.2, §2; *Pesiqta Rabbati* 31.5; for moral factors in delay, *b. Niddah* 13b; *b. Sanhedrin* 97b; *Song of Songs Rabbah* 4.8, §3; *Pesiqta Rabbati* 33.6; for correlation with divine sovereignty, *Sipra Behuqotai* pq. 8.269.2.3.

137. See John of Damascus, *Orthodox Faith* 2.29, differentiating God's antecedent will from his consequent will.

138. See McClymond, *The Devil's Redemption*.

identifies Jesus with the Old Testament Lord—that is, Israel's God (1 Cor. 1:8; 2 Cor. 1:14; Phil. 1:6, 10; 2:16).

While the warning of imminence urges us to remain always ready, it does not, as some have supposed, refer to the beginning of the great tribulation. The **day of the Lord** is the day when God judges, the day of his judgment, his anger, and destruction (Isa. 13:6, 9, 13; 34:8; Jer. 46:10; Lam. 2:22; Ezek. 30:3; Joel 1:15; 2:1, 31; Amos 5:18–20; Obad. 15; Zeph. 1:7–9, 18; 2:2–3; Mal. 4:5; 1 Cor. 5:5), so this is also the "day of judgment" mentioned in 2 Pet. 2:9; 3:7.

The passing of the heavens and the burning and unraveling of the elements leave neither time nor place for tribulation; it is not the tribulation but Christ's return in glory for which we look.[139] Still, this need not rule out phases in God's plan (e.g., as in a premillennial reading of Rev. 20:4–6). A prophet could speak of the earth being destroyed in one breath and then speak of the nations' conversion at that time in the next (Zeph. 3:8–9). What this passage and scores of others do rule out is the common modern idea that God is not really angry about sin, the ways we reject his mercy and mistreat others.

Combined with **elements**, the term translated as **destroyed** (*lyō*) in 3:10 sometimes could mean "come apart," but it clearly means **destroyed** in 3:11–12.[140] This expression might not rule out recycling the matter, but at least it must be purged fairly thoroughly, by **burning** (3:10, 12).[141] For an ancient audience, the term **elements** (*stoicheia*) would designate not the periodic table but rather what were considered (most commonly) the four rudimentary principles of earth, water, air, and fire itself (the former two dominating earth, the latter, lighter two dominating the heavens). The idea is that even the most basic components of matter will be purged, perhaps to replace the perishable (cf. 1:4; 2:12, 19) with the imperishable. (Alternatively, commentators often apply **elements** here to sun, moon, and stars, though this is not the term's usual sense; cf. Isa. 34:4.)

Although the variant reading that **the works in it will be** "burned up" could make sense, that **the works in it will be found**, or "laid bare" (NIV), makes sense too. The idea here is that nothing will be hidden from God at the judgment; all will come to light (cf. Matt. 10:26–27 // Luke 12:2–3; 1 Cor. 4:5). This is why we must seek to be "found" blameless when he comes (2 Pet. 3:14).

139. See discussion in Brown and Keener, *Not Afraid*.

140. Although Aristotle held the heavens indestructible, he rejected the eternality of the elements (*Heavens* 3.6, 304b23–305a32). For "coming apart," cf. perhaps *Sibylline Oracles* 3.80–83; 8.337.

141. Most New Testament texts may depict renewal, though 2 Pet. 3 sounds more extreme. See varied discussions in Stephens, *Annihilation or Renewal?*; Adams, *Stars Will Fall* (esp. 200–235); Juza, *Future of the Cosmos*.

Live in Light of His Coming (3:11–18)

> [3:11]**Given that all these things will be destroyed like this, what sort of people is it necessary for you to be, living holy and reverent lives?** [12]**This means living expectantly for and being diligent to bring quickly the coming of the day of God. Because of that day the heavens will be destroyed by burning and the elements will melt while burning.**

Living in 3:11 involves living in light of eternity—how our present lives will look after the perfect, purified world replaces the present perishable one. We should consider how our lives would look in light of realities a billion years from now, rather than for momentary pleasures (cf. Heb. 11:25–26) or relief (2 Cor. 4:16–18). As I make my daily and hourly choices, I want to weigh them in light of how I would look back on them from the vantage point of eternity.

Holy means consecrated to God, living for Christ's service because we belong to him and his purposes rather than our own (or someone else's). In light of eternity to come, it makes no sense to live for any other purpose. On being **reverent** (reverence, piety, godliness), see comment on 1:3, 6–7.

The word *prosdokaō*, translated as **living expectantly for** in 3:12, recurs in 3:13 and 3:14, a key theme of this section (cf. perhaps "waiting for" and "hoping in" the Lord in the prophets; e.g., Isa. 40:31; Hosea 12:6; Mic. 7:7; Hab. 2:3; Zeph. 3:8). The **coming** (3:12) is the coming denied by mockers because it has not yet happened (3:4). How may we be **diligent to bring quickly** his coming? The cognate noun for **bring quickly** (*speudō*) is *spoudē*, used in 1:5 for "effort" (there I translate "zealously"); another related verb (*spoudazō*) is used for being "zealous" in 1:10 and 1:15. Since his delay involves patience, waiting for more to be saved (3:9, 15), the key contribution we make is evangelism, especially toward reaching those who have had little exposure to the good news about Christ. The **day of God** (3:12) is simply another way of speaking of the day of the Lord (Rev. 16:14), the day when God reveals himself fully and he alone is judge.

In one Greek story, the sky and earth catch fire as an inept charioteer fails to control the sun chariot. In another story, Zeus destroys the earth by flood rather than by fire because the entire cosmos was someday fated to be destroyed by fire.[142] More relevant, Stoics expected the universe to be resolved back into primeval fire, though for them this was a periodic cycle of destruction and rebirth (unlike the biblical picture of an ultimate judgment).[143] Given the new

142. Ovid, *Metamorphoses* 1.253–61.

143. See discussion in Keener, *Acts*, 2:1110–11. Stoics allowed for periodic cataclysmic floods (Seneca, *Natural Questions* 3.27.1; 3.28.7; 3.29.1; 3.30.3, 7) as well as conflagration (Seneca, *Benefits* 4.8.1). For cyclical renewal, see Cornutus, *Greek Theology* 17, §28.11; Seneca,

heavens and new earth in 3:13, however, the primary background here must be Isa. 65:17, a newness that plainly follows the Lord judging the world with fire (66:15–16, 22–24; cf. Zeph. 1:18; 2 Pet. 2:6).

> **3:13 But we live in expectation for what he has promised, new heavens and a new earth, in which righteousness dwells.**

Most people in antiquity experienced injustice, not least including inequitable distribution of food and a judicial system heavily slanted toward people of rank. But **righteousness** characterizes the promised coming world (e.g., Isa. 11:4–5; 60:17; 61:11; Jer. 23:5–6; 33:15–16). Righteousness will dwell there, so human oppression (cf. 2 Pet. 2:5, 21) will stop; with sin ended, paradise will be restored (Gen. 2:10–17; Isa. 11:6–10; Rev. 22:1–3). The righteous have a foretaste of that righteous world in our lives now, through the righteousness of Christ (2 Pet. 1:1; cf. 2 Cor. 5:17; Gal. 6:15). Jewish tradition celebrated the promise of **new heavens and a new earth** (cf. Isa. 65:17; 66:22) frequently.[144] In Scripture, all creation celebrates God's coming to judge the world and put things right (Pss. 96:11–13; 98:7–9; cf. Rom. 8:19–22).

> **3:14 Therefore, loved ones, since you live in expectation for these things, be diligent to be found spotless and blameless in peace.**

In 3:12, we "diligently hasten" (*speudō*) the day of God; in 3:14, we "diligently live" (*spoudazō*) in readiness for it. Since we eagerly wait for a new world of righteousness (3:13), we should live righteously in the present (3:14). Since all works in earth will be "found" (*heuriskō*; 3:10), we must be diligent to be **found** (*heuriskō*; 3:14) righteous: God knows and will bring to light all our works. Just as Jesus is a spotless and blameless lamb (1 Pet. 1:19), so in 2 Pet. 3:14 must we be **spotless** (*aspilos*) and **blameless** (*amōmētos*). This is the opposite of the false teachers who are "spots, stains" (*spilos*) and "blameworthy, blemished" (*mōmos*) (2:13). (Cf. Eph. 5:27, where Christ at his coming will present to himself a church that has no "spot" [*spilos*] and is "blameless" [*amōmos*].)

Dialogues 6.26.6–7; Epictetus, *Discourses* 2.1.18; 3.13.4; Plutarch, *Common Conceptions* 31, *Moralia* 1075B; Lucian, *Philosophies for Sale* 14; Marcus Aurelius, *Meditations* 4.46; Diogenes Laertius, *Eminent Philosophers* 9.1.7; against it, Philo, *Eternity of the World* 85; Tatian, *Address to the Greeks* 6. For reversion to original chaos, see Lucan, *Civil War* 1.72–74; *2 Baruch* 3.7. For Jewish eschatological fire, see *Sibylline Oracles* 3.54, 73–74, 84–86, 760–61; 4.43, 161, 176–78; 5.211–13; *1 Enoch* 1.6; *1QRule of the Community* (1QS) 2.8; *1QHodayot*[a] (1QH[a]) 14.21. For a fluid connection, note the rivers or lakes of fire in *1 Enoch* 14.19, 22; 17.4–5; *Sibylline Oracles* 2.196–203; 3.54, 84–85.

144. For example, *1 Enoch* 72.1; 91.16; *Jubilees* 1.29; 4.26; *2 Baruch* 44.12.

> **3:15And recognize that our Lord's patience is for salvation, just as our beloved brother Paul wrote you according to the wisdom God gave him.**

Our Lord's patience is for salvation in the sense that by delaying his coming he allows more and more people space for repentance (3:9). Peter does not specify in which letter or letters Paul conveys this wisdom to Peter's audience. (It is clear in 3:16 that Peter knows of multiple letters of Paul. Since they may have been collected in stages, however,[145] it is not clear how many letters Peter knows.) If 2 Peter shares the same audience as 1 Peter, it may address groups of churches in Asia Minor (1 Pet. 1:1), just as some of Paul's letters apparently do (Gal. 1:2; 3:1; Eph. 1:1). If 2 Peter shares the same provenance as 1 Peter (1 Pet. 5:13), it may be from Rome. Paul's **wisdom** about divine delays to allow more to be saved appears especially in Rom. 11:11, 25–32. Using a divine passive, Peter indirectly attributes Paul's **wisdom** to God,[146] presumably by the Spirit (cf. 1 Cor. 12:8; Eph. 1:17; Wis. 9:17; *1 Enoch* 49.3).

> **3:16Paul talks about these matters in all his letters. There are some points hard to understand in his letters. Uninstructed and unstable people distort those points, just as they do with the rest of the Scriptures, for their own destruction.**

Paul's Greek is usually simpler than that of 2 Peter, but Paul would agree that **some** of his **points** are **hard to understand**, if only because they involve matters of the Spirit (1 Cor. 2:13–3:2) or sometimes delve too deeply into exegesis for a biblically illiterate audience.[147] Moreover, his use of genitives is often ambiguous (e.g., think of the ongoing debate today concerning whether Paul's *pistis Christou* means "faith in Christ" or "Christ's faithfulness"), his use of the article

145. See Aune, *Literary Environment*, 205; Gamble, "Canonical Formation," 185–86. Paul probably kept copies of his own letters (Richards, "Codex"), but the earliest collection available may have been a partial version left at Corinth. From an early period, Christians acknowledged the inspiration of Paul's letters (*1 Clement* 47.3; cf. 1 Cor. 7:40) and cited them (Polycarp, *To the Philippians* 3.2; 11.2; Ignatius, *To the Romans* 4.3; *To the Ephesians* 12.2).

146. Compare Exod. 36:1–2; 1 Kings 4:29; 5:12; 1 Chron. 22:12; 2 Chron. 1:10, 12; Prov. 2:6; Eccles. 2:26; Dan. 1:17; 2:21–23; 1 Esd. 4:60; Sir. 43:33; 45:26; 51:17; Wis. 7:7; 9:4; *1 Enoch* 5.8; 82.2; *1QRule of the Community* (1QS) 4.22; Mark 6:2; Luke 21:15; Acts 7:10; James 1:5.

147. As perhaps in Galatians, where he addresses esp. gentile converts yet must counter biblically literate rivals (see Keener, *Galatians*, 13–14, 31); analogously, cf. Heb. 5:11–6:3. Critics deplored the "obscurity" of Jesus's teaching (Macarius Magnes, *Apocriticus* 4.8–19) (though Jesus's use of sage-like riddles was deliberate); for preference for clarity in normal rhetoric, see Dionysius of Halicarnassus, *Thucydides* 40; *Second Letter to Ammaeus* 2; Fronto, *Marcus Caesar* 3.1; Diogenes Laertius, *Eminent Philosophers* 7.1.59.

and prepositions inconsistent, and his otherwise praiseworthy use of literary variation could confuse some.[148] Still, a work's difficulty could also be attributed to its profundity.[149]

From Peter's perspective, Paul wrote in all his letters **about these matters** (3:16) at least including salvation and eschatology (3:15; for analogous hyperbole, see Acts 3:24); certainly, these themes are prominent in the earliest letters collected (most of which are accepted as authentic by nearly all scholars). **Uninstructed** refers not to lack of education generally (which could be said of Peter in Acts 4:13) but to those who did not understand basic principles of the good news about Jesus.

The **unstable** (*astēriktos*) are vulnerable to false teachers (2:14). The **unstable** distort Scripture (3:16); in 3:17, Peter warns his audience against being moved by their lawless error and so losing their own "stability" (*stērigmos*). As in 1:12, Peter is addressing those already "established" (the cognate verb *stērizō*) in the truth. That the **unstable distort Scriptures**, including Paul's letters, reminds us that people can prove almost anything they want from Scripture and make it sound plausible if they ignore context. Satan himself does this in Matt. 4:6 // Luke 4:10–11, where he tries to counter Jesus's more contextual use of Scripture (Matt. 4:4, 7, 10 // Luke 4:4, 8, 12, using Deut. 6:13, 16; 8:3).

What seems extraordinary is that 2 Peter already ranks Paul's letters among the Scriptures; apostolic memoirs carry the same authority as Old Testament Scriptures (2 Pet. 1:16–21; 3:2; cf. 1 Tim. 5:18). Peter has already affirmed the divinely moved character of Scripture in 1:20; already Jesus (e.g., Mark 10:8–9; 12:10, 24; 14:49; John 5:39) and his movement (e.g., Rom. 1:2; 1 Cor. 15:3–4; Gal. 3:8; 2 Tim. 3:16–17) had borrowed from the preexisting Jewish consensus respect for the special authority of a canon of sacred writings (e.g., 2 Kings 23:21; 2 Chron. 23:18; 25:4; Ezra 3:2; Dan. 9:13). Among the first Christian writings accepted as canonical by second-century Christians were the Gospels and Paul's letters. Peter already recognizes Paul's letters as such, just as others so treated Jesus's teachings (1 Cor. 9:13–14; 1 Tim. 5:18).

Peter has already spoken about **destruction** (*apōleia*; 3:16) on false teachers: they deny the master who bought them (2:1), misleading others (2:3); they, their followers, and the world they have corrupted will face destruction (3:7).

> [3:17]**Since you know about this in advance, loved ones, guard yourselves, so the error of lawless people doesn't lead you away and make you fall from your secure foundation.**

148. Anderson, *Ancient Rhetorical Theory*, 240. For the *pistis Christou* debate, see Bird and Sprinkle, *Faith of Jesus Christ*; for my approach, see Keener, *Galatians*, 177–83.

149. So Cicero, *Ends* 4.1.2; Diogenes Laertius, *Eminent Philosophers* 9.1.12–13.

The wicked twist Scripture, and Peter's ideal audience must guard against such error (3:17) and grow (3:18). Just because someone quotes verses does not mean that their teaching is faithful to Scripture. Although they were the minority even in their own day, slaveholder and Nazi theologians illustrate the life-and-death dangers of irresponsible biblical interpretation.[150]

> [3:18]**Instead, grow in the grace and knowledge of our Lord and Savior Jesus Christ. May he receive the honor, both now and forever!**[151] **Amen.**

The alternative to falling backward is growing forward (Heb. 5:11–6:8). Peter has already proposed disciplines to enable us to **grow** (see 1:5–7), the pursuit of which keep us from falling (1:8–11; cf. Heb. 6:1–8).[152] Our ability to pursue such growth rests in the divine virtue that God has already given us in Christ (2 Pet. 1:3–4). What we today call progressive sanctification may be more biblically designated as growing in grace and knowing Christ.

Grace refers to God's generosity, unmerited yet inviting a response of grateful loyalty. **Knowledge** likely includes not only knowledge *about* Jesus but also a covenant relationship *with* him (as in the prophets: Isa. 19:21; Jer. 22:16; 24:7; 31:34; Hosea 2:20; see comment on 2 Pet. 1:2). We recognize that God has welcomed us by his unearned favor, and we live in light of the reality of his working in our lives.

Ancient letters did not typically close with doxologies, but some early Christian letters meant to be read in assemblies did so (see esp. Rom. 16:25–27; Jude 24–25; *1 Clement* 65.2). Doxologies honored God; in this context, the attribution of such honor to Jesus (3:18) indicates his deity, returning to Peter's opening affirmation in 1:1 (cf. Rev. 1:5–6).

150. For some Aryan theologians serving the Reich church, see Heschel, *Aryan Jesus*; on slaveholder versus abolitionist theologians, see Usry and Keener, *Black Man's Religion*, 101–9; for perceptive African American readings from the relevant eras, see Bowens, *Readings of Paul*.

151. Literally, "to the day of eternity / the [coming] age," meaning "forever" (cf. Sir. 1:2; 18:10). To God, even forever may be like a day (2 Pet. 3:8).

152. On "progress" in ancient philosophy and pedagogy, see Keener, *Galatians*, 81.

Jude

Introduction

To keep within space constraints, I cite only a fraction of my research here, but I include what I believe is most useful for following, preaching, and teaching the text. As noted in the introduction to 1 Peter, I supply my own translations for 2 Peter and Jude. My translation here leans more toward interpretive paraphrase (since this is a commentary) than I would actually encourage in a stand-alone Bible translation per se.

Authorship and Date

The name "Judah" gets translated into English many different ways in different parts of the Bible (Judah, Judas, Jude). I distinguish here between the author (whom I call Judah) and the letter (which, following anglophone convention, I call Jude).

Since Judah does not claim any special designation except by the name of his brother, there is little reason for anyone to doubt the tract's claim to be authored by someone named Judah. Pseudepigraphers sought the explicit mantle of illustrious predecessors, but Judah does not elaborate or boast in his identity. Not surprisingly, Judah was quite a common Jewish (lit., *Ioudaios*, i.e., Judah-ite or Judah-ish) name. More contested is the question as to *which* Judah he is; the text is not explicit, but the most probable guess—since "Judah" or "James" without qualification likelier than not suggests the best-known one—is that this Judah is Jesus's brother (Mark 6:3).[1] Judah may have acquired some of his excellent facility

Scripture quotations in the commentary on Jude are the author's own unless otherwise noted.

1. Some regard Jesus's "brothers" as his cousins or, on the premise of the virgin birth, his half brothers. Whether such circumstances might factor into the author not mentioning being a brother

in Greek after becoming a church leader, and even likelier he would have available assistance for drafting the formal letter.[2] Regardless of authorship, the letter's date is uncertain (Judah was likely the youngest brother [cf. Mark 6:3], and we do not know his longevity); some suggest a date later in the first century (cf. Jude 17).

Content

Judah's letter is so brief that it would require only a single sheet of papyrus. Unlike most of Paul's letters, this one is closer to the average size of letters in antiquity.[3] Against some earlier scholars who treated Jude's polemic as being against later Gnosticism, Jude addresses a (probably) diaspora Jewish Christian audience heavily influenced by Judean apocalyptic ideas.[4] The author seems most familiar with Judean theological source material (for example, *1 Enoch*) despite the letter being composed in Greek. The current occasion for writing is the infiltration of and influence on the church by those who live values contrary to Jesus's teaching and lordship (vv. 3–4). The concern here is less explicitly false "teachers" (as explicitly in 2 Pet. 2:1) than a wider danger of infiltrators introducing apostasy (e.g., Jude 4, 21–23).[5] Nevertheless, some false prophecy seems involved (dreaming in v. 8; cf. Balaam in v. 11). Jude affirms charismatic experience from God's Spirit (v. 20), but he recognizes that experiences that undermine biblical morality are not genuinely from God.

Polemic against the false voices simultaneously guards community boundaries, more clearly defining the in-group's social-theological identity. For example:[6]

Bad guys	Good guys
They complain and speak against God-appointed authority.	You follow true words.
They will face judgment.	You persevere to salvation.
They lack the Spirit.	You should pray in the Spirit.

Although some of Jude's denunciations were standard polemic, attention to ancient rhetoric demonstrates that their specificity suggests genuine concerns regarding the matters denounced.[7]

---

of Jesus is uncertain (cf. 1 Cor. 9:5; Gal. 1:19; James 1:1). James also avoids specifying a possible fraternal relationship with Jesus (James 1:1).

2. For Judah as author, see discussion in Bauckham, *Jude, 2 Peter*, 14–16; G. Green, *Jude and 2 Peter*, 2–9.

3. For short letters, see Cicero, *Letters to Atticus* 12.53.

4. See Eybers, "Letter of Jude."

5. See Bateman, "2 Peter and Jude."

6. See similarly Mbuvi, *Jude and 2 Peter*, 57, 119.

7. See G. Green, *Jude and 2 Peter*, 22, explaining Quintilian, *Institutes of Oratory* 2.4.22.

Canonicity

Jude was popular in the second century, by the end of which it was accepted as canonical. That Jude explicitly *quotes* at least one noncanonical source should warn interpreters not to neglect taking into account extrabiblical background when reading the Bible.[8] But many in Jerome's day (though not Jerome himself) questioned its authority because of its use of noncanonical sources; in the Reformation period, so did Calvin and some other Reformers and Catholic scholars. Jude appears in all Bibles, however, and it has functioned canonically for the universal church through the ages. Some church fathers accepted Jude as canonical but therefore concluded that *1 Enoch* (or at least *1 Enoch* 1.9, which it quotes) was inspired. The Judean Qumran sect may have already treated *1 Enoch* and similar works as canonical or quasi-canonical, though the more public Pharisaic stream apparently reacted strongly against the work. Unlike the rest of Christendom, the Ethiopian Orthodox Church (which alone preserved the whole of *1 Enoch*) treated *1 Enoch* as part of its canon.

The Jewish myths protested in Titus 1:14 could include those in *1 Enoch*. Still, Titus 1:12 (just two verses earlier) quotes a Greek poet, so *quoting* or using sources does not necessarily mean that the author is treating them as if they are canonical. Indeed, a standard element of debate rhetoric included citing an ancient authority—whenever possible from the opponent's repertoire of authorities. If Judah addresses false prophets enamored with extrabiblical traditions such as those in *1 Enoch*, he may counter them by applying to them Enoch's prophecy of their damnation. Judah agrees with at least this point in *1 Enoch*! (It could be like Christians today citing a point in the Qur'an that supports their case when challenging Muslims.)

Judah does not balk at citing extrabiblical stories about biblical characters (vv. 9, 14–15). These stories were familiar to his audience and illustrated his point. Quoting them no more makes them canonical than Paul quoting Greek poets conferred such a status on them (Acts 17:28; 1 Cor. 15:33; Titus 1:12). Whether Judah believed them to be true stories is another question. Perhaps he did, but his use of illustrations, like Paul's, does not require this approach (consider Jesus's use of parables). Judah nowhere uses a standard Scripture citation formula for these quotations (such as, "As it is written"), although "prophesied" may suggest that he takes at least the lines he quotes to be genuinely inspired (so also Bede). (Some scholars today argue that apocalyptic writers such as the author of *1 Enoch* often believed that God was leading their writing.)

8. For tools for this at a popular level, see Keener, *Bible Background Commentary*. For learning background, see Ferguson, *Backgrounds of Early Christianity*; Green and McDonald, *World of the New Testament*.

Jude is very applicable for combatting errors today. Lisa Fields started the Jude 3 Project, addressing apologetic questions in the African American community. Spirit-filled Ghanaian Anglican theologian Emmanuel Kwasi Amoafo wrote his dissertation to elucidate principles in Jude relevant for helping charismatic churches in Africa.[9] Likewise, Sri Lankan Pentecostal scholar Danny Moses applies his careful exegesis of Jude to current issues in Asia.[10]

Outline

1. Judah's introduction (1–4)
2. Warning examples (5–7)
3. Disrespect for heavenly powers (8–10)
4. False promises and doom (11–13)
5. Enoch's prophecy (14–16)
6. Persevering in the faith (17–23)
7. Praise to God (24–25)

Recommended Resources

For recommended resources on Jude, see the introduction to 2 Peter.

Judah's Introduction (1–4)

> **1From: Judah, slave of Jesus Christ and brother of Jacob.**
> **To: Those whom God has called, who are loved in God the Father and preserved for Jesus Christ.**
> **2May mercy and peace and love be multiplied to you!**

Most translations render the Greek name *Ioudas* here as "Jude." It is, however, the same name translated "Judas" elsewhere, the Greek version of the Old Testament *Yehudah*, normally rendered in English as **Judah**. Likewise, most English translations render the Greek name *Iakōbos* as "James," even though in the Greek version of the Old Testament *Iakōbos* everywhere renders the Hebrew name *Ya'akob*, which English versions render as **Jacob**.

As the ancestral name of the Jewish people and the name of one of the Maccabee brothers, **Judah** was a very common Jewish name—the fourth most common male name in Judea and Galilee in this era. Not surprisingly, then,

9. See now Amoafo, *Stand Up for the Gospel*, offering a model of useful contextualization.
10. Moses, *Contending for the Faith*.

Jesus had two disciples named Judah (Luke 6:16; John 14:22). Obviously, the present **Judah** is not Judas Iscariot, who quickly came to a bad end (Matt. 27:5; Acts 1:18); the other disciple is more likely the *son* of a certain Jacob rather than his brother ("son of" is the more common sense of the Greek phrase in Luke 6:16; Acts 1:13). Another Jesus-follower was "Judah-born-on-the Sabbath" (Acts 15:22).

Because our **Judah** introduces himself simply as the brother of **Jacob**, however, he is presumably the well-known Judah who was brother of the early church's best-known Jacob,[11] the one who led the community of believers in Jerusalem (Acts 12:17; 15:13; 21:18; Gal. 1:19; 2:9), a brother of Jesus (Gal. 1:19). The church knew that Jesus's half brothers were leaders (Acts 1:14; 1 Cor. 9:5), with **Jacob** at their head. Correspondingly, the Gospels also name two of Jesus's brothers **Jacob** (James) and **Judah** (Mark 6:3).

But **Judah** knows that what characterizes him most is what also characterizes the rest of us: he is a **slave of Jesus Christ**. Although slavery was considered a lower status than freedom, being the slave of someone prominent, like the emperor, could in some cases give one more status and power than senators. Scripture had long called Moses and the prophets servants of YHWH. Being a **slave of Jesus Christ** is a great honor.

Just as God **called** Abraham and Israel (Isa. 51:2), God has **called** Jesus's people (Rom. 9:24; 1 Cor. 1:9; Gal. 1:6; 5:8; 1 Thess. 2:12; 5:24; 2 Thess. 2:14; 2 Tim. 1:9; 1 Pet. 2:21; 3:9; 5:10; 2 Pet. 1:3). We cannot take credit for our salvation; it is God's gift to us in Christ. As God saved Israel because he **loved** them (Deut. 7:8), so has he done with us (Jude 1). This calling also assures us of our perseverance (Rom. 8:30). In a letter full of warnings against being led astray, Judah reminds us that we are **preserved** (*tēreō*) for Jesus (Jude 1; cf. v. 24) and invited to keep ourselves (v. 21, using *tēreō*), while the wicked are kept for judgment (vv. 6, 13, again *tēreō*).

For the blessing in Jude 2, see comment on 1 Pet. 1:2. Judah frames his letter with blessing, praise, and the language of **love** and **mercy** (vv. 2, 21). His audience must persevere in God's "love" (v. 21), watching out for those who infiltrate their "love" meals (v. 12). Writers could pair **mercy** with **peace** in blessing prayers (Gal. 6:16; 1 Tim. 1:2; 2 Tim. 1:2; 2 John 3); like the peace blessing (*shalom*, "May it be well with you"), the mercy blessing is also a Jewish form.[12] (Jude often arranges material in sets of three.) The audience continues to await Jesus's "mercy" at his coming (v. 21) and must show "mercy"

11. The same methodological assumption we would use in classics (see Finamore and Dillon, introduction to *De Anima*, 1).

12. See the letter greeting in *2 Baruch* 78.3; in prayers, *Jubilees* 1.20; *Psalms of Solomon* 4.25; with "mercy," *Jubilees* 22.9.

on others struggling to persevere (vv. 22–23). For **multiplied**, see comment on 1 Pet. 1:2.

> **[3]Loved ones, I've been so eager to write to you about the salvation we share.[13] In this connection, I need to write warning you to contend hard for the faith that was entrusted once-for-all to those consecrated for God. [4]I need to write this because certain people have stealthily snuck in [among you]. They were already written about for this verdict of judgment a long time ago. Irreligious, they corrupt our God's graciousness into an excuse for unrestrained license and deny our only master and lord, Jesus Christ.**

Writing to those "loved" in Christ (v. 1), Judah addresses them also as his **loved ones** (v. 3) at other key transitions (vv. 17, 20), an address also favored in 2 Peter (1:17; 3:1, 8, 14, 17; cf. 3:15). **The faith** refers to the message about Jesus (Acts 6:7; Gal. 1:23; 1 Tim. 3:9) received by faith (Eph. 1:13). When writing something controversial, writers sometimes justified their project by appeals to various factors, one of the key ones being necessity,[14] thus **need** in verse 4.

The language of **contend** (also 1 Tim. 6:12; 2 Tim. 4:7) is originally a Greek athletic metaphor, adopted widely in Greek-speaking Judaism. It communicates strenuous effort.[15] Abusing the biblical teaching of God's sovereignty, some eighteenth- and early nineteenth-century churchgoers refused to even convert, waiting for God to convert them. Scripture, by contrast, urges us to trust God's invitation enough to act on it.

That the faith was delivered **once-for-all**[16] means not that it is not for today but that it came to us in a strategic time and way as history climaxed in Jesus the Messiah. Early Christians for good reason required genuinely canonical books of the New Testament to come from the circle of those who knew Jesus and to be theologically consistent with other such works. Jesus and his message are the standard for deciding the New Testament canon. Although the canon is established, the ministry of the Spirit remains ongoing; prophesying is as much for this "last days" era as is salvation by calling on the Lord's name (Acts 2:17–21). Yet continuing prophecy, too, must remain grounded securely in the message of Jesus (1 Cor. 12:3; 1 John 4:1–3; Rev. 19:10).

13. Appeals to shared agreement were common (e.g., *Rhetorica ad Alexandrum* 1.1422a.2–3; 2.1424a.11; Gal. 2:15–16).

14. Anderson, *Greek Rhetorical Terms*, 17.

15. See Pfitzner, *Agon Motif*, chap. 3. *Agōn* language appears more than ninety times each in Philo and Josephus; note the idea in 4 Macc. 16:16; *4 Ezra* 7.92, 127; 12.47; *2 Baruch* 15.8.

16. See also Polycarp, *To the Philippians* 7.2.

Sometimes critics refused to dignify enemies by naming them, calling them only **certain people** (v. 4).[17] Paul speaks of false brothers who have been "snuck in" secretly by others (Gal. 2:4), but the false teachers here have **snuck in** by themselves. That they act secretly means that they are not always obvious: Wolves may look like sheep (Matt. 7:15; Rev. 13:11) and sometimes even start out as such (Acts 20:29–30). We should neither endorse nor denounce anyone's ministry prematurely (1 Tim. 5:19–22), though this means that some wolves go largely undetected in the short run (1 Cor. 4:5; 1 Tim. 5:24). We cannot know private details in the lives of even many of our friends, but when reports come to light we must evaluate them and, when information is sufficient, act accordingly. We must listen to unfamiliar teaching with appropriate wariness, open to correction from Scripture (cf. Acts 17:11) but careful to check Scripture in context. Those advancing what seem to be new ideas must bear the burden of proof.

Whereas Judah writes to his audience (v. 3) only now, these subversives were **written about** [or, "designated"] **. . . a long time ago** (v. 4). Just as God "called" his consecrated ones (v. 1), he already knew about these ungodly people far in advance—even writing in Scripture about this kind of apostate (vv. 5–7; for heavenly books, cf. Dan. 7:10; *1 Enoch* 108.7; Luke 10:20; Rev. 20:12). The **verdict of judgment** (*krima*) is consistent with the "judgment" (*krisis*) in verses 6, 9, and 15.

The term that I render here as **irreligious** [*asebēs*] merely designates those who do not respect deity; Jude returns to their irreligion in verses 15 and 18 (cf. 2 Pet. 2:5–6; 3:7). God's **graciousness** (*charis*; "generosity," undeserved, kind gift-giving)[18] forgives and transforms us; true grace is the *antithesis* of an excuse to sin. In verse 4, the term *aselgeia* (also 2 Pet. 2:2, 7, 18), rendered here as **unrestrained license,** involves lack of self-restraint, most often sexually (cf. Jude 6–7). Ancients were well aware that the undisciplined could turn liberty into an excuse for license, whether politically or morally.[19] It is possible to **deny** Jesus (and thus be denied as his own [Matt. 10:33 // Luke 12:9; 2 Tim. 2:12]) by deeds as well as words (Titus 1:16).

Although few preachers would openly say, "All is forgiven, so sin as much as you want," some people do treat forgiveness that way.[20] Dangerously, some claim that those once forgiven will be saved no matter what they do afterward (contrast Titus 1:16). We normally think ill of those who exploit others' love for their own ends, and we consider codependent the exploited ones who let them keep doing it. But God is a just judge who knows the heart, and his love is ready to help us win victory over our temptations, not continue to indulge them.

17. For example, Aeschines, *Ctesiphon* 1; Dio Chrysostom, *Orations* 40.8–9; 47.20–23; 51.3; Lucian, *How to Write History* 17.

18. See Barclay, *Paul and the Gift*; Harrison, *Language of Grace*.

19. For example, Livy, *History of Rome* 5.6.17; 27.31.6; Phaedrus, *Fables* 1.2.1–3.

20. See warnings in Brown, *Hyper-Grace*.

APPLICATION

A Shared Faith

Recognizing that God's Spirit is with us, we often work for our groups of churches without thinking much about other churches. There are, however, important benefits of being connected with other churches that share our faith. The body of Christ consists of all believers, and Jesus gave his life to make us one body (Eph. 2:13–16). We don't have to agree with one another on every detail or element of style to be committed to one another in love. There is no overarching structure that connects all churches; Christ's love must do that.

In terms of structure, however, there are parts of our mission that churches can do better together, in cooperation, and that is why we have networks and denominations. Again, most of these do not require agreement on every detail, but we can work together for the common good, especially our common mission to reach the world for Christ. Such larger networks also allow for various members to specialize and provide resources for the larger movement.

One particularly important benefit of connections with other churches is accountability. The early apostolic church had to deal with false teachers; one important way to know who was true and who was false was to identify who was in unity with the apostles who learned from Jesus himself (1 John 4:6). Obviously, that first generation of apostles is long gone, but we still have the faith that they entrusted to the church (Jude 3), the content of which is preserved for us in Scripture. Many people do not know Scripture well enough to know who speaks in accordance with it and who does not, but movements can enforce some theological and moral standards that individual churches cannot. When someone moves to a new city and looks for a new church, they can expect certain things from certain churches because they know that "brand." They can trust that cooperating leaders will help screen out immoral or unorthodox leaders if they discover them. Conversely, people may mistrust other "brands" that are less careful in providing discipline for errant leaders. We can protect the apostolic faith better together than alone, not as a matter of prejudice against other Christian movements, but as a matter of joining with some we trust for our common mission and mutual accountability.

Warning Examples (5–7)

> **[5]Now even though you already know all the examples I'm going to share, I want to remind you: The Lord[21] saved once-for-all a people from the land of Egypt, but he later destroyed those who did not believe [him]. [6]And so with angels who did not keep their own sphere of authority but left their own habitation: The Lord has kept them in eternal chains in darkness, reserved for judgment on the great day. [7]Likewise, Sodom and Gomorrah and the surrounding cities acted like those angels, committing sexual immorality and chasing after a different kind of flesh. Thus they present themselves as an example of suffering the punishment of eternal fire.**

Judah provides three examples of destruction, two of them regarding those who already knew the truth yet disobeyed it. The first example is Israel (v. 5). God graciously redeemed his people from Egypt before he gave them commandments (Exod. 20:2); he saved them not because of their righteousness (Deut. 9:4) but because he loved them and made a promise to their ancestors (Deut. 7:7–8). Yet most of his people rebelled and died in the wilderness, receiving God's free grace only to squander it in the end. The prophets promised a new exodus of salvation (Isa. 11:16; 51:10–11; Jer. 23:7–8; Hosea 11:11; Mic. 7:15; Zech. 10:10), but apostasy is possible even in the time of the new exodus (Heb. 3:12–4:11). Instead of **Lord** (v. 5), some early sources read "Jesus"; if one accepts that reading, Jude attributes God's action in the exodus directly to Jesus (cf. 1 Cor. 10:4).

Judah points out that Israel's **once-for-all** salvation (v. 5) did not preclude Israelites' subsequent destruction. The faith was also entrusted to God's consecrated ones "once-for-all" (v. 3), but that does not guarantee that every individual will persevere to salvation. Sometimes people speak of salvation "once-for-all" as if their past embrace of God's graciousness guarantees that they will be saved whether or not they persevere. Judah's point is the opposite: It is possible for those who have experienced new life in Christ to turn from the faith and face destruction.

The second example, fallen angels (v. 6), requires fuller comment. Here, too, were those who knew what was right and should have remained secure in God's favor, but they rebelled and are damned. The biblical text in view is Gen. 6:2–4, where sons of God had intercourse with human women. The ancient world was replete with stories of gods and spirits impregnating mortal women, as

21. The variant reading "Jesus" here also has significant textual support, but the matter is debated.

church fathers also recognized.[22] While scholars debate the precise meaning of Gen. 6, all agree that the dominant first-century Judean understanding of that passage was that fallen angels impregnated human women.[23] Most other Jewish sources about this fall depend on the fundamental storyline found in the second-century-BC work *1 Enoch*, a work that Judah soon goes on to quote explicitly in verse 14.

The Greek term *archē*, rendered here as **sphere of authority**, can mean "rule," "ruler" or "realm," a sense sometimes elsewhere associated with angelic powers (Rom. 8:38; Eph. 6:12). (For those angels acting outside "the mandate of their authority," see *Jubilees* 7.21.) Then again, *archē* can mean "first," so here it might mean something more like their "original assignment." Either way, their original dwelling was supposed to be in heaven (*1 Enoch* 15.7), but they abandoned their assigned domain (12.4; 15.3)—something that errorists of Judah's day were also doing if they were trying to meddle in the heavens (2 Pet. 2:10–11; Jude 8–9).

Judah twice uses the term *tēreō* ("keep") in verse 6: These angels did not **keep** to their place, so the Lord has **kept** them in chains, reserving them for the final judgment. Judah's Enoch-familiar audience would understand the idea. In *1 Enoch* 10.4–6, 12–13, for example, the Lord orders fallen angels to be bound in darkness until "the great day of judgment," when they will be cast into eternal fiery torment.[24] Commentators note that the specific term for **darkness** (*zophos*) here often refers to that of the netherworld, the abode of the dead.[25] **The great day** is the "great day of the Lord" (Joel 2:1, 31; Zeph. 1:14; Mal. 3:22; cf. Rev. 6:17; 16:14), the day of judgment. **The great day** phrase is also popular in *1 Enoch* (10.6; 19.1; 22.11; 54.6; 84.4).

Judah's third example is that of Sodom and Gomorrah. Other Judean interpreters linked together the examples of the sexual sins of the "fallen angels" tradition and that of Sodom.[26] While Sodom did not fall away from a state of salvation (though even they had a witness [Gen. 14:14–24]), this case illustrates the depravity of the apostates that merits damnation. Both earlier biblical prophets

22. For example, Aeschylus, *Prometheus Bound* 645–56; Justin Martyr, *First Apology* 5.

23. See *1 Enoch* 6.1–2; 69.5; 106.13–14; *Jubilees* 4.22; 5.1; 7.21; *4QAges of Creation A* (4Q180) f1.7–8; see comment on 1 Pet. 3:19; 2 Pet. 2:4.

24. Compare *Jubilees* 5.6; *Sibylline Oracles* 1.102–3. Another section of *1 Enoch* finds no inconsistency between the wicked dead being in darkness and their being in flames (103.8). Chains and darkness apply to the wicked in Wis. 17:2, 17.

25. For example, Homer, *Iliad* 15.191; 23.50; *Odyssey* 11.55, 155. Still, this is by no means the exclusive use of *zophos*; cf. primeval darkness in Menander Rhetor, *Treatises* 2.17, 438.20–24; depressing darkness in Aretaeus, *Therapeutics of Acute Diseases* 1.2 (Adams, pp. 143, 387). For the netherworld's darkness, see Pseudo-Apollodorus, *Bibliotheca* 1.1.2; Sallust, *War with Catiline* 52.13; Lucian, *Downward Journey* 2.

26. *Jubilees* 20.5; later, *Testament of Naphtali* 3.4–5.

(Isa. 1:9–10; 3:9; Jer. 23:14; Ezek. 16:46; Amos 4:11) and Jesus (Matt. 10:15 // Luke 10:12) used Sodom also as an analogy to warn sinning Israel.[27] Sodom's destruction prefigures that of the wicked at the end (Luke 17:28–29; Rev. 20:9). God also destroyed **the surrounding cities** of the plain (Gen. 19:25–29), Admah and Zeboiim (Deut. 29:23; Hosea 11:8).

Jewish tradition continued to recall Sodom's sexual immorality (*Jubilees* 16.5–6; 20.5). The men of Sodom were ready to gang rape fellow males, but the focus here does not appear to be on their same-sex predilections, which would hardly be described as seeking **a *different* kind of flesh**. Also, while Scripture and Jewish tradition clearly condemned same-sex intercourse (Lev. 18:22; 20:13; in the New Testament, most extensively Rom. 1:26–27), sometimes including that of Sodom (Philo, *Life of Abraham* 135–36), ancient comments about Sodom's wickedness often focus on their neglect of the needy (Ezek. 16:49), pride (Ezek. 16:49–50; Sir. 16:8), and mistreatment of strangers (Wis. 19:15–17; Josephus, *Jewish Antiquities* 1.194). Mistreatment of strangers was the antithesis of hospitality (cf. that of Abraham in Gen. 18:1–8 and of Lot in Gen. 19:1–8).

Their pursuit of **a different kind of flesh,**[28] then, probably refers to their inversion of the angels' sin in Jude's previous verse: although the Sodomites did not know it, they were lusting for (and hoping to gang rape) angels (Gen. 19:1, 4). Since demons were believed to mislead false prophets, the connection between fallen angels (Jude 6–7) and the false prophets that Judah might imply (vv. 11, 19) is likely close.

Although Sodom was not still burning,[29] the language of **eternal fire** points to what awaits those who pursue wickedness like they did (cf. the same expression in Matt. 18:8; 25:41; *Sibylline Oracles* 8.401; for the **punishment of eternal fire**, see also 4 Macc. 9:9; 12:12). Jewish people often envisioned Gehinnom, the abode of the damned, as fiery. In some conceptions, the wicked might burn temporarily and then be either rehabilitated or consumed, but in the harshest understanding of Gehinnom, they would be tormented forever. Drawing on the language of Isa. 66:24, both John the Baptist (Matt. 3:12 // Luke 3:17), and Jesus (Mark 9:48) spoke of "unquenchable fire."

27. Elsewhere, see *Jubilees* 20.6; 36.9–10; Targum Isaiah on 1:10. Sodom rebelled despite blessings (*Sipre Deuteronomy* 43.3.5; Targum Pseudo-Jonathan on Gen. 19:24) and epitomized evil (*t. Shabbat* 7.23; Targum Isaiah on 1:10).

28. For blending of "natures," see Libanius, *Description* 21, on the chimera. Even some gentiles disdained sex across such categories (Philostratus, *Life of Apollonius* 6.40), or counted them "against nature" (Artemidorus, *Onirocritica* 1.80). God's ideal was for husband and wife to become "one flesh" (Gen. 2:24).

29. Though interpreters believed that evidence of its burning persisted, as in Josephus, *Jewish War* 4.484–85; esp. Wis. 10:7.

Disrespect for Heavenly Powers (8–10)

> **[8]But in the same way, these people by their dreaming defile the flesh, reject authority, and speak with hostility against the glorious ones. [9]Yet the archangel Michael, when he was contending with the devil over Moses's corpse, did not dare to pronounce a hostile judgment against him. Instead, he just said, "May the Lord rebuke you!" [10]But these people speak with hostility against things they don't understand. Meanwhile, they're destroyed by the things they know only—like reasonless animals—by instinct.**

Just as Judah linked together the above examples (cf. "likewise" in v. 7), he connects them closely with the apostates of his day: **in the same way** (v. 8). Although not always, the anonymous phrase **these people** (*houtoi*; vv. 8, 10, 12, 16, 19) was often contemptuous in antiquity. The grammar here suggests that **dreaming** leads to all of the following three sins. In the LXX, the language of **dreaming** normally refers to prophetic dreams; false prophets could likewise appeal to their "prophetic" dreams to justify sin (Deut. 13:1–5; Jer. 23:25–32; 27:9; 29:8; Zech. 10:2). Even apocalyptic visionaries recognized that the wicked might appeal to their visionary dreams for idolatry.[30] Such false prophets lack the true Spirit (Jude 19–20).[31]

Some voices today that claim to be prophetic put too much stock in their dreams. As God warned in Jeremiah's day, "Let the prophet who has a dream tell the dream, but let the one who has my word speak my word faithfully. What has straw in common with wheat? says the Lord" (Jer. 23:28 NRSV). Learning from Jack Deere and my African wife, I began paying attention to my dreams. But I have also had to learn to discern which are prophetic dreams infused by the Holy Spirit (and among those, fairly clear messages from God versus conditional what-if scenarios) and which are just free association of memories or the product of indigestion. Not all dreams are prophetic, and claims that reject what God has already spoken in Scripture must be rejected.

These dreamers may **defile the flesh** with sexual perversion (cf. "flesh" in v. 7) or more generally (v. 23). Certainly, the language of "defiling" oneself was considered appropriate to fallen angels' intercourse with women (*1 Enoch* 9.8; 12.4; 15.3–4; 69.5) and to Sodom's sexual sins "in their flesh" (*Jubilees* 16.5). It

30. See *1 Enoch* 99.8. Gentiles occasionally had stories of gods impregnating women initially in dreams or sleep (Aeschylus, *Prometheus Bound* 645–56; Philostratus, *Heroicus* 45.3). Compare later rabbinic concern about the night demoness Lilith abducting those who sleep alone (*b. Shabbat* 151b). The medical writer Aretaeus, however, associates dreams and shameless sexual behavior with mania (*Causes and Symptoms of Chronic Diseases*, book 1, chap. 6, p. 61.20–22).

31. For the connection, see Lampe, "Grievous Wolves," 260.

could also apply more generically to sexual sin (*Sibylline Oracles* 2.279; more generally, Philo, *Special Laws* 1.257).

The **authority** (*kyriotēs*) that they reject might be that of angels (cf. vv. 6–7), since some other early Christians applied the term to angelic rulers (Eph. 1:21; Col. 1:16), and the following illustration reflects disrespecting ranks that God established (Jude 9–10; cf. 2 Pet. 2:10–11). Alternatively, the **authority** in view, being singular, could be that of *the* aforementioned "Lord," Jesus (v. 4). These examples could also illustrate the wider principle of rejecting authority, like Korah in verse 11.

Judah gets more specific with **the glorious ones**. Greeks viewed stars and other heavenly bodies (cf. v. 13) as gods, but Jewish people viewed them as angels; such heavenly luminaries could be described in terms of glory (1 Cor. 15:41; cf. Dan. 12:3).[32] **Glorious ones** also appears as a title for angels in *1QHodayot^{a}* (1QH^{a}) 18.10. **Glorious** also means "honorable," fitting the context of respecting their rank (Jude 9–10).

Judah may be criticizing some Judeans' practice of directly cursing Satan.[33] Nevertheless, many other Judeans, like Judah himself, disagreed with the practice. This might be the case already in the pre-Christian work Sirach: "When an ungodly person curses an adversary [Gk. *satanas*], he curses himself" (21:27 NRSV). Later rabbis told the story of Pelimo, who used to go around saying, "An arrow in Satan's eyes!" But one day Satan caught Pelimo in a particularly vulnerable spot, and warned, "You should just say, 'The Merciful rebuke Satan!'" (*b. Qiddushin* 81ab).[34] Later rabbis protested cursing Satan (again with "An arrow in Satan's eyes!") by pointing out that this was "a challenge [to Satan] to contend with him" (*b. Menahot* 62a). Talk about inviting trouble! Other Jews complained about those who defy both God and heavenly stars—that is, angels (*1 Enoch* 46.7).

The problem here is people so arrogant that they act as if they have authority over angels. Perhaps they do so because they realize that God gave people a special role in his plan (1 Pet. 1:12), that angels serve his purposes for them (Matt. 18:10; Heb. 1:14), or that someday we will judge angels (1 Cor. 6:3; cf. 11:10). But ruling angels is for the future, not the present. In Heb. 1:14, God sends angels for our sake, but we do not send them; while on earth, our Lord

32. Also, e.g., *PGM* 1.200. Most interpreters do see them as angelic powers here (e.g., Carr, *Angels and Principalities*, 129–30).

33. *1QWar Scroll* (1QM) 13.1–2, 4; *4QCurses* (4Q280) f2.2; *4QBlessings^{a}* (4Q286) f7.2.2.

34. This is also the formula preferred in *Life of Adam and Eve* 39.1; *b. Qiddushin* 29b–30a; Aramaic incantation texts in Isbell, *Aramaic Incantation Bowls* 10.5–6; 24.14; 35.2–3; 42.10–11. God directly rebukes Satan's angels in *1QWar Scroll* (1QM) 14.10; the same term appears for rebuking Satan in Targum Zechariah on 3:2; *b. Qiddushin* 81b (so Jastrow, *Dictionary of the Targumim*, 261).

himself would have asked his Father for angelic help rather than commanding them directly (Matt. 26:53; cf. 4:6, 11). Indeed, the fringe charismatic practice of "sending" angels to accomplish one's bidding[35] is not only not biblical; it resembles the magical use of spirits in many cultures. Hebrews 1:14 says not "sent to render service *at the command of*" but rather "sent to render service *for the benefit of*." Likewise, in Ps. 91:11, guardian angels remain subject to God's command rather than ours ("*He* will command his angels concerning you"); placing them at our discretion seems closer to how Satan uses the passage in Matt. 4:6 // Luke 4:10–11.

Practitioners of magic invoke spirits, and Jewish practitioners of magic often invoked angels;[36] people often invoked deities or spirits to grant curses. Westerners sometimes arrogantly and without research dismiss the reality of curses and the intelligence of those who believe in them. Assuming that such ethnocentric thinkers can accept criticisms as readily as bestowing them, they should not take too much offense when some of us with actual experience with such curses (e.g., in our connections in Africa, where my wife is from) dismiss their pontifications as uninformed. An unmerited curse lacks access (Prov. 26:2), and God can turn a curse into a blessing (Num. 23:11; 24:10; Deut. 23:5; 2 Sam. 16:12; Neh. 13:2; Ps. 109:28). But Balaam (see Jude 11) recognized that a curse would become efficacious if Israel sinned (Num. 31:8, 16; Josephus, *Jewish Antiquities* 4.157). Those who wished to subdue God's people might thus hope to first subvert their morals.[37] The wise should not give the devil access by their misbehavior (Eph. 4:25–32, esp. 4:27).

I render *blasphēmeō* as **speak with hostility** in verses 8 and 10 to retain the connection with **hostile** (*blasphēmia*) speech in verse 9: Even the greatest archangel knows better than to speak personally against the devil (himself a slanderer, a key sense of *diabolos*, "devil"), but these boastful people speak arrogantly against angels as if God has authorized them to do so. God has indeed authorized us as the ground forces to cast out demons; we are not, however, the air force authorized to directly engage heavenly powers. To deal with those entities, we pray to God (2 Pet. 2:10–11; cf. Dan. 10:12–13, 20–21).[38]

35. See Hagin, *I Believe in Visions*, 126; Hagin, *Prayer Secrets*, 20; Capps, *The Tongue*, 57; K. Copeland, *Laws of Prosperity*, 104.

36. See the well-documented discussion in Estrada, "Blaspheming Angels," esp. 753–57. See also Keener, *Miracles*, 1:239n157, 247; 2:771, 793n38, 811, 846; Peters, *Ecstasy and Healing*, 61. Magical texts invoke Michael in *CIJ* 2.109, §876; *PGM* 1.301; 3.405; 7.1012–13; 44.1–18. Objects of curses also could become objects of invocation in magic (Frankfurter, *Religion in Roman Egypt*, 112–15; cf. 54).

37. See Jdt. 5:20–21; 11:10; *4QFlorilegium* (4Q174) f1–2.1.8–9; Rev. 2:14. Later rabbis deemed this a far greater sin than direct murder (e.g., *Sipre Deuteronomy* 252.1.4).

38. In principle, an exception might be possible if commanded by God to prophesy to them, like God commands Ezekiel to prophesy to mountains (Ezek. 36:1, 6) or peoples; but this is not the biblical norm for prayer.

The **archangel Michael** was Israel's guardian prince.[39] As the highest named angel in Scripture, he also came to be viewed as one of the chief archangels.[40] Treating him as the defending angel of the Lord in Zech. 3:1, some traditions paired him off against Satan.[41]

Jesus often rebuked demons (e.g., Mark 1:25; 9:25), but **rebuke** here echoes Zech. 3:2, where God (possibly speaking through his angel [3:1]) declares to Satan, "The **Lord** rebuke you!" Judah apparently believes that such a confrontation happened more than once, however. The specific source that Jude quotes here is now lost,[42] but the storyline has survived from snippets in various sources: Satan as the accuser (cf. Zech. 3:1) apparently claimed the right to Moses's body by accusing Moses of murder. Michael knew better, but rather than disrespecting Satan's angelic rank, Michael appealed to the Lord himself.[43]

Michael defeating the devil

39. Dan. 10:21; 12:1; *1 Enoch* 20.5; 71.3; *1QWar Scroll* (1QM) 17.7–8; *3 Enoch* 44.10.

40. *1 Enoch* 9.1; 24.6; 71.3; *4QWords of Michael ar* (4Q529) f1.1; *Sibylline Oracles* 2.214–20; *Testament of Abraham* recension A, passim; 2.2; 4.9 B; *Life of Adam and Eve* 25.2; *2 Enoch* 22.6; 33.10; *Genesis Rabbah* 78.1; for other archangels, see *1 Enoch* 79.6; *4 Ezra* 4.36; *2 Baruch* 59.11; *2 Enoch* 20.1; 21.3.

41. See *1QWar Scroll* (1QM) 17.5–7; Rev. 12:7; later, *Exodus Rabbah* 18.5. For Michael as the angel of the Lord, see Targum Pseudo-Jonathan on Gen. 32:25; 38:25; Exod. 24:1; *Exodus Rabbah* 2.5. Some later rabbis also treated him as the fourth figure in Nebuchadnezzar's furnace (*Genesis Rabbah* 44.13; *Song of Songs Rabbah* 1.12, §1; for Gabriel, see *Exodus Rabbah* 18.5).

42. Most scholars attribute this to the lost ending of *Testament of Moses* (see Bauckham, *Jude, 2 Peter*, 65–76; G. Green, *Jude and 2 Peter*, 80; differently, Charlesworth, *Pseudepigrapha and the New Testament*, 75–77).

43. Sources varied as to Moses's death (Loewenstamm, "Death of Moses," 194–208) and why he needed to be buried outside the land (186–93). The Lord buried Moses in an unknown location (Deut. 34:6; Pseudo-Philo, *Biblical Antiquities* 19.12). In later tradition, Moses rebuked the angel of death (e.g., *Avot of Rabbi Nathan* 12 A), and God had to take Moses directly (*Sipre Deuteronomy* 305.3.3).

Not unlike some online "experts" today, the impious people here pontificate on matters beyond their knowledge (v. 10). Indeed, these sinners' only knowledge, Judah charges, is limited to that shared with animals (cf. Ps. 49:20), such as how to have intercourse. Ancient thinkers often contrasted reasoning ability in humans with its lack in animals.[44] To the extent that humans did not practice reason, however, philosophers viewed them as beasts (see comment on 2 Pet. 2:12).[45] Regarding right and wrong ways to do spiritual warfare, see comment on 1 Pet. 4:1; 5:9.

False Promises and Doom (11–13)

> **[11]It will be so terrible for them! That's because they've followed in Cain's path and expended themselves for pay as in Balaam's error and perished in Korah's rebellion.**

It will be so terrible (v. 11) is a translation that attempts to find a modern English equivalent for the Semitic expression *ouai*, "woe!" The opposite of a blessing, it can mean "Alas!" but often functions as a pronouncement of judgment. It is common in the later LXX books (some sixty times), and also in extant Greek portions of *1 Enoch*.

Jewish sources often use **Cain** (v. 11) as an example of evil, especially because he murdered his brother.[46] Ancients considered the murder of a brother one of the most heinous sins.[47] Tradition developed this negative view of Cain further. Since he killed his brother with a stone, his house later collapsed so its stones could kill him (*Jubilees* 4.31–32); later sources claim that he suffered a new plague every hundred years (*Testament of Benjamin* 7.3–5). He was covetous (Josephus, *Jewish Antiquities* 1.52–59) and a lover of self (Philo, *Worse Attacks the Better* 32, 78). He denied future retribution (Targum Neofiti 1 on Gen. 4:8; Targum Pseudo-Jonathan on Gen. 4:8), but he would be eternally lost (Philo, *Posterity of Cain* 39). Some Jewish sources name him alongside Balaam as an example of the wicked and damned (*Avot of Rabbi Nathan* 41 A; *Numbers Rabbah* 20.6).

The term translated as **error** (*planē*; v. 11) can mean "wandering from the path," consistent with the earlier mention of Cain's **path**. Balak enticed **Balaam** with the promise of wealth (Num. 22:17; Deut. 23:4; Neh. 13:2). Balaam had a great gift spiritually, yet without character to match it. Both with Balaam and

44. For example, Cicero, *Duties* 1.4.11.

45. For example, Epictetus, *Discourses* 1.3.7, 9.

46. Gen. 4:8; *1 Enoch* 22.7; *Jubilees* 4.2–4, 31; Wis. 10:3; Heb. 11:4; 1 John 3:12. For one survey, see Chempakassery, "Cain."

47. For example, Justin, *Epitome* 28.2.10; Horace, *Epodes* 7.17–20; Plutarch, *Cicero* 10.2; Apuleius, *Metamorphoses* 10.8.

BIBLICAL BACKGROUND

Jewish Traditions About Balaam

Jewish sources treat Balaam as the prototypical false prophet.[a]

- Jewish sources contrast Balaam the false or pagan prophet with Moses as a pious prophet.[b]
- They understood him as a special prophet of the gentiles[c] and sometimes as a gentile philosopher.[d]
- Epitomizing Balaam as a figure of extreme wickedness (later rabbis call him "Balaam the wicked"),[e] Jewish sources consigned him to hell.[f]
- Others commented on Balaam's donkey being wiser than he;[g] Philo allegorized Balaam to signify foolish people.[h]

a. See *4QList of False Prophets ar* (4Q339) f1.1–2. For Jewish traditions about Balaam, see also Greene, "Balaam Figure."

b. For example, *Sipre Deuteronomy* 357.18.1–2; *Numbers Rabbah* 14.20; *Ecclesiastes Rabbah* 2.15, §2; Targum Neofiti 1 on Gen. 27:29; also Targum Pseudo-Jonathan on Gen. 27:29; Targum Pseudo-Jonathan on Num. 24:9. See Remus, "Moses and the Thaumaturges." Compare contrasts with Abraham in *m. Avot* 5.19; *Genesis Rabbah* 55.9. Israel's prophets expected judgment soon, but Balaam later (*Pesiqta Rabbati* 41.3).

c. *Sipre Deuteronomy* 343.6.1; *b. Bava Batra* 15b; *Exodus Rabbah* 32.3.

d. *Genesis Rabbah* 65.20; 93.10; *Exodus Rabbah* 30.20; *Leviticus Rabbah* 5.3; *Lamentations Rabbah* proem 2; *Pesiqta Rabbati* 20.1. Some even identified him with Laban the Aramean (Targum Pseudo-Jonathan on Num. 22:5; 31:8; Targum 1 Chronicles on 1:43).

e. *B. Berakhot* 7a; *b. Avodah Zarah* 4a; *b. Sanhedrin* 105b; *Exodus Rabbah* 20.5. He was thus like a chamber pot, "a vessel full of urine" (*Numbers Rabbah* 20.6).

f. For example, *m. Avot* 5.19; *Exodus Rabbah* 30.24; *Numbers Rabbah* 14.1.

g. *Genesis Rabbah* 93.10.

h. Philo, *Cherubim* 32; *God Is Unchangeable* 181.

with prominent figures today, Jesus's warning is not that we will know them by their gifts, but that we will know them by their fruits (Matt. 7:15–16). Unable to curse Israel so long as they served God, Balaam counseled Israel's enemies to entice Israel to commit sexual immorality so that they would become curse-worthy (Num. 31:16).[48] The false teaching promoting immorality here likewise renders Israel vulnerable to sin (cf. similarly Rev. 2:14).[49]

Similar to the arrogant rebels referenced in this letter, Korah's **rebellion** included a claim of equality with Moses and Aaron, disrespecting God-ordained

48. Also Josephus, *Jewish Antiquities* 4.157; Pseudo-Philo, *Biblical Antiquities* 18.13.

49. Leading someone to sin was worse than committing murder, because sin also alienates from the life of the coming world (*Numbers Rabbah* 21.4).

authority (Num. 16:1–3; Sir. 45:18). Korah and some of his followers **perished** when the ground swallowed them (Num. 16:31–34). Judgment on Korah naturally functioned as a warning to later generations.[50] Tradition associated his rebellion with opposing the law.[51] Although later rabbis debated whether Korah held a place in the coming world, most held that he would not.[52]

> **[12]These are the ones who are stains [or, "reefs"][53] in your love gatherings, feasting themselves without reverence. They are like shepherds who pasture only themselves. They're waterless clouds blown along by winds. They're like trees in the fall without fruit, twice dead, uprooted. [13]They're like wild waves of the sea, foaming up their shameful acts; like wandering stars for whom netherworld darkness has been reserved forever.**

Love gatherings designates the early church's gathering around meals; the term was clearly understood this way already in the second century.[54] Although eventually separated from the Lord's Supper, in the first century they were the same meal (1 Cor. 10:21; 11:20–22). Greeks often invited friends to dine with them; well-to-do Romans invited their clients. Unlike Roman dinners, however, the Christian one should transcend status boundaries (1 Cor. 11:21–22) and should reveal believers' unity as Christ's body (10:16–17; 11:29).

Pagan banquets were notorious for sexual excesses (see comment on 1 Pet. 4:3), and the idea of **love** and **love gatherings** was easily perverted.[55] Pagan banquets were even more notorious for drunkenness and gluttony (thus perhaps here, **feasting themselves**), also condemned by early Christians (e.g., Rom. 13:13; Gal. 5:21; 1 Pet. 4:3; 2 Pet. 2:13; cf. already Isa. 5:22; 28:1).

Eating meals together established covenant relationships. In small house-church gatherings as in most Greco-Roman associations, members knew one another intimately, so they may need Judah's help in drawing proper theological and moral boundaries. That the errorists feast themselves **without reverence**

50. As in e.g., *4QInstruction^g* (4Q423) f5.1.

51. Pseudo-Philo, *Biblical Antiquities* 16.1; Targum Pseudo-Jonathan on Num. 16:1–2.

52. *M. Sanhedrin* 10.3; *b. Bava Batra* 74a; *b. Sanhedrin* 109b–110a; *Numbers Rabbah* 18.13.

53. The Greek word *spilas* could signify a "reef," an image that fits clouds in verse 12 and esp. waves in verse 13. Subsurface reefs endangered ships (Acts 27:41), and this is the term's most common meaning (e.g., Homer, *Odyssey* 3.298; 5.401, 405; Josephus, *Jewish War* 3.420). Its rarer, perhaps figuratively extended, sense of "stain" (cf. the cognate *spilos*), however, might make more sense with love feasts, and it connects with verse 23, where *spiloō* applies to what is stained by the flesh. For what it is worth, it also corresponds better with its early reapplication in 2 Pet. 2:13.

54. For example, Ignatius, *To the Smyrnaeans* 8.2; Tertullian, *Apology* 39.16. Compare an earlier Roman description of an intimate banquet as "charity" or "love" (Valerius Maximus, *Deeds and Sayings* 2.1.8).

55. On perversion of the idea, see Maximus of Tyre, *Orations* 18.3; 19.4; 21.3.

BIBLICAL BACKGROUND

Background of the Lord's Supper

Jesus dined with sinners interested in his message (Luke 5:29-32; 15:1); the early Lord's Supper probably welcomed prospective believers as well as current ones. People who claimed to follow Christ and dishonored his name, however, might face stricter discipline and exclusion (1 Cor. 5:9–13; 2 Thess. 3:6; cf. 2 John 9–11). The Lord's Supper spiritually reenacts Jesus's last supper with his disciples, reminding us of the price Jesus paid for us to belong to him in a sort of new exodus (Mark 14:22–24). The Last Supper was in turn a Passover meal, a commemoration (Exod. 12:14; 1 Cor. 11:24–25) of God's earlier act of redemption in the first exodus (Exod. 24:8; Zech. 9:11; Mark 14:24). Just as baptism envelops us with water, embodying our immersion into Christ, so ingesting the Lord's Supper signifies our taking Christ into us. That is, both rites underline our identification with and participation in Christ (cf. 1 Cor. 10:16).

Christians differ on the particulars of the Lord's Supper, differences that sometimes have been expressed violently. Luther, for example, broke fellowship with Zwingli over his different understanding. Misunderstandings go back to the earliest period, when outsiders accused Christians of cannibalism for eating the "flesh" of Jesus. Because our sharing in the Lord's Supper embodies our participation in Christ's body, however, it invites us not to division but to unity with others who depend on Christ alone for salvation (1 Cor. 10:16–17; 11:27–30).

would be relevant to the Lord's Supper (1 Cor. 11:27–30) but may also suggest their hardness against the Spirit's conviction; they feel no guilt or shame for their behavior (cf. Ps. 36:2; Isa. 3:9; 1 Cor. 5:1–2).

Shepherds who pasture only themselves is an image that evokes Ezek. 34:2–10; note 34:2: "It will be terrible for the shepherds who pasture only themselves! Shouldn't the shepherds be pasturing the sheep?" (AT). The Old Testament uses shepherds as an image for leaders of Israel, and the New Testament applies the title also to leaders of God's people (Eph. 4:11); see discussion at 1 Pet. 5:2. God is angry with shepherds who exploit his flock (Jer. 23:1–2; Ezek. 34:10).

Judah now turns to images from nature. **Waterless clouds** are worthless, promising farmers hope for their crops only in vain; compare Prov. 25:14: "Clouds and wind without rain: that's someone who lies about having given a gift" (AT). (Clouds and waves were also known for transience, as in *2 Baruch* 82.8–9.) Being

blown along by winds leaves no rational sense of direction (Eph. 4:14; James 1:6). Many **trees** bear fruit in summer, with some continuing in early fall (note esp. the autumn grape vintage), but fruit trees still fruitless in the fall might be dead and fit to be **uprooted** (cf. Matt. 3:10 // Luke 3:9; Mark 11:13–14, 20; Luke 13:6–9). Like waterless clouds, they hold false promises for the future. Although some associate their being **twice dead** only with the second death,[56] it probably evokes the former believers' return to their preeternal life state (cf. Rom. 8:13).[57]

Wild waves are particularly dangerous (LXX Wis. 14:1), and they may be **foaming** (cf. Ps. 46:3; Hab. 3:15) against reefs (a possible sense of *spilas* in v. 12). Here they are **foaming up** filth; compare Isa. 57:20: "The wicked are like the tossing sea . . . ; its waters toss up filth and mud" (AT).[58] From a moral perspective, sins are all truly **shameful acts**; in ancient Mediterranean honor-shame culture, even a normal sense of decency would fail to restrain a shameless person (i.e., one who would act shamefully).

The term for **wandering** (*planētēs*) recalls Balaam's "error" (*planē*) in verse 11. From a geocentric standpoint, the seven known "planets" became so named because observers viewed them as **wandering stars**, since their "orbit" over the earth differed from that of normal stars. Jewish people viewed angels as **stars**, and rebellious angelic stars (esp. seven [*1 Enoch* 18.13]) as going astray (*1 Enoch* 21.6; cf. 80.6). Their straying included them impregnating women (*1 Enoch* 86.3–4), as in verse 6. Imprisoning such *luminaries* in **darkness** (v. 6) sounds ironic (cf. *1 Enoch* 88.1). Now, **netherworld darkness** [*zophos*] **has been reserved** [*tēreō*] for these sinners as it was for the fallen angels in verse 6 (also using *zophos* and *tēreō*). Some other Jewish traditions also associated damnation with darkness.[59]

Enoch's Prophecy (14–16)

> **[14]Concerning these sinners, Enoch, the seventh from Adam, prophesied. He said, "Look! The Lord comes[60] with his holy myriads [15]to**

56. Rev. 2:11; 20:6, 14; 21:8; Targum Neofiti 1 on Deut. 33:6; Targum Isaiah on 22:14; 65:6, 15; Targum Jeremiah on 51:39, 57.

57. Pythagoreans also treated apostates as dead (Burkert, "Craft Versus Sect," 18).

58. This image is echoed in *1QHodayot*[a] (4QH[a]) 10.14–16. Some suggest an association with Aphrodite, goddess of sexual love. Greeks associated her with an origin in sea foam (Hesiod, *Theogony* 188–98; Cornutus, *Greek Theology* 24, §45.3–4; Macrobius, *Saturnalia* 1.8.6; Aristaenetus, *Erotic Letters* 1.7.13–14, 17; Libanius, *Speech in Character* 18.3), but "foam" had far wider connotations than Aphrodite (cf. Mark 9:18–20; Luke 9:39), and her name could also be associated with "folly" (*aphrosynē*) and being "foolish" (*aphrōn*), as in Cornutus, *Greek Theology* 24, §45.5–7.

59. *1 Enoch* 103.7; *Psalms of Solomon* 14.9; 15.10; see also Matt. 8:12.

60. The sense is likely future, as in the wording in extant texts of *1 Enoch*, but Jude may employ the aorist verb to highlight it, to render a Semitic idiom, or to stress that the promise is as good as accomplished.

execute judgment against everyone and to convict every person concerning all their impious acts that they have impiously done, and concerning all the resistant words that impious sinners have spoken against him." [16]These are fault-finding complainers, pursuing their own desires. They talk big, seeking to profit by acting impressed with others.

Judah's earlier allusions to the Enoch story (esp. in v. 6) culminate in an actual citation here from *1 Enoch* 1.9.[61] Later rabbis often played down Enoch, probably polemically,[62] but he remained popular in most early Jewish circles.[63] In context, *1 Enoch* 1.9 refers to the coming of God for judgment; Jude may apply it to Jesus coming for judgment. If the false prophets and their followers appeal to Enoch, Judah can deftly cite Enoch as prophesying their own damnation.

Others had also noted that Enoch was **seventh from Adam.**[64] Perhaps Judah finds special significance in Enoch being **seventh**; many regarded seven as a special number.[65] Perhaps, however, Judah merely labored to distinguish the Enoch of Gen. 5:18–24 from others with (in the original languages) the same name (e.g., Gen. 4:17–18; 46:9; 1 Chron. 1:33).

Myriads is literally "ten thousands," but *myrias* often functioned as a number beyond counting, appropriate for angels (LXX Deut. 33:2; Dan. 7:10; Heb. 12:22; Rev. 5:11). Zechariah prophesied that God would come with all his **holy** ones (Zech. 14:5), applied in the New Testament to angels (Mark 8:38) and possibly also to believers (1 Thess. 3:13). Years ago, I had to challenge a Bible study leader who claimed that the Lord would come here with "myriads of himself," and that we would all become Jesus. He reached this dangerously nonsensical conclusion because the Greek text of verse 14 says "myriads of him," and the

61. More of Judah's quotation matches the surviving Greek version than the Ethiopic version; this could indicate his familiarity with especially the Greek version, but while the Ethiopic version is more complete, the Greek version may reflect an earlier text type at points. Regarding the Aramaic, see Knibb, *Ethiopic Book of Enoch*, 59–60. Jude may also adapt or remember this text in light of his knowledge of an Aramaic version.

62. For example, *Genesis Rabbah* 25.1; but contrast the positive approach associated with the minority voice of Rabbi Ishmael in *3 Enoch*.

63. Note "Enoch the righteous" in *Testament of Levi* 10.5; *Testament of Judah* 18.1; *Testament of Dan* 5.6; *Testament of Benjamin* 9.1, following *1 Enoch* 1.2; 15.1. Earlier, Enoch was clearly popular in Essene-like circles (*1 Enoch*; *Jubilees* 4.22; 10.17; 19.27; *1QGenesis Apocryphon* [1Q20] 2.19–24; *4QEnoch^g ar* [4Q212]).

64. *1 Enoch* 60.8; *Jubilees* 7.39; *4QPrayer of Enosh (?)* (4Q369) f1.1.10; *Life of Adam and Eve* 51.9. Without enumeration, see Gen. 5:3–18.

65. For example, Pliny the Elder, *Natural History* 2.4.12; 2.6.32–41; Dio Chrysostom, *Orations* 72.12; Aulus Gellius, *Attic Nights* 3.10; Apuleius, *Metamorphoses* 11.1; Macrobius, *Saturnalia* 1.19.15; *4QSongs of Sabbath Sacrifice^d* (4Q403) f1.1.2–9; f1.2.27; Philo, *Creation* 99–100, 111–39; *Life of Abraham* 28; *Special Laws* 2.56–62. So Enoch as the seventh being the most loved in *Pesiqta of Rab Kahana* 23.10.

study leader did not understand that "of him" (*autou*) is the normal Greek way to say "his." The moral of the story is that while interlinear Bibles are useful for learning Greek vocabulary, novices should be careful about their conclusions until they have learned some Greek grammar. While my role there was not as a leader for the Bible study (and some protested that I was being divisive), I had to challenge his claim. Nothing should be allowed to detract from the Lord's honor. As far in the future as the Bible reveals, we will always remain the Lord's servants, serving him alone (Rev. 22:3–4).

The term translated as **resistant** (*sklēros*) comes directly from *1 Enoch* 1.9 and normally means "harsh" or "hard" (as in hardness of heart). The condemnation in *1 Enoch* picks up in 5.4–5: "You . . . have spoken proud and harsh words with your unclean mouth against his majesty. You hard of heart!" (see also 16.3; 27.2).[66] Note also sinners' hard words in *1 Enoch* 101.3; 102.6.

On acting **impiously**, see comment on verse 4 (where, however, I rendered the term as "irreligious"); the term indicates disrespect toward deity. Of all the defiant words against authority (vv. 8–11), the worst are those **spoken against him** (v. 15). Judah then expounds about their hostile speech: they are **complainers** (v. 16). Although the passage's word for **fault-finding** (*mempsimoiros*) does not occur in the Greek version of the Old Testament, the Jewish philosopher Philo uses it for Israel's complaints against God in the wilderness (*Life of Moses* 1.181). Meanwhile, cognates of the word translated as **complainers** (*gongystēs*) are common in the Greek Old Testament to refer to the same offense, and the idea is even more common. The agitators are like those who complained about God's gracious provision in the wilderness, and thus were punished (Exod. 16:7–12; 17:3; Num. 11:1; 14:27–29; 16:41; 17:10; Ps. 106:25; 1 Cor. 10:10). Just as God's people complained because of their desires for different food (Num. 11:4; Pss. 78:29–30; 106:14), so, too, do these sinners pursue their own desires. Sometimes we need to wrestle with God in prayer, but this differs from complaining about him to others. The Spirit-filled life on the whole is one of gratitude toward God, not complaining against him (Eph. 5:18–20; 1 Thess. 5:18–19).

While grumbling about God and his agents, the agitators flatter others to their faces; this catering to people rather than God confirms their impiety (noted in vv. 4, 15, 18). A flatterer seeks their own good rather than that of the person they flatter (Prov. 28:23; 29:5). This behavior includes false prophets who just tell people what they want to hear (Isa. 30:10; Jer. 14:13–16; Mic. 3:5). Whether with prophecies or just compliments, the cunning can still manipulate hearers, especially where our sense of inadequacy makes us too vulnerable (although *true* words of encouragement are always welcome; Prov. 12:25; 15:4; Eph. 4:29).

66. Translation in Knibb, *Ethiopic Book of Enoch*, 65.

PENTECOSTAL INTEREST

Should All Prophecies Be Positive?

Some say that all prophecies today, as opposed to many in the Old Testament, should be positive. But this is not biblical, even if one narrows the pool of evidence to the New Testament. The clearest New Testament examples of prophecies appear in Acts, where they involve impending suffering: coming famine (11:28) or arrest (21:11). The next clearest are the letters to the seven churches in Revelation (2:1–3:22), which include both encouragements and warnings; five churches receive corrections and reproofs. In one case, this includes the removal of a church's lampstand (2:5), meaning its end as a church. I once had to prophesy these same words to an apparently vibrant church, to my own dismay. I did not understand why the Lord would say it to this church and not to many other ones that I thought were worse off. This one seemed to be failing only on the matter that the Lord pointed out—in this case, lack of outreach. But within a year this church ceased to exist.

We do not have the right to choose what the Lord wants to say. The idea of prophetic declarations as positive confessions, without the Lord's Spirit leading the prophecy, risks significant danger. As Lam. 3:37 warns, "Who is there who speaks and it comes to pass, unless the Lord has commanded it?" (NASB). What people often call "prophetic declarations" are really blessings—prayers—not predictions per se.

Paul likewise addresses deceptive flattery in Rom. 16:18. Most ancient moralists agreed on this point, denouncing flattery as harmful.[67] Ancient moralists and orators accepted moral **profit** as a positive criterion for decisions, but the idea here is immoral **profit** by exploiting others (cf. the idea in 2 Cor. 2:17; 4:2; 2 Pet. 2:3).

Persevering in the Faith (17–23)

> **[17]But you, loved ones, should remember what the apostles of our Lord Jesus Christ foretold. [18]They told you that in the final time there will be**

67. For example, Cicero, *Friendship* 25.94–26.99; *Duties* 1.26.91; Epictetus, *Discourses* 1.9.20; 1.12; 4.6.33; 4.7.24; Plutarch, *Education of Children* 17, *Moralia* 13B; Juvenal, *Satires* 3.86–87; 4.65–72; Wis. 14:17; Josephus, *The Life* 367; *Pseudo-Phocylides* 91.

mockers pursuing their own impious desires. [19]These mockers are divisive and this-worldly; they lack the Spirit.

Judah transitions in verses 17 and 20 with **But you**. In contrast to those who speak impiously (vv. 8–16), Judah's audience should take heed of godly words (v. 17), be renewed (vv. 20–21), and help pull others out of the error (vv. 22–23). By **apostles** (v. 17) Jude might mean the Twelve (e.g., Luke 6:13) or a somewhat broader group (e.g., 1 Cor. 9:5; 15:7). Various apostles warned about end-time evils (e.g., 2 Thess. 2:10–11; 1 Tim. 4:1; 2 Tim. 3:1–5; 1 Pet. 4:17; 1 John 2:18–19), much of which they learned about from Jesus (Mark 13:9–23). That some **foretold** God's truth about the future encourages hearers to trust that God remains in control of it (Isa. 45:21; John 13:19; 14:29; 16:4);[68] compare also our modern saying (based on a Latin proverb), "Forewarned is forearmed."

For **the final time** (v. 18), see comment on 2 Pet. 3:3; the particular phrase here is closest in wording to 1 Pet. 1:20. Like similar phrases elsewhere in the New Testament, this expression refers to the present era between Jesus's comings as an eschatological time, the period of the outpouring of the prophetic Spirit (Acts 2:17–18).

The apostles' prediction of **mockers pursuing their own impious desires** (v. 18) is being fulfilled in the complainers pursuing their own desires (v. 16). In recent years, the church has experienced plenty of scandals from those within the church exposed for exploiting God's people for their own desires. Some were predictable, but others were shocking (cf. 1 Tim. 5:24). Ravi Zacharias seemed balanced in his teaching, but his private life included sexual exploitation. Before Mike Bickle's sexual exploitation of spiritual dependents came to light, I relished the privilege of my brief visit with him; my friend Sam Storms, in an intimate small group with Bickle for years, felt every reason to trust him fully. The unexpected truth devastated the many genuine people of prayer in the International House of Prayer movement. Sometimes God uses for the sake of others individuals who are sinning (Judg. 16:1–3, 9, 12; 1 Sam. 19:20–24), but sooner or later truth comes out (Num. 32:23; 1 Tim. 5:24).

In verse 19, the Greek term *apodiorizō* (**divisive**) means to "mark off by dividing or separating."[69] Some people like to nitpick theological points just to assert their superiority over others; I was fairly argumentative by the time I finished Bible college, including on fine points of eschatology. I still enjoy deep Bible discussions exploring views—provided we act as brothers and sisters—and there's nothing like a few hot-button issues to keep theological students awake.

68. Note the idea also in *Jubilees* 1.6; *Sibylline Oracles* 3.816–18.
69. BDAG 110.

But my experience of practical ministry made me much less arrogant and argumentative. When we're in an academic silo or a narrow circle lacking much fellowship with other Christians, we can major on minors and demean fellow believers inappropriately. For Christians active in the world—for example, in secular jobs or studies or neighborhoods—our shared unity in Christ becomes paramount. We recognize that we need all the support we can get!

Such separatism marks not only cults but even some fundamentalist Christians who practice extra "degrees" of separation. For example, many fundamentalists rejected Billy Graham because he worked with Catholics and mainline Protestants to share the gospel. John MacArthur's statements about the vast majority of charismatics in the world being unsaved fall into this category of separatism. (Since he has criticized charismatic teachers for not naming more names of those who promote error, hopefully he will not protest me naming him.) His anticharismatic conferences and well-funded global literature distribution have sown much division in Christ's body, and I believe that God will someday call him and his circle to account for the damage caused by their divisive approach. At the same time, some of his critiques about excesses are valid, and if charismatics simply close ranks against him and defend those who should be challenged, that is also a form of separatism. The body of Christ needs not reactionary voices but biblically sound, balanced voices. Charismatic authors such as Michael Brown and Paul King have provided faithful continuationist critiques.[70] It is not divisive to challenge error, especially in a gentle way (2 Tim. 2:24–25) but vocally when necessary (e.g., 1 Tim. 1:20; 2 Tim. 2:17).

I use **this-worldly** (v. 19) to translate *psychikos* (NIV: "who follow mere natural instincts"). The term *psychikos* comes from *psychē*, which in Jude simply means "person" (v. 15). Paul, however, contrasts *psychikos* (regarding humans in themselves) with *pneumatikos* (empowered by God's Spirit) (1 Cor. 2:13–3:1; 15:44–46). This description carries forward the depiction of the apostates' merely bestial character (Jude 10) (the LXX applies *psychē* to animals [e.g., Gen. 1:20–30; 9:4]). They might claim to be more spiritual (this would be *pneumatikos*), but they **lack** God's **Spirit**.

Divisiveness and this-worldliness—common as they are in much of the church—characterize those who **lack the Spirit** (v. 19). Such lack of the Spirit contrasts with those of us who can grow stronger in the way of the Spirit by "praying by the Holy Spirit" (v. 20). Because Scripture often associates the Spirit's activity with prophetic empowerment, this emphasis also fits into Judah's concern for false prophets versus genuine apostolic teaching.

70. King, *Is It of God?*; Brown, *Playing with Holy Fire*.

> **[20]But you, loved ones, build yourselves up in your holiest faith, praying by the Holy Spirit. [21]In this way, keep yourselves in God's love, awaiting our Lord Jesus Christ's mercy for eternal life. [22]Show mercy to those who are questioning. [23]Rescue others by snatching them from the fire. When you show mercy on yet others, do so with fear, hating even their garment stained by the flesh.**

It is important to **build yourselves up**. Some critics play down prayer in tongues, insisting that because Paul emphasizes what edifies the wider body of Christ, he demeans tongues as what merely builds up oneself (1 Cor. 14:4). This is like arguing that we should study Scripture only for sermon preparation and never for personal devotion. Judah is clear that we should in fact fortify our faith, and one way to do this is by praying empowered by the Holy Spirit (v. 20).

One of the biblically explicit forms of **praying by the Holy Spirit**, in fact, is praying in tongues.[71] While Paul describes this practice as praying with one's own spirit (1 Cor. 14:13–15), it, like the gift of praying the interpretation, is a gift from God's Spirit (12:7–11), indicating that the Spirit may move us in prayer whether in tongues or in our own language. Given Acts 1:14, Jude the brother of Jesus surely was present at Pentecost when Jesus's followers first began to pray in tongues.[72]

Ephesians teaches that we can worship by the Spirit (5:18–21), which probably helps inform what Paul means by prayer in or by the Spirit in Eph. 6:18. This worship includes Spirit-inspired songs (1 Cor. 14:15, 26; probably the meaning of "spiritual songs" in Eph. 5:19; Col. 3:16), as in Old Testament prophetic temple worship (1 Chron. 25:2–3). Worship inspired by the Spirit is a key mark that distinguishes genuine Christian worship from mere ritual (John 4:23–24; Phil. 3:3), although the Spirit can work through prepared, formal structures as well as spontaneous ones (1 Chron. 25:1–6).

Scholars debate whether Rom. 8:26–27 refers to tongues. Both sides offer strong evidence,[73] but I suspect that it is something deeper and less articulate than tongues (the Greek term *alalētos*, used in 8:26, means "unutterable, unspeakable"). At times I have heard "tongues" that do not sound like a language (though I have heard some languages like that too), but if they are genuine prayer to God, they are at the very *least* groanings by the Spirit that should not

71. Many scholars find that focus here. See, e.g., Menzies, *Speaking in Tongues*, 135 (noting also Dunn and Bauckham).

72. Pointed out by Amoafo, *Stand Up for the Gospel*, 164. Amoafo also addresses abuses and more broadly the importance of Spirit-led prayer (164–71).

73. For tongues here, see Fee, *Listening to the Spirit*, 107–20; Fee, *God's Empowering Presence*, 575–86; Menzies, *Speaking in Tongues*, 139–46. For a wider reference not limited to tongues, see Storms, *Romans*, 123–24.

be despised. In Acts, tongues illustrate empowerment for cross-cultural mission (1:8; 2:4);[74] no longer is Hebrew the exclusive holy language, but every language is now consecrated for worship and honoring Christ. Absent or at least never explicit in the Old Testament, tongues appear in the New Testament because this is where God's people go global.

Keep yourselves (v. 21) complements God keeping us ("preserved" [v. 1]) and contrasts with those kept for judgment (vv. 6, 13). To **keep yourselves in God's love** might resemble the teaching in John 15:10: "If you keep my commands, you'll stay in my love, just as I kept my Father's commands and I stay in his love" (AT). **God's love** here probably is in Greek a subjective genitive; that is, it refers to God's love for us, because we remain his children who remain in him.

As opposed to those who care only about the natural things of this age (v. 19), we are **awaiting our Lord Jesus Christ's mercy for eternal life** (v. 21). This is end-time expectation, as in Rom. 8:23–25; Titus 2:13. We who already experience God's mercy in Christ (v. 2) should have confidence in his end-time **mercy** (v. 21; cf. Matt. 5:7; 2 Tim. 1:18). Receiving **mercy** (v. 21) is also related to showing **mercy** (vv. 22–23; cf. Matt. 6:12 // Luke 11:4; Matt. 5:7; 18:33; Mark 11:25).

The usual meaning of *diakrinō* (which I render as **questioning**) involves making distinctions (the sense of "doubting" is not attested before the New Testament). In verse 9 it has to do with disputing; in verse 22, then, it might continue that idea of questioning or it might involve divisions, doubting, or wavering. Those so designated here seem to be believers whose faith is nevertheless on the edge. Our culture is good at raising questions; leaders telling those struggling with questions to ignore those questions is not helpful. God may not answer all our questions in this life, but he does provide answers for many of them, especially if we commit ourselves to patiently seeking them—starting from reverence for God that is the beginning of knowledge (Prov. 1:7). We should welcome sincere inquirers, whether simply wondering or doubting, to ask their questions, and then help them find answers. But not everyone has honest questions. Harder cases appear in verse 23.[75]

Rescue (v. 23) translates the verb *sōzō* ("save"), and their position in **the fire** suggests that they are further gone than those mentioned in verse 22: Like the Sodomites consumed by fire (v. 7), they are now lost, but unlike them, they may still be rescued. The image might recall God's mercy in the Old Testament: He snatched Israel like a log from the fire (Amos 4:11, comparing them to Sodom

74. Keener, *Between History and Spirit*, 239–45; Keener, "Tongues as a Sign."

75. For kindness and various degrees of reachability, see also Seneca, *To Lucilius* 29.1–7 (in Malherbe, *Moral Exhortation*, 28–29); Marcus Aurelius, *Meditations* 9.11; *b. Sanhedrin* 37a. In contrast to New Testament teaching (Matt. 18:12–14; Luke 22:32; Gal. 4:19; James 5:19–20; 1 John 5:16–17), *1QRule of the Community* (1QS) 10.20–21 simply rejects apostates wholesale.

and Gomorrah). More relevantly, the Lord refers to the high priest as a log snatched from the fire (Zech. 3:2) in the same passage where he declares, "The Lord rebuke you, Satan!" and replaces the priest's filthy garments (Zech. 3:2–5; cf. Jude 9, 23b).

The third group (assuming the likeliest textual reading)[76] is further still. While not unreachable, they themselves risk contaminating others if we are not careful. Therefore, we approach them **with fear, hating even their garment stained by the flesh** (v. 23). A garment could contract and communicate ritual impurity until washed (e.g., Lev. 15:5–27; cf. Gen. 35:2; Isa. 64:6; Zech. 3:3–5) or burned (Lev. 13:52), an image here applied to moral contagion. (Here the term for **garment** [*chitōn*], in contrast to the LXX verses just mentioned, normally specifies the inner tunic worn next to the skin.) People of the Spirit can, like Jesus, be agents of purity rather than being rendered impure (Mark 5:27–34), but we need to be careful and aware of our vulnerabilities (Gal. 6:1). Thus, one of my Nigerian PhD students shared about his cousin who became very effective in casting out demons. Nevertheless, in challenging hostile powers without adequate biblical foundations in her own life she eventually lost her own sanity, perhaps from challenging forces in the wrong ways (cf. Jude 8).

Hating is appropriate for what is disgusting to God (Exod. 18:21; Pss. 97:10; 101:3; 119:104, 128; Rev. 2:6), though here, in contrast to some Old Testament passages, hating sin does not justify hating the sinners (Pss. 26:5; 31:6; 119:113; 139:21–22).[77]

Stained may evoke "stains" in verse 12, if that reading is correct there. On **flesh**, see comment on 2 Pet. 2:10.

Praise to God (24–25)

> **[24]To the one able to preserve you from falling away and to enable you to stand before his glory, blameless and with celebration: [25]To the only God, our savior, through Jesus Christ our Lord, be glory, majesty, power, and authority, before all time and now and through all the ages to come! Amen!**

For the doxology, see comment on 2 Pet. 3:18. In verse 24, the Greek term for **preserve** (*phylassō*) differs from that in verse 1, but the idea is the same. Judah

76. See Metzger, *Textual Commentary*, 725–26. Jude has as many as twenty triplets (Aune, *Literature and Rhetoric*, 473). Still, the earliest text is quite debatable here.

77. For hating what God hates, see also *1QRule of the Community* (1QS) 1.4; 4.24; *Damascus Document*[a] (CD) 2.15; *1QHodayot*[a] (1QH[a]) 4.36; *1 Enoch* 48.7; for hating the wicked, *1QRule of the Community* (1QS) 1.10.

frames his letter with trust that God will preserve his hearers' faith, underlining this letter's emphasis on perseverance. The fundamental benediction of Num. 6:24–26 includes the prayer for God to "keep" his people (6:24).

For **falling away** (v. 24), see comment on 1 Pet. 2:8. The image of avoiding stumbling fits with **enable you to stand** (a connection obscured in the otherwise helpful rendering in the NIV and the ESV). On **blameless**, see comment on 2 Pet. 3:14.[78]

Monotheists would not dispute **the only God** (cf. Deut. 6:4); for **God** as **our Savior**, see, for example, Isa. 45:15, 21. The ancient rhetoric of praise often lavished various honor terms on the one being praised, especially a deity. God is worthy of our praise!

78. For God keeping one blameless, compare a Jewish tradition about Abraham as "blameless" in Wis. 10:5.

Bibliography

Abelson, Joshua. *The Immanence of God in Rabbinical Literature*. 2nd ed. Hermon, 1969.

Achtemeier, Paul J. *1 Peter*. Edited by Eldon Jay Epp. Hermeneia. Fortress, 1996.

Adams, Edward. *The Stars Will Fall from Heaven: "Cosmic Catastrophe" in the New Testament and Its World*. Library of New Testament Studies 347. T&T Clark, 2007.

Alcorn, Randy. *Heaven*. Tyndale, 2004.

Amoafo, Emmanuel Kwasi. *Stand Up for the Gospel: Getting the Church Back on Track*. Oasis, 2022.

Anderson, R. Dean, Jr. *Ancient Rhetorical Theory and Paul*. Rev. ed. Contributions to Biblical Exegesis and Theology 18. Peeters, 1999.

———. *Glossary of Greek Rhetorical Terms Connected to Methods of Argumentation, Figures, and Tropes from Anaximenes to Quintilian*. Contributions to Biblical Exegesis and Theology 24. Peeters, 2000.

Aretaeus, the Cappadocian. *The Extant Works*. Edited and translated by Francis Adams. London, 1856.

Arius Didymus. *Epitome of Stoic Ethics*. Edited by Arthur J. Pomeroy. SBL Texts and Translations 44, Graeco-Roman Series 14. Society of Biblical Literature, 1999.

Assemblies of God. "Divine Healing." https://ag.org/Beliefs/Position-Papers/Divine-Healing.

Aune, David E. *The New Testament in Its Literary Environment*. Library of Early Christianity 8. Westminster, 1987.

———. *The Westminster Dictionary of New Testament and Early Christian Literature and Rhetoric*. Westminster John Knox, 2003.

Baer, Jonathan R. "Perfectly Empowered Bodies: Divine Healing in Modernizing America." PhD diss., Yale University, 2002.

Balch, David L. "Household Codes." In *Greco-Roman Literature and the New Testament: Selected Forms and Genres*, edited by David E. Aune. Society of Biblical Literature Sources for Biblical Study 21. Scholars Press, 1988.

———. *Let Wives Be Submissive: The Domestic Code in 1 Peter*. Society of Biblical Literature Monograph Series 26. Scholars Press, 1981.

Barclay, John M. G. *Paul and the Gift*. Eerdmans, 2015.

Barr, George K. "The Structure of Hebrews and of 1st and 2nd Peter." *Irish Biblical Studies* 19 (1997): 17–31.

Bateman, Herbert W., IV. "'Memories' About the Old Testament in Jewish and Christian Tradition Inform 2 Peter and Jude, Part 1." *Journal of the Evangelical Theological Society* 67 (2024): 103–12.

Bauckham, Richard. Jesus and the *Eyewitnesses: The Gospels as Eyewitness Testimony*. 2nd ed. Eerdmans, 2017.

———. *Jude, 2 Peter*. Word Biblical Commentary 50. Word, 1983.

Baum, Armin D. "Content and Form: Authorship Attribution and Pseudonymity in Ancient Speeches, Letters, Lectures, and Translations—A Rejoinder to Bart Ehrman." *Journal of Biblical Literature* 136 (2017): 381–403.

Bede. *Commentary on the Seven Catholic Epistles*. Monastic Study Series 30. Gorgias, 2010.

Berding, Kenneth. *Polycarp and Paul: An Analysis of Their Literary and Theological Relationship in Light of Polycarp's Use of Biblical and Extra-Biblical Literature*. Supplements to Vigiliae Christianae 62. Brill, 2002.

Bird, Michael F., and Preston M. Sprinkle, eds. *The Faith of Jesus Christ: Exegetical, Biblical, and Theological Studies*. Paternoster; Hendrickson, 2009.

Bowens, Lisa M. *African American Readings of Paul: Reception, Resistance & Transformation*. Eerdmans, 2020.

———. *An Apostle in Battle: Paul and Spiritual Warfare in 2 Corinthians 12:1–10*. Wissenschaftliche Untersuchungen zum Neuen Testament 2/433. Mohr Siebeck, 2017.

Brown, Michael L. *Hyper-Grace: Exposing the Dangers of the Modern Grace Message*. Charisma House, 2014.

———. *Our Hands Are Stained with Blood: The Tragic Story of the "Church" and the Jewish People*. Rev. ed. Destiny Image, 2019.

———. *Playing with Holy Fire: A Wake-Up Call to the Pentecostal-Charismatic Church*. Charisma House, 2018.

Brown, Michael L., and Craig S. Keener. *Not Afraid of the Antichrist: Why We Don't Believe in a Pretribulation Rapture*. Chosen Books, 2019.

Bruce, F. F. *The Message of the New Testament*. Eerdmans, 1981.

Burkert, Walter. "Craft Versus Sect: The Problem of Orphics and Pythagoreans." In *Self-Definition in the Greco-Roman World*, edited by Ben F. Meyer and E. P. Sanders. Vol. 3 of *Jewish and Christian Self-Definition*. Fortress, 1982.

Byrskog, Samuel. *Story as History, History as Story: The Gospel Tradition in the Context of Ancient Oral History*. Mohr Siebeck, 2000. Reprint, Brill, 2002.

Cao, John Sanqiang. "'I Knew I Would Pay a Price for My Faith': China Releases Missionary After Seven Years." Interview by C. J. Wu. *Christianity Today*, May 10, 2024. https://www.christianitytoday.com/2024/05/john-cao-prison-china-missionary-myanmar-faith/.

Capps, Charles. *The Tongue, a Creative Force*. Harrison House, 1976.

Carr, Wesley. *Angels and Principalities: The Background, Meaning and Development of the Pauline Phrase hai archai kai hai exousiai*. Society for New Testament Studies Monograph Series 42. Cambridge University Press, 1981.

Charlesworth, James H. *The Old Testament Pseudepigrapha and the New Testament: Prolegomena for the Study of Christian Origins*. Society for New Testament Studies Monograph Series 54. Cambridge University Press, 1985.

Chempakassery, Philip. "Cain in the Bible and Outside." *Bible Bhashyam* 30, no. 2 (2004): 123–47.

Chimtom, Ngala Killian. "Nigerian Christians Slaughtered in Christmas Attacks." *Crux: Taking the Catholic Pulse*, December 28, 2023. https://cruxnow.com/church-in-africa/2023/12/nigerian-christians-slaughtered-in-christmas-attacks.

Copeland, Gloria. *God's Will for Your Healing*. Kenneth Copeland Ministries, 1972.

Copeland, Kenneth. *The Laws of Prosperity*. Kenneth Copeland Publications, 1974.

Curtis, Heather D. *Faith in the Great Physician: Suffering and Divine Healing in American Culture, 1860–1900*. Johns Hopkins University Press, 2007.

Davies, W. D., and Dale C. Allison. *A Critical and Exegetical Commentary on the Gospel According to Saint Matthew*. 3 vols. International Critical Commentary. T&T Clark, 1988–97.

Dayton, Donald W. *Theological Roots of Pentecostalism*. Hendrickson, 1987.

Donelson, Lewis R. *I & II Peter and Jude: A Commentary*. New Testament Library. Westminster John Knox, 2010.

Dunn, James D. G. *Romans*. 2 vols. Word Biblical Commentary 38A, 38B. Word, 1988.

———. *The Theology of Paul the Apostle*. Eerdmans, 1998.

Edwards, Mark J., ed. *Galatians, Ephesians, Philippians*. Ancient Christian Commentary on Scripture, New Testament 8. InterVarsity, 1999.

Elliott, John H. *1 Peter: A New Translation with Introduction and Commentary*. Anchor Bible 37B. Doubleday, 2000.

Estrada, Rodolfo Gavan, III. "Blaspheming Angels: The Presence of Magicians in Jude 8–10." *Journal of the Evangelical Theological Society* 63 (2020): 739–58.

Eybers, I. H. "Aspects of the Background of the Letter of Jude." *Neotestamentica* 9 (1975): 113–23.

Fee, Gordon. *The Disease of the Health and Wealth Gospels*. Reprint, Regent College Publishing, 1985.

———. *God's Empowering Presence: The Holy Spirit in the Letters of Paul*. Hendrickson, 1994.

———. *Listening to the Spirit in the Text*. Eerdmans, 2000.

Ferguson, Everett. *Backgrounds of Early Christianity*. 3rd ed. Eerdmans, 2003.

Finamore, John F., and John M. Dillon. Introduction to *De Anima: Text, Translation, and Commentary*, by Iamblichus. Philosophia Antiqua 42. Brill, 2002.

Flusser, David. *Judaism and the Origins of Christianity*. Magnes, 1988.

Forbes, Christopher. "Comparison, Self-Praise, and Irony: Paul's Boasting and the Conventions of Hellenistic Rhetoric." *New Testament Studies* 32 (1986): 1–30.

Frankfurter, David. *Religion in Roman Egypt: Assimilation and Resistance*. Princeton University Press, 1998.

Frankl, Viktor E. *Embracing Hope: On Freedom, Responsibility and the Meaning of Life*. Beacon, 2024.

———. *From Death-Camp to Existentialism: A Psychiatrist's Path to a New Therapy*. Translated by Ilse Lasch. Beacon, 1959.

Gamble, Harry Y. "Canonical Formation of the New Testament." In *Dictionary of New Testament Background*, edited by Craig A. Evans and Stanley E. Porter. InterVarsity, 2000.

Gardner, Jane F. *Women in Roman Law and Society*. Indiana University Press, 1986.

Gathercole, Simon. *Defending Substitution: An Essay on Atonement in Paul*. Acadia Studies in Bible and Theology. Baker Academic, 2015.

Gilmour, Michael J. *The Significance of Parallels Between 2 Peter and Other Early Christian Literature*. Academia Biblica 10. Society of Biblical Literature, 2002.

Gorman, Michael J. *Inhabiting the Cruciform God: Kenosis, Justification, and Theosis in Paul's Narrative Theology*. Eerdmans, 2009.

Green, Gene L. *Jude and 2 Peter*. Baker Exegetical Commentary on the New Testament. Baker Academic, 2008.

Green, Joel B. *1 Peter*. Two Horizons New Testament Commentary. Eerdmans, 2007.

Green, Joel B., and Lee Martin McDonald, eds. *The World of the New Testament: Cultural, Social, and Historical Contexts*. Baker Academic, 2013.

Greene, J. T. "The Balaam Figure and Type Before, During, and After the Period of the Pseudepigrapha." *Journal for the Study of the Pseudepigrapha* 8 (1991): 67–110.

Hagin, Kenneth E. *I Believe in Visions*. Revell, 1972.

———. *Prayer Secrets*. Kenneth Hagin Ministries, n.d.

———. *What Faith Is*. Kenneth Hagin Ministries, 1978.

Hansen, G. Walter. *Abraham in Galatians—Epistolary and Rhetorical Contexts*. Journal for the Study of the New Testament Supplement Series 29. Sheffield Academic, 1989.

Harrison, James R. *Paul's Language of Grace in Its Graeco-Roman Context*. Wissenschaftliche Untersuchungen zum Neuen Testament 2/172. Mohr, 2003.

Hengel, Martin. *The Atonement: The Origins of the Doctrine in the New Testament.* Translated by John Bowden. Fortress, 1981.

Heschel, Susannah. *The Aryan Jesus: Christian Theologians and the Bible in Nazi Germany.* Princeton University Press, 2008.

Ibraheem, Mariam, with Eugene Bach. *Shackled: One Woman's Dramatic Triumph over Persecution, Gender Abuse, and a Death Sentence.* Whitaker House, 2022.

Isbell, Charles D. *Corpus of the Aramaic Incantation Bowls.* Society of Biblical Literature Dissertation Series 17. Scholars Press, 1975.

Jastrow, Marcus. *Dictionary of the Targumim, Talmud Babli, Yerushalmi, and Midrashic Literature.* Judaica, 1971.

Jeter, Hugh. *By His Stripes: A Biblical Study on Divine Healing.* Gospel Publishing House, 1977.

Jobes, Karen H. *1 Peter.* Baker Exegetical Commentary on the New Testament. Baker Academic, 2005.

Johnson, Luke Timothy. "The New Testament's Anti-Jewish Slander and Conventions of Ancient Rhetoric." *Journal of Biblical Literature* 108 (1989): 419–41.

Juza, Ryan. *The New Testament and the Future of the Cosmos.* Pickwick, 2020.

Kadushin, Max. *The Rabbinic Mind.* 3rd ed. Bloch, 1972.

Keener, Craig S. *Acts: An Exegetical Commentary.* 4 vols. Baker Academic, 2012–15.

———. *Between History and Spirit: The Apostolic Witness of the Book of Acts.* Cascade Books, 2020.

———. "A Comparison of the Fruit of the Spirit in Galatians 5:22–23 with Ancient Thought on Ethics and Emotion." In *The Language and Literature of the New Testament: Essays in Honor of Stanley E. Porter's 60th Birthday*, edited by Lois K. Fuller Dow, Craig A. Evans, and Andrew W. Pitts. Brill, 2016.

———. *1 and 2 Corinthians.* New Cambridge Bible Commentary. Cambridge University Press, 2005.

———. *1 Peter: A Commentary.* Baker Academic, 2021.

———. *Galatians: A Commentary.* Baker Academic, 2019.

———. *Gift and Giver: The Holy Spirit for Today.* Baker Academic, 2001.

———. *The Gospel of Matthew: A Socio-Rhetorical Commentary.* Eerdmans, 2009.

———. "Human Stones in a Greek Setting—Luke 3.8 // Matthew 3.9; Luke 19.40." *Journal of Greco-Roman Christianity and Judaism* 6 (2009): 28–36.

———. *The IVP Bible Background Commentary: New Testament.* 2nd ed. InterVarsity, 2014.

———. *The Mind of the Spirit: Paul's Approach to Transformed Thinking.* Baker Academic, 2016.

———. *Miracles: The Credibility of the New Testament Accounts.* 2 vols. Baker Academic, 2011.

———. "Paul and Spiritual Warfare." In *Paul's Missionary Methods: In His Time and Ours*, edited by Robert L. Plummer and John Mark Terry. IVP Academic, 2012.

———. *Paul, Women, and Wives: Marriage and Women's Ministry in the Letters of Paul.* Hendrickson, 1992.

———. *Romans.* New Covenant Commentary Series. Cascade Books, 2009.

———. *Spirit Hermeneutics: Reading Scripture in Light of Pentecost.* Eerdmans, 2016.

———. "Transformation Through Divine Vision in 1 John 3:2–6." *Faith & Mission* 23, no. 1 (Fall, 2005): 13–22.

———. "Transformed Thinking in Paul's Letters." *Doon Theological Journal* [Dehradun, India] 13, nos. 1–2 (2016): 5–24.

———. "The Unridden Donkey Colt—Mark 11:2 in Light of Equine Development and Pedagogy." *Bulletin for Biblical Research* 32 (2022): 17–40.

———. "Why Does Luke Use Tongues as a Sign of the Spirit's Empowerment?" *Journal of Pentecostal Theology* 15 (2007): 177–84.

———. "Youthful Vigor and the Maturity of Age: Peter and the Beloved Disciple in John 20–21." In *Rediscovering John: Essays on the Fourth Gospel in Honour of Frédéric Manns*, edited by L. Daniel Chrupcala. Studium Biblicum Franciscanum Analecta 80. Edizioni Terra Santa, 2013.

Keener, Craig S., and Médine Moussounga Keener. *Impossible Love: The True Story of an African Civil War, Miracles, and Love Against All Odds.* Chosen Books, 2016.

Keener, Craig S., and Glenn Usry. *Defending Black Faith: Answers to Tough Questions About African-American Christianity.* InterVarsity, 1997.

Kelly, J. N. D. *A Commentary on the Epistles of Peter and Jude.* Thornapple Commentaries. Baker, 1981.

Kim, Jintae. "The Concept of Atonement in Early Rabbinic Thought and the New Testament Writings." *Journal of Greco-Roman Christianity and Judaism* 2 (2001–5): 117–45.

———. "The Concept of Atonement in Hellenistic Thought and 1 John." *Journal of Greco-Roman Christianity and Judaism* 2 (2001–5): 100–116.

King, Paul L. *Is It of God? A Biblical Guidebook for Spiritual Discernment.* 2 vols. Bridge-Logos, 2019; Paul King Ministries, 2021.

Kloppenborg, John S. "Associations, Christ Groups, and Their Place in the Polis." *Zeitschrift für die neutestamentliche Wissenschaft* 108 (2017): 1–56.

Knibb, Michael A. *The Ethiopic Book of Enoch: A New Edition in the Light of the Aramaic Dead Sea Fragments.* 2 vols. In consultation with Edward Ullendorff. Clarendon, 1978.

Kyle, Richard. *The Last Days Are Here Again.* Baker, 1998.

Lampe, G. W. H. "'Grievous Wolves' (Acts 20:29)." In *Christ and Spirit in the New Testament: Studies in Honor of C. F. D. Moule*, edited by Barnabas Lindars and Stephen S. Smalley. Cambridge University Press, 1973.

Larsen, Matthew D. C. *Gospels Before the Book.* Oxford University Press, 2018.

Lauterbach, Jacob Z., ed. and trans. *Mekhilta de-Rabbi Ishmael: A Critical Edition, Based on the Manuscripts and Early Editions, with an English Translation, Introduction, and Notes*. 2 vols. 2nd ed. Jewish Publication Society, 2004.

Lewis, C. S. *The Great Divorce*. Macmillan, 1946.

Loewenstamm, Samuel E. "The Death of Moses." In *Studies on the Testament of Abraham*, edited by George W. E. Nickelsburg Jr. Society of Biblical Literature Septuagint and Cognate Studies 6. Scholars Press, 1976.

Malherbe, Abraham J. "'Gentle as a Nurse': The Cynic Background to I Thess. ii." *Novum Testamentum* 12 (1970): 203–17.

———. *Moral Exhortation: A Greco-Roman Sourcebook*. Library of Early Christianity 4. Westminster, 1986.

Marshall, I. Howard. *Kept by the Power of God: A Study in Perseverance and Falling Away*. Epworth, 1969. Reprint, Bethany Fellowship, 1974.

Marshall, Paul A. *Their Blood Cries Out: The Worldwide Tragedy of Modern Christians Who Are Dying for Their Faith*. Word, 1997.

Marshall, Paul, Lela Gilbert, and Nina Shea. *Persecuted: The Global Assault on Christians*. Nelson, 2013.

Mbuvi, Andrew M. *Jude and 2 Peter*. New Covenant Commentary Series. Cascade Books, 2015.

McClymond, Michael J. *The Devil's Redemption: A New History and Interpretation of Christian Universalism*. 2 vols. Baker Academic, 2018.

Menzies, Robert P. *Speaking in Tongues: Jesus and the Apostolic Church as Models for the Church Today*. CPT, 2016.

Metzger, Bruce M. "Literary Forgeries and Canonical Pseudepigrapha." *Journal of Biblical Literature* 91 (1972): 3–24.

———. *A Textual Commentary on the Greek New Testament*. Corrected ed. United Bible Societies, 1975.

Moses, Danny. *Contending for the Faith: A Commentary on Jude*. Published by the author, 2021.

Nettleton, Todd. *When Faith Is Forbidden: 40 Days on the Front Lines with Persecuted Christians*. Moody, 2021.

Opp, James. *The Lord for the Body: Religion, Medicine, and Protestant Faith Healing in Canada, 1880–1930*. McGill-Queen's University Press, 2005.

Oropeza, B. J. *Apostasy in the New Testament Communities*. 3 vols. Cascade Books, 2011.

O'Rourke, John J. "Roman Law and the Early Church." In *The Catacombs and the Colosseum: The Roman Empire as the Setting of Primitive Christianity*, edited by Stephen Benko and John J. O'Rourke. Judson, 1971.

Panahi, Naghmeh Abedini. *I Didn't Survive: Emerging Whole After Deception, Persecution, and Hidden Abuse*. Whitaker House, 2023.

Peters, Larry. *Ecstasy and Healing in Nepal: An Ethnopsychiatric Study of Tamang Shamanism*. Undena, 1981.

Pfitzner, Victor C. *Paul and the Agon Motif: Traditional Athletic Imagery in the Pauline Literature*. Supplements to Novum Testamentum 16. Brill, 1967.

Pomeroy, Sarah B. *Goddesses, Whores, Wives, and Slaves: Women in Classical Antiquity*. Schocken Books, 1975.

Rapske, Brian M. *The Book of Acts and Paul in Roman Custody*. Vol. 3 of *The Book of Acts in Its First Century Setting*. Edited by Bruce W. Winter. Eerdmans; Paternoster, 1994.

Reese, Ruth Anne. *2 Peter & Jude*. Two Horizons New Testament Commentary. Eerdmans, 2007.

Remus, H. "Moses and the Thaumaturges: Philo's *De Vita Mosis* as a Rescue Operation." *Laval théologique et philosophique* 52, no. 3 (1996): 665–80.

Reyes, Erlinda T. "A Theological Framework on Non-Healing in the Pentecostal Perspective." ThM thesis, Asia Pacific Theological Seminary, 2007.

Richards, E. Randolph. "The Codex and the Early Collection of Paul's Letters." *Bulletin for Biblical Research* 8 (1998): 151–66.

———. *Paul and First-Century Letter Writing: Secretaries, Composition and Collection*. InterVarsity, 2004.

———. *The Secretary in the Letters of Paul*. Wissenschaftliche Untersuchungen zum Neuen Testament 2/42. Mohr, 1991.

Robinson, John A. T. *Redating the New Testament*. Westminster; SCM, 1976.

Roseveare, Helen. "Counting the Cost: Loving the Lord with Heart, Soul and Strength." *World Christian*, November 1986, 36–39.

Rowe, Galen O. "Style." In *Handbook of Classical Rhetoric in the Hellenistic Period, 330 B.C.–A.D. 400*, edited by Stanley E. Porter. Brill, 1997.

Schaefer, Kurt C. *Husband, Wife, Father, Child, Master, Slave: Peter Through Roman Eyes*. Wipf & Stock, 2018.

Shank, Robert. *Life in the Son: A Study of the Doctrine of Perseverance*. Rev. ed. Bethany House, 2024.

Sidebottom, E. M. *James, Jude, and 2 Peter*. New Century Bible Commentary. Attic, 1967.

Slater, Thomas B. "The Misnomer of 'Catholic' (or 'General') Letters." In *Afrocentric Interpretations of the New Testament Epistles Hebrews, James, Jude, Peter, John, and Revelation: Things That Black Scholars See That White Scholars Do Not*, edited by Thomas Bowie Slater. Mellen, 2021.

Smith, Shively T. J. *Strangers to Family: Diaspora and 1 Peter's Invention of God's Household*. Baylor University Press, 2016.

Sorabji, Richard. *Emotion and Peace of Mind: From Stoic Agitation to Christian Temptation*. Oxford University Press, 2000.

Stephens, Mark B. *Annihilation or Renewal? The Meaning and Function of New Creation in the Book of Revelation*. Wissenschaftliche Untersuchungen zum Neuen Testament 2/307. Mohr Siebeck, 2011.

Storms, Sam. *Romans*. Word and Spirit Commentary on the New Testament. Baker Academic, 2024.

Tamfu, Dieudonné. *2 Peter and Jude*. Africa Bible Commentary Series. HippoBooks, 2018.

Thiede, Carsten Peter. "A Pagan Reader of 2 Peter: Cosmic Conflagration in 2 Pet 3 and the *Octavius* of Minucius Felix." *Journal for the Study of the New Testament* 26 (1986): 79–96.

Trebilco, Paul R. *Jewish Communities in Asia Minor*. Society for New Testament Studies Monograph Series 69. Cambridge University Press, 1991.

Usry, Glenn, and Craig S. Keener. *Black Man's Religion: Can Christianity Be Afrocentric?* InterVarsity, 1996.

Uytanlet, Samson L. *2 Peter and Jude: A Pastoral and Contextual Commentary*. Asia Bible Commentary Series. Langham Global Library, 2023.

Verner, David C. *The Household of God: The Social World of the Pastoral Epistles*. Society of Biblical Literature Dissertation Series 71. Scholars Press, 1983.

Voice of the Martyrs. *I Am N: Inspiring Stories of Christians Facing Islamic Extremists*. With Mikal Keefer. Edited by Sheryl Martin Hash. Rev. ed. VOM Books, 2024.

Weima, Jeffrey A. D. *Neglected Endings: The Significance of the Pauline Letter Closings*. Journal for the Study of the New Testament Supplement Series 101. JSOT Press, 1994.

Wilson, Dwight. *Armageddon Now! The Premillenarian Response to Russia and Israel Since 1917*. Baker, 1977.

Winter, Bruce W. *Seek the Welfare of the City: Christians as Benefactors and Citizens*. First-Century Christians in the Graeco-Roman World. Eerdmans; Paternoster, 1994.

Witherington, Ben, III. *Jesus, Paul, and the End of the World: A Comparative Study in New Testament Eschatology*. InterVarsity, 1992.

Wolfson, Harry Austryn. *Philo: Foundations of Religious Philosophy in Judaism, Christianity, and Islam*. 2 vols. 4th rev. ed. Harvard University Press, 1968.

Wright, N. T. *The Resurrection of the Son of God*. Vol. 3 of *Christian Origins and the Question of God*. Fortress, 2003.

Wurmbrand, Richard. *Tortured for Christ: The Complete Story*. VOM Books, 2020.

Wurmbrand, Sabrina. *The Pastor's Wife*. VOM Books, 2023.

Yancey, Philip. *Rumors of Another World: What on Earth Are We Missing?* Zondervan, 2003.

Index of Authors

Index of Scripture and Other Ancient Sources

Proverbs

Ecclesiastes

Isaiah

Jeremiah

1 Corinthians

2 Corinthians

Galatians

Philemon

Hebrews

James

1 Peter

2 Peter

Old Testament Pseudepigrapha

2 Baruch

1 Enoch

2 Enoch

3 Enoch

4 Ezra

Jubilees